Confronting Child Sexual Abuse

KNOWLEDGE TO ACTION

Anne M. Nurse

LEVER PRESS

Lever Press (leverpress.org) is a publisher of pathbreaking scholarship.
Supported by a consortium of liberal arts institutions focused on, and
renowned for, excellence in both research and teaching, our press is grounded
on three essential commitments: to be a digitally native press, to be a peer-
reviewed, open access press that charges no fees to either authors or their
institutions, and to be a press aligned with the ethos and mission of liberal
arts colleges.

The complete manuscript of this work was subjected to a partly closed ("single
blind") review process. For more information, please see our Peer Review
Commitments and Guidelines at https://www.leverpress.org/peerreview

DOI: https://doi.org/10.3998/mpub.12085149
Print ISBN: 978-1-64315-032-1
Open access ISBN: 978-1-64315-033-8

Published in the United States of America by Lever Press, in partnership with
Amherst College Press and Michigan Publishing

Contents

Member Institution Acknowledgments

Lever Press is a joint venture. This work was made possible by the generous support of Lever Press member libraries from the following institutions:

Adrian College
Agnes Scott College
Allegheny College
Amherst College
Bard College
Berea College
Bowdoin College
Carleton College
Claremont Graduate
    University
Claremont McKenna College
Clark Atlanta University
Coe College
College of Saint Benedict /
    Saint John's University
The College of Wooster

Denison University
DePauw University
Earlham College
Furman University
Grinnell College
Hamilton College
Harvey Mudd College
Haverford College
Hollins University
Keck Graduate Institute
Kenyon College
Knox College
Lafayette College Library
Lake Forest College
Macalester College
Middlebury College

Morehouse College
Oberlin College
Pitzer College
Pomona College
Rollins College
Santa Clara University
Scripps College
Sewanee: The University of the
    South
Skidmore College
Smith College
Spelman College
St. Lawrence University

St. Olaf College
Susquehanna University
Swarthmore College
Trinity University
Union College
University of Puget Sound
Ursinus College
Vassar College
Washington and Lee
    University
Whitman College
Willamette University
Williams College

PREFACE

On a beautiful Saturday in the fall of 2013, I woke up angry. My alarm had gone off at a painfully early hour so that I could drive to a neighboring town for a training session. I suppose it was my own fault that I had to get up. In a moment of maternal guilt, I had signed up to drive a field trip for my eight-year-old son's class. That was clearly the wrong move. A few days later, the school called to let me know that I was ineligible to drive because I was not "certified," meaning that I had not attended a required three-hour training course about child sexual abuse (CSA), nor had I taken a required background check. These demands seemed ridiculous to me, and I was particularly galled because my child was attending a Catholic school. Having followed the unfolding of the priest sex scandal in the early 2000s, I felt that I was paying for the "sins of the fathers." Shouldn't they be the ones getting up early to attend a training and not me?

Of course, the training was not the first time I had thought about CSA. As the mother of three children, sexual abuse was on my list of fears. This was partly because close friends had shared the anguish they had experienced as a result of being abused as children. I had also thought about CSA because I am a Catholic. I felt outraged about my church's response to the widespread abuse of children by priests and sadness for the many victims. Strangely, however, I had not thought much about CSA in my professional role as a criminologist. For over twenty-five years, I had studied juvenile prisons and their impact on individuals and society, interviewing hundreds of incarcerated and paroled young men. I had also taught for years in a maximum-security juvenile facility. This work put me in contact with youth who were incarcerated for sex crimes against children, yet I had not studied or thought too deeply about the issue. Perhaps this was because I found it to be an upsetting topic and just wanted to avoid it.

Due to my inattention to CSA, I arrived at the prevention training program that morning with little idea of what to expect. I chatted somewhat awkwardly with the other participants while we waited for a cup of tepid coffee. Like me, most were parents wanting to volunteer in their children's classrooms, although I also met coaches and teachers. We found common ground in our annoyance about being forced to attend the training. Finally, we were instructed to assemble on folding chairs. We spent the next couple of hours watching videos about CSA and having directed discussions. I would like to say that the session was outstanding, but that would be an overstatement. At the same time, it was much more interesting and emotional than I expected and, by the time I walked out the door, I had settled on a new direction for my research. The session made me realize that not only was CSA affecting thousands of our nation's children and families, it was a topic rife with misconceptions and fear. I suddenly saw that my own anxiety about my children's safety and my seeming unwillingness to think sociologically about CSA offenders offered a personal challenge. Could I step back from such an emotional topic and think clearly about CSA, its effects, and the policies we put in place to stem it?

The training session sent me on a frenzied odyssey of discovery. Right after my return home, I started reading the academic literature to see whether anyone had conducted an evaluation assessing the efficacy of adult prevention training. Even though over two million Americans had participated in the particular program I attended, there had been no scientific study of its effects. I asked the bishop of my diocese if I could conduct such a study, and he eventually approved my request. For the next two years, I explored participants' base level of knowledge about CSA, whether the training taught them new information, and whether they retained that information over time. I also investigated whether the training increased protective behaviors. After publishing the results of my evaluation, I moved on to read other researchers' work on a wide range of topics related to CSA. These included the psychology of offenders, the impact of abuse on victims, and the effect of different public policies on the prevalence of CSA.

In terms of policy, I learned that the legal system, as well as most organizations, have made significant changes regarding CSA punishment and prevention over the last thirty years. This makes it a particularly appropriate moment for us to step back and think critically about our CSA prevention efforts. Although recent high-profile cases of serial abuse in various organizations (like USA Gymnastics) may make it difficult to believe, the official rate of CSA has been on the decline for more than thirty years.[1] Perhaps this means that our policies have been working. Or it may mean that some policies are working while others are useless or even harmful. Even more distressing, it is possible that the rate is declining for some reason that has nothing to do with our efforts. Because CSA prevention efforts are expensive, time consuming, and have an impact on many people's lives (not to mention on our ability to sleep in on a Saturday morning), it is in all of our best interest to figure out the truth. This book is intended for readers who want to learn more about both CSA and the efficacy of prevention.

---

1. David Finkelhor, Kei Saito, and Lisa Jones, "Updated Trends in Child Maltreatment, 2018" (University of New Hampshire: Crimes against Children Research Center, 2020), http://www.unh.edu/ccrc/pdf/CV203%20-%20 Updated%20trends%202018_ks_df.pdf.

A NOTE ABOUT LANGUAGE

As I was writing this book, I thought a lot about language and its impact. An experiment conducted by social psychologists many years ago illustrates the importance of word choice. The researchers showed participants a film of a car crash and then, a week later, they asked half of the group to recall the film; had there been broken glass when the two cars "smashed" into each other? The other half of participants were asked the same question, except the cars were described as "colliding" rather than "smashing." The people in the smash group were more likely to recall broken glass than the people in the collision group. The funny part is that both groups had seen the same film, and there wasn't any broken glass at all.[2] It appears that language is so powerful it can induce memory. "Smashed" is such a strong word it practically screams "broken glass!"

Words are particularly important with an emotional and upsetting topic like CSA. What should the people who commit CSA be called? And what should we call the children who experience that abuse? Starting first with those who commit CSA, the Urban Institute, a well-respected research think tank, argues that we should avoid words like *felon* and *offender*, especially when we are talking about people who have served their time and have returned to their communities.[3] The Urban Institute's reasoning is that, no matter how horrible a crime a person has committed, they are still human. Terms like *offender* suggest that people's only identity is criminal, so they recommend the use of "people first" language. For example,

---

2. Elizabeth F. Loftus and John C. Palmer, "Reconstruction of Automobile Destruction: An Example of the Interaction between Language and Memory," *Journal of Verbal Learning and Verbal Behavior* 13, no. 5 (October 1974): 585–89.

3. Cameron Okeke and Nancy G. La Vigne, "Restoring Humanity: Changing the Way We Talk about People Touched by the Criminal Justice System," Urban Institute, November 29, 2018, https://www.urban.org/urban-wire/restoring-humanity-changing-way-we-talk-about-people-touched-criminal-justice-system.

we can say "people with a felony" or "people who have committed CSA." This kind of "people first" recommendation is not new. People with disabilities, for example, have long argued against being called "the disabled" for similar reasons. In this text, I generally try to follow the Urban Institute's recommendations when discussing people who have served their time. I use the term *offender* when referring to a person who is actively committing abuse or who is serving time in prison for CSA.

Turning to children who suffer abuse, there is also debate. Some use the term *victim* while others prefer *survivor*. The advocacy group Rape, Abuse, and Incest National Network (RAINN) cautions that individual preference is important, and that it is best to ask people what terminology they prefer.[4] This is obviously not an option in this book since I rarely refer to particular individuals. RAINN itself uses the term *victim* when they are talking about someone who has recently suffered abuse and the term *survivor* for people who have been engaged in the recovery process for some period of time. Another option is people-first language, like *people who have suffered CSA*. The reasoning behind the use of this more cumbersome term is the same as discussed above: people who have suffered CSA are much more than the abuse they have experienced. In this text, I try to follow RAINN's suggestion and use *victim* if I am talking about abuse and its immediate aftermath and *survivor* when time has passed.

PSYCHOLOGICAL PROCESSES THAT CAN IMPACT OUR UNDERSTANDING OF CHILD SEXUAL ABUSE

In this section, I briefly introduce two psychological mechanisms that may be impactful while reading this book. The first, confirmation bias, threatens the ability to accept information that

---

4. RAINN, "Key Terms and Phrases," RAINN, 2019, https://www.rainn.org/articles/key-terms-and-phrases.

Figure I. Confirmation Bias. Source: The Upturned Microscope by Nik Papageorgiou. May 2017. https://theupturnedmicroscope.com/comic/logical-fallacies-confirmation-bias/

contradicts preexisting beliefs. The second, defensive attribution, leads people to distance themselves from victims. I found it was useful to know about both of these psychological phenomenon as I learned about CSA.

Warren Buffett has been quoted as saying that "what the human being is best at doing is interpreting all new information so that their prior conclusions remain intact."[5] This is a succinct definition of confirmation bias. Confirmation bias is the human tendency to look for (or notice, or weigh more heavily) information that

5. Tomas Chamorro-Premuzic, "How the Web Distorts Reality and Impairs our Judgement Skills," *Guardian*, May 13, 2014, https://www.theguardian.com/media-network/media-network-blog/2014/may/13/internet-confirmation-bias.

supports our previously held beliefs. It also leads us to ignore (or fail to notice, or underweigh) information that contradicts those beliefs. It is hard to notice when we engage in confirmation bias because it is usually unconscious.[6]

There has been a significant amount of research conducted on confirmation bias. In one experiment, people were asked to read a detailed crime scenario and determine the guilt or innocence of the suspect. Once they had made their initial decision, they were allowed to request additional information from a list of twenty options. For example, they could ask for an interview of a particular witness. The investigation options were crafted so that half looked like they would provide incriminating evidence, and the other half looked like they would provide exculpatory evidence. As you might expect from the definition of confirmation bias, the people who thought the suspect was guilty requested investigations that would help support that position. It was the opposite for those who thought the suspect was innocent.[7] This shows that people prefer to confirm their beliefs than to consider evidence that does not support those beliefs.

How might confirmation bias affect our thinking about CSA? It makes our attitudes about offenders and victims difficult to change, regardless of what they are. As I was writing this book, I sometimes struggled when I found evidence that went against something I had always believed. The box below includes some tricks that I found useful for working against my mind's desire to confirm preexisting beliefs.

---

6. Raymond S Nickerson, "Confirmation Bias: A Ubiquitous Phenomenon in Many Guises," *Review of General Psychology* 2, no. 2 (1998): 175–220, http://psy2. ucsd.edu/~mckenzie/nickersonConfirmationBias.pdf.

7. Eric Rassin, Anita Eerland, and Ilse Kuijpers, "Let's Find the Evidence: An Analogue Study of Confirmation Bias in Criminal Investigations," *Journal of Investigative Psychology and Offender Profiling* 7 (2010): 231–46, https://www. researchgate.net/publication/230268983_Let's_Find_the_Evidence_An_Ana logue_Study_of_Confirmation_Bias_in_Criminal_Investigations.

Combatting Confirmation Bias

An article in *Psychology Today*[8] provides a set of questions to ask after receiving new information. The questions might even be useful while reading this book.

1. Which parts did I automatically agree with?
2. Which parts did I ignore or skim over without realizing?
3. How did I react to the points I agreed or disagreed with?
4. Did what I read/hear confirm any ideas I already had? Why?
5. What if I thought the opposite of those ideas?

Confirmation bias is one important psychological mechanism that can affect our views of CSA. Defensive attribution is another. It is a common tool that our minds use to try and calm us about scary topics. It involves minimizing our own perceived level of risk by attributing blame to victims. For example, researchers looked at how people react to the thought of a car accident. They told study participants a story about a responsible young man who had recently bought a used car. He parked it on hill and it later rolled away. While the young man might have failed to engage the parking brake, the car's brakes were also later found to be very rusted.

After setting up the story, the researchers divided the study participants into four groups and each group heard a different ending. In one, the car rolled a short distance, suffering only minimal damage. In the second, the car rolled all the way down a hill and hit a stump, totaling the car. In the third, the car rolled all the way down the hill and hit a grocery store, causing minimal damage to the car and to the store. Finally, in the fourth, the car hit the grocery store and was totaled. The impact also caused minor injuries to a child who was in the store, as well as significant injuries

---

8. F. Diane Barth, "How Confirmation Bias Affects You Every Single Day," *Psychology Today* (blog), December 31, 2017, https://www.psychologytoday.com/us/blog/the-couch/201712/how-confirmation-bias-affects-you-every-single-day.

to the grocer. The researchers found that the greater the damage incurred, the more likely the study participants were to blame the young man. They did not want to believe that the brakes in their own car might rust and cause major damage, so they preferred to believe the young man had failed to set the brake. People's tendency toward defensive attribution gets stronger as possible negative outcomes get scarier.[9]

It is easy to understand why people engage in defensive attribution when they hear about cases of CSA. None of us wants to believe that abuse could happen to someone we love. As a result, when I read about a teacher who molests a child over several months, I might say, "My kid would have told me if his teacher had touched him in that way." Similarly, if there is a report on television about a child who was abused by his neighbor, I could say, "I never would have let my child play over at that person's house." While defensive attribution functions to make us feel better, it can also cloud our judgement about the reality of CSA and our own risk level.

FRAMING AND CHILD SEXUAL ABUSE

One of the ways that people receive and interpret knowledge about CSA involves "framing." A "frame" refers to the way people define, construct, and interpret events. It might be helpful to think about frames in terms of jigsaw puzzles. When doing a puzzle, one does not try to fit pieces together randomly. If you are like me, you start by looking for edge pieces. While I am certainly aware that there are other distinguishing features of the puzzle pieces, I force my brain to concentrate on seeing edges. After I have the edges done, I often focus on particular colors—or I look for the shape of a piece I need. These strategies are like frames: they highlight particular aspects of reality to make a huge amount of information

---

9. Elaine Walster, "Assignment of Responsibility for an Accident," *Journal of Personality and Social Psychology* 3, no. 1 (1966): 73–79, http://www.elainehatfield.com/uploads/3/4/5/2/34523593/12._hatfield_1966.pdf.

manageable and coherent. It's similar when telling a story; there are a million details that could be included but the story is shaped to emphasize particular themes or frames. Below are two examples.

> **Examples of Frames**
>
> Example One: The media is going to run a story about illegal drug use. One frame could portray drug use as a public health problem, suggesting that users are victims who need medical help. Alternately, the media could frame the issue as a criminal justice problem. In that case, they would portray users as law breakers who should be locked up.[10]
>
> Example Two: Laws about same-sex marriage were changed recently in the United States. In the run-up to the change, many media outlets published stories about the topic. One frame envisioned same-sex marriage as a threat to hetero-sexual marriage. This frame suggested that the solution was to continue to define marriage as between one man and a woman. Another frame, however, portrayed same-sex marriage as an issue of equal rights. This frame pointed toward legalization as the proper solution.[11]

In the examples in the box, frames provide parameters for thinking about drug use and same-sex marriage. The frames also lead us to favor particular solutions.[12] It is important to understand framing

---

10. David L. Altheide and R. Sam Michalowski, "Fear in the News: A Discourse of Control," *Sociological Quarterly* 40, no. 3 (1999): 475–503, https://scholar.google.com/scholar?hl=en&as_sdt=0%2C36&q=Fear+in+the+News%3A+A+Discourse+of+Control&btnG=.

11. Deirdre M. Warren and Katrina R. Bloch, "Framing Same-Sex Marriage: Media Constructions of California's Proposition 8," *Social Science Journal* 51, no. 4 (2014): 503–13.

12. Altheide and Michalowski, "Fear in the News," https://scholar.google.com/scholar?hl=en&as_sdt=0%2C36&q=Fear+in+the+News%3A+A+Discourse+of+Control&btnG=

in relation to CSA. In chapter 1, I discuss how the media and various social movements frame CSA and show that their choices have a serious impact on our understanding of victims, offenders, and solutions. In chapters 4 and 5, I discuss how politicians frame CSA to support particular policies and laws. Chapter 7 covers how various organizations (like the Catholic Church) frame CSA in their prevention training. Finally, I employ frames myself throughout this book. While reading, think about how I am framing CSA and how that might impact your opinions.

Does a story's frame really affect our thoughts? Research suggests that the answer is *yes*, but it turns out that it is not a straightforward process. People are not just robots, blindly taking in what they are handed. Frames direct feelings, but people also react to stories based on many other factors, including their own previous experiences, the experiences of people they know, and information obtained from other sources.

To test how framing affects thinking, researchers presented undergraduates at a state university with one of four versions of a news story. The story was about anticipated budget cuts, some of which would impact state universities (including their own). One version of the story did not have a strong frame, it just contained basic facts about budget cuts. The second version employed a "conflict frame" that focused on two grassroots organizations that disagreed with each other about whether the budget cuts were necessary or advisable. The human-interest framing of the story focused on a high-level state employee who was retiring from his job because he was frustrated with figuring out how to equitably distribute limited money to the universities. The final frame, the "consequences frame," explicitly stated that state university tuition would need to be increased because of budget cuts. After the students were presented with one of the four stories, they were asked to list the thoughts and feelings they experienced while reading.[13]

---

13. Vincent Price, David Tewskbury, and Elizabeth Powers, "Switching Trains

The study showed that the way stories are framed affects how people interpret information. For example, the students who read the story that emphasized consequences were more likely to think about tuition increases. Those who read the story with the conflict frame tended to think about politics or interest groups. At the same time, the students were also able to think outside their story's frames. For example, some members of the human-interest group thought about the possibility of tuition increases even though it was not emphasized in what they read. Surprisingly, those who read the story that lacked a strong frame were even more likely than other groups to think about tuition increases. This suggests that frames can push people toward thinking in particular directions as well as distract them from thoughts they would have in the absence of the frame.

Another interesting finding from the study involved how students' personal characteristics affected their interpretation of the state budget story. Both residency status (whether the student was from within the state or out of it) and social class made a difference in what students thought about as they read the stories. This indicates that reactions to frames are at least partly shaped by who we are and our own particular interests. Finally, the experiment showed that frames affect support for particular policies. Specifically, the students in the consequences condition were more likely than those in other groups to support placing a limit on tuition increases.[14]

---

of Thought: The Impact of News Frames on Readers' Cognitive Responses," *Communication Research* 24, no. 5 (1997): 481–506, https://www.researchgate.net/publication/247687811_Switching_Trains_of_ThoughtThe_Impact_of_News_Frames_on_Readers'_Cognitive_Responses.

14. Price, Tewskbury, and Powers, "Switching Trains of Thought," 481–506, https://www.researchgate.net/publication/247687811_Switching_Trains_of_ThoughtThe_Impact_of_News_Frames_on_Readers'_Cognitive_Responses.

THE ORGANIZATION OF THE BOOK

As described, this book is designed to provide information and spark discussion about CSA, allowing readers to take an active role in policy discussions. The first section focuses on knowledge about CSA. We start with an examination of common beliefs and attitudes. What do people know about CSA and how do they interpret that knowledge? It turns out that social forces, including the media and social movements, are important players in shaping perceptions. Sociologists sometimes call this process the "social construction of knowledge," to highlight that our understanding of issues like CSA is not developed in isolation. Instead, people rely on others for information, and their framing of that information influences how it is interpreted. Chapter 1 of this book explores how knowledge about CSA has been constructed across time in the United States. While I discuss particular historical moments when public attention has been focused on CSA, I also talk about general trends in public and media discourse.

The next two chapters present a summary of what research has revealed about CSA. Researchers from a wide variety of fields have worked to understand the how, what, who, where, and why of CSA. It turns out that some of their findings match common beliefs, but others do not. Chapter 2 focuses on how researchers define CSA and their estimates of its prevalence. It also summarizes what the general public knows about the harms that abuse causes to victims, their families, and their communities. Chapter 3 looks at the research findings about the characteristics of victims and offenders and describes what is known about the causes of CSA.

In the second section of the book, I look at CSA prevention, starting with the approach of the criminal justice system. This system is primarily focused on preventing identified offenders from abusing children anymore. Chapter 4 considers how the criminal justice system responds in the wake of an CSA allegation. How are cases investigated, prosecuted, and sentenced? Chapter 5 considers legal measures applied to known offenders who live in the community. These include sex-offender registries, restrictions on housing, and civil confinement. Both chapters take a deep dive into the research that evaluates whether or not particular criminal justice measures work to prevent CSA. They also ask if there have been unintended consequences associated with those measures.

The criminal justice system is not the only group working on CSA prevention. Child-serving organizations—such as day-care centers, schools, nonprofits, and churches—have also put measures in place to reduce CSA. Unlike the criminal justice system, however, these organizations' primary goal is to stop abuse before it starts. Chapter 6 looks at how organizations have tried to achieve this through mandatory background checks, employee/volunteer screening tests, and rules about how adults should interact with children. Chapter 7 focuses on the prevention training organizations provide, both for adults (like the session I attended through the Catholic Church) and for children. What is learned in these programs? Are they an effective way to prevent abuse?

The final chapter of the book pulls together the contents of the earlier chapters to look to the future. Given what is known about CSA, what is the best course of action for the legal system, organizations, and families? The chapter is organized into approaches that work, those that don't, and those that hold promise. While I have included a number of suggestions for large-scale change, I also present ideas for individuals who want to get involved in prevention efforts.

WHY ARE THERE SO MANY FOOTNOTES AND LINKS IN THIS BOOK?

One of the goals of this book is to be transparent about the sources of the information I use when I draw conclusions. I also want to help readers obtain original sources whenever possible. For this reason, I have put a clickable link in the footnotes when a referenced source is freely available to the public. Unfortunately, much academic research is held behind paywalls and is not free unless one has a university affiliation. I do not provide links for these paywall sources. If you are interested in finding one of the unlinked sources, you should first try Google Scholar (https://scholar.google.com/). Many sources become publicly accessible after a set period of time, and it is always worth checking to see if the one you are looking for has become available recently. The local public library is another way to access sources; many give their patrons access to academic databases. It should also be noted that sources sometime move or become unavailable to the public so not all the links I provide may work.

I conclude each chapter with a few suggestions for further reading. Sometimes I have referenced the books in the chapter, but other times they are about topics that are not covered. For example, human trafficking is related to CSA, but it is not a focus in the text. Instead, I have suggested reading for people who would like to learn more. Most of the recommended books will be available through the public library. Used and new copies are also for sale through major online booksellers.

A NOTE TO SURVIVORS OF CHILD SEXUAL ABUSE

Many people who pick up this book will have a deep understanding of the pain caused by CSA because they have experienced it themselves or they love someone who has been abused. Over the course of this project, I had the opportunity to talk with a lot of survivors. With their help, I learned how devastating such an experience can be, and I also learned how, with tremendous strength and bravery, many people who have experienced CSA refuse to let it define them.

If reading this book causes you to become uncomfortable, upset, or depressed, please reach out for help. Here are links to a couple of resources:

1. RAINN has a website with a lot of resources at https://www.rainn.org/about-rainn, or you can call 800-656-HOPE (4673) to be routed to your local sexual assault helpline.
2. Stop It Now! has a webpage with links to all sorts of support services. Some are for specialized groups (like men who were abused as children or partners of people who were abused as children): https://www.stopitnow.org/help-guidance.

There are also some outstanding books about healing from CSA. I list just a couple here:

1. Mike Lew, *Victims No Longer: The Classic Guide for Men Recovering from Sexual Child Abuse* (New York: Harper Perennial, 2004).
2. Wendy Maltz, *The Sexual Healing Journey: A Guide for Survivors of Sexual Abuse* (New York: William Morrow Paperbacks, 2012).

A NOTE TO ANYONE WHO HAS COMMITTED OR IS THINKING ABOUT COMMITTING CHILD SEXUAL ABUSE

Our society does not make it easy for people to seek help if they have sexual impulses toward children, but it can be done. If you are engaging in, or thinking about engaging in, sexual contact with a child, you can contact a therapist in your area who specializes in sexual issues. You need to know that disclosure laws vary by state and, in many areas, therapists are required to report past or planned CSA to authorities. It may be possible, however, to enter treatment for sexual thoughts about children without revealing any past or planned activity. There is a website that summarizes state laws on mandatory reporting. You can find it here: https://www.childwelfare.gov/topics/systemwide/laws-policies/state/. Further, the American Psychological Association provides a listing of therapists by specialty and location at https://locator.apa.org/.

There are a number of organizations that provide support for people struggling with attraction to children. Try starting with the webpage of the Blue Rock Institute at http://www.bluerockinsti tute.com/. It has lots of information and resources. There is also a confidential helpline available through Stop It Now! at https:// www.stopitnow.org/help-guidance/help-services. The helpline staff are able to address a wide range of issues that face victims, but they are also equipped to help people with sexual feelings for children. Parents United International is an organization that offers support groups for members of families (including people who have offended against their own children). Their website can be found at http://parents_united.tripod.com/Chapters/PUI.htm.

SECTION ONE

KNOWLEDGE

CHAPTER ONE

THE SOCIAL CONTEXT OF CHILD SEXUAL ABUSE

Reading a book to learn more about child sexual abuse and its prevention is commendable. Child sexual abuse (CSA) is a very emotional and upsetting topic, and parts of this book may be hard to read. I suspect, however, that you have chosen to read this because you know that CSA has a profound impact on individuals, families, and society at large. Perhaps you are a teacher, parent, or coach who wants to protect the kids in your care. Or maybe you are working in criminal justice and want to get a better understanding of CSA and its prevention. Or it's possible that you just want to be an informed citizen who can contribute to the debate about the best policy responses to CSA. Regardless of your purpose, the book is designed to provide readers with a wide range of current information from fields that include psychology, sociology, communications, criminology, and political science. When done reading, you should have a good sense of why and how CSA occurs, what its costs are, and which prevention strategies work.

While this book draws on research from many disciplines, its approach is primarily sociological. Sociology is a critical perspective, questioning commonly held assumptions about the way the world works. In broad terms, sociologists are interested in how the organization of society impacts individual lives. One example is how people choose careers. Does one simply choose an area that matches their talent, or do race and gender have an impact? Do friends and family make a difference? Sociologists aren't suggesting that people are merely robots—certainly choices are made among various career options—and people can work toward changing social structures as well. I might, for example, join a social movement looking to make more occupations open to women. The point is that sociologists ask about how individual choices, actions, and beliefs are affected by interactions with others and by the social context in which one lives.

What does it mean to approach the topic of CSA sociologically? First, a sociological perspective calls on us to interrogate our own assumptions. This is because, as discussed in the preface, knowledge about CSA is socially constructed. In other words, the interactions had with other people—like teachers, family members, or the media—guide people toward particular beliefs. This does not necessarily mean those beliefs are wrong, but sociology demands deep investigation before accepting beliefs as truth. Second, a sociological perspective towards CSA focuses on trends rather than individual cases. The advantage to this approach is that it provides a big-picture view of CSA. What does a typical case look like? Are particular categories of children more at risk? Is CSA increasing or decreasing? Third, a sociological perspective considers how the organization of society plays a role in when, why, and how CSA occurs. Psychological explanations are certainly important, and I will cover them at some length, but they tell only one part of the story. A sociological perspective suggests that all individual action is affected by social factors.

Let's start by taking a short quiz:

> Answer the following questions on the following scale:
>
> 1=I am *very sure* this is **false.**
>
> 2=I *am somewhat sure* this is **false**
>
> 3=Neutral or don't know
>
> 4=I am *somewhat sure* this is **true**
>
> 5=I am *very sure* this is **true**
>
> 1. Most sex offenders were sexually abused as children. (pg. 90)
> 2. Children who change their mind about the abuse probably lied at first (pg. 84)
> 3. Boys are less likely than girls to be emotionally traumatized by the experience of abuse. (pg. 71)
> 4. Most sexual abusers are homosexual. (pg. 44)
> 5. Child sexual abuse takes place mainly in poor families. (pg. 78)
> 6. Adolescents and even preadolescents are sometimes sex offenders. (pg. 87)
> 7. Penalties should be increased for sex offenders. (pg. 133)

The questions in the quiz are derived from scales that measure CSA knowledge and attitudes.[1] The answers are in later chapters, although clicking the linked questions will also provide them. I assume that readers already know something—maybe a lot—about CSA. Where did that knowledge come from? Research suggests that the primary source of CSA information for most is

---

1. Craig Windham and Patricia Hudsen, *Study of Past Participants in the Protecting God's Children Program* (Tulsa, OK: Virtus Program, 2010); Martine Hébert, Francine Lavoie, and Nathalie Parent, "An Assessment of Outcomes Following Parents' Participation in a Child Abuse Prevention Program," *Violence and Victims* 17, no. 3 (2002): 355–72; Steven J Collings, "Development, Reliability, and Validity for the Child Sexual Abuse Myth Scale," *Journal of Interpersonal Violence* 12, no. 5 (1997): 665–74.

the internet, magazines, newspapers, and other media outlets.[2] As discussed in chapter 7, however, an increasing number of people also get information from prevention training programs provided by schools, churches, and other organizations. On an even larger scale, various social movements work to bring attention to abuse. Of course, some of the most important knowledge about CSA comes through interactions with other people. Sometimes people might talk about the topic directly, but silence about abuse also carries meaning. This chapter covers all of these intertwined social forces and looks at how they have come to define what many know and believe about CSA. As you read, you may recognize some of the forces that drive your own responses.

WAVES OF ATTENTION TO CHILD SEXUAL ABUSE

For most of US history, people simply didn't talk about child abuse. This was partly because children were considered the property of their parents. This gave parents a wide berth to do as they pleased with them. Starting in the late 1800s, however, certain acts, like extreme beating, became socially unacceptable. The idea that abuse could and did occur within families began to grow. Mary Ellen McCormick was a young girl in New York City who was repeatedly beaten by her foster mother. The abuse was so severe, a church worker sought to remove her from her home. When social work organizations refused to intervene, her case was presented to the Society for the Protection of Animals. Ultimately, Mary Ellen was moved out of her home and her case became the inspiration for the founding of the first Society for the Protection of Children in 1874.[3]

---

2. Stacey Katz-Schiavone, Jill S. Levenson, and Alissa R. Ackerman, "Myths and Facts about Sexual Violence: Public Perceptions and Implications for Prevention," *Journal of Criminal Justice and Popular Culture* 15, no. 3 (2008): 291–311, https://www.researchgate.net/profile/Jill_Levenson/publication/267256472_Myths_and_Facts_About_Sexual_Violence_Public_Perceptions_and_Implications_for_Prevention/links/5592face08ae5af2b0eb6774.pdf.

3. Stephen J. Pfohl, "The 'Discovery' of Child Abuse," *Social Problems* 24, no. 3 (1977): 310–23.

As part of the growing awareness of child welfare, social workers began to recognize cases of child sexual abuse and brought them to the attention of the legal system and the media. Interestingly, the temperance movement also pushed for the recognition of incest and other types of abuse as a social problem. Temperance advocates believed that if men stopped drinking, they would abuse women and children less.[4] In reality, however, the attention that reformers paid to incest paled in comparison to their attention to prostitution. Prostitution was understood to be the way that most men and, subsequently, their wives got sexually transmitted diseases. Although there were also many cases of gonorrhea in young girls, most medical professionals declared them to be a result of nonsexual transmission (toilet seats and soiled bedsheets, for example). Incest was defined as an aberration, most frequently found among the lower classes, and many reformers simply refused to acknowledge that it could be the cause of so much sexually transmitted disease.[5] Interest in incest waned even further after 1920 as the problem was largely reframed as one of weak mothers and sexually provocative daughters. Incest continued to be portrayed as rare, and girls and women who accused their family members were seen as liars.[6]

A second period of attention to incest, also sparked by social activism, began in the 1970s. The nascent women's liberation movement identified the abuse of women and children as a key issue. Along with domestic violence and marital rape, activists called attention to incest. In "consciousness raising groups,"

4. Linda Gordon, "The Politics of Child Sexual Abuse: Notes from American History," *Feminist Review* 28 (1988): 56–64, https://www.jstor.org/stable/1394894?seq=1.

5. Lynn Sacco, *Unspeakable: Father-Daughter Incest in American History* (Baltimore, MD: Johns Hopkins University Press, 2009).

6. Rachel Devlin, "'Acting Out the Oedipal Wish': Father-Daughter Incest and the Sexuality of Adolescent Girls in the United States, 1941–1965," *Journal of Social History* 38, no. 3 (2005): 609–33, https://muse.jhu.edu/article/180434/pdf?casa_token=gbntdQsUM5QAAAAA:WbLkoAPvcEv6fUJoNgllKxc4sDDF51ySA-dpKevfcoPVH_ikQ2OVfkxrtittoOHPfOgwWKOfIA.

women got together and talked about their childhood experiences. For many, it was the first time they were able to put words to what had happened to them. The media paid attention and began to take sexual violence much more seriously. Reporters relied less on sexist myths to explain abuse than they had in the past. This wave of media attention reached a group of people who had no access to other sources of information about CSA.[7] Most of the media coverage during this period framed incest as an important problem that society had denied for too long.[8]

Public interest in incest continued into the 1980s with the publication of a number of popular novels. These included *Flowers in the Attic* (1979), *The Hotel New Hampshire* (1981), and *The Color Purple* (1983). All three were later adapted into movies. There were also made-for-TV movies such as *Something about Amelia* (1984), which focused on a middle-class thirteen-year-old girl who was being sexually abused by her father. Over time, however, coverage of incest gradually decreased as the public's attention was drawn to other issues.[9] For example, events at the McMartin preschool located in Manhattan Beach, California, began to dominate the headlines. In September 1983, a mother of a two-year-old boy told the police that she believed her son was being abused by his teacher Raymond Buckey. The police responded by sending a letter to all school parents detailing the accusations of sexual abuse and requesting leads to other victims. This letter caused many panicked parents to talk to their children and call the police to report suspicions of abuse.

---

7. Jenny Kitzinger, "Media Coverage of Sexual Violence against Women and Children," in *Women and Media: International Perspectives*, ed. Karen Ross and Carolyn M. Byerly (Hoboken, NJ: Wiley-Blackwell, 2004), 13–38.

8. Katherine Beckett, "Culture and the Politics of Signification: The Case of Child Sexual Abuse," *Social Problems* 43, no. 1 (1996): 57–76, https://www.researchgate.net/profile/Katherine_Beckett/publication/249985363_Culture_and_the_Politics_of_Signification_The_Case_of_Child_Sexual_Abuse/links/596fc1a4a6fdccc6c96c1407/Culture-and-the-Politics-of-Signification-The-Case-of-Child-Sexual-Abuse.p.

9. Sacco, *Unspeakable*.

Ultimately, a social worker was hired to interview the children and criminal charges were extended to include Virginia McMartin, who owned the school, as well as five other women who were teachers (charges against the latter five were dropped before the case went to trial).[10]

As the McMartin case progressed, children and parents made new allegations, including animal sacrifice, satanic rituals, orgies, and the use of underground tunnels to abuse children. Today, these accusations may seem bizarre, but they made more sense in the context of the 1980s. The founding of the Church of Satan in San Francisco in 1966 set off a media firestorm, and the public began to believe that satanism posed a real threat to the United States. By the time of the McMartin case, there was a significant antisatanist movement composed of various groups, including fundamentalist Christians and anticult activists. These groups generated media coverage about satanism.[11] Satanism, however, was not the only issue creating cultural anxiety during the 1970s and 1980s. Increasing numbers of mothers were entering the workforce, and critics of this rapid social change stoked fears that day care could result in lasting damage to children.[12] In some ways, the McMartin case represented the convergence of perceived threats to both the traditional family and to Christianity.

In the end, both Buckey and McMartin were exonerated—largely because the jury questioned the tactics that had been used to interview the children (for a description of these tactics, see chapter 3). The closing of the McMartin case, however, did not put an end to fears of satanic activity. Other day-care centers faced

---

10. Edgar W Butler et al., *Anatomy of the McMartin Child Molestation Case* (Lanham, MD: University Press of America, 2001).

11. James T. Richardson, Joel Best, and David Bromley, "Satanism as a Social Problem," in *The Satanism Scare*, ed. Richardson, Best, and Bromley (New York: Routledge, 1991), 3–17.

12. Mary deYoung, "The Devil Goes to Daycare: McMartin and the Making of a Moral Panic," *Journal of American Culture* 20, no. 1 (1997): 19–25, https://blogs.baruch.cuny.edu/eng2150rv/files/2019/03/The-Devil-Goes-to-Daycare.pdf.

allegations, and there were many more rumors about children being kidnapped by satanic cults. National television shows (such as *20/20*) covered the supposed satanic threat, and local papers often reported on rumors of satanic activity. By graphically covering these stories, the media contributed to an air of fear.[13]

During the same period that the McMartin investigation was taking place, public attention was drawn to a second issue involving CSA. Repressed memory was based on the idea that people who suffer extremely traumatic events can unconsciously protect themselves by repressing their memories. Therapists reported that these memories could surface on their own years later or that they could be extracted by a psychologist. One of the first legal tests of this idea came in the widely reported 1990 case of George Franklin Sr., a California man whose daughter accused him of abusing and murdering her friend. While the murder had occurred more than twenty years earlier, the daughter claimed that she had repressed the memory of it. Franklin was convicted on the basis of her testimony and was sentenced to life in prison.[14] Following Franklin's case, many other people came forward, claiming repressed memories of childhood sexual abuse.

One of the primary ways that people came to know about repressed memory was a book called *Courage to Heal* by Ellen Bass and Laura Davis. Published in 1988, the book was intended to help women who had experienced sexual abuse. It strongly validated the idea of repressed memories by saying, "If you are unable to remember any specific instances like the ones mentioned above but still have a feeling that something abusive happened to you, it probably did."[15] The authors encouraged women to delve deeply

---

13. Jeffrey Victor, "Satanic Cult Rumors as Contemporary Legend," *Western Folklore* 49, no. 1 (1990): 51–81.

14. Associated Press, "Memory Issue Prompts Retrial in Murder Case," *New York Times*, November 21, 1995, https://www.nytimes.com/1995/11/21/us/memory-issue-prompts-retrial-in-murder-case.html.

15. Ellen Bass and Laura Davis, The Courage to Heal: A Guide for Women

into their memories, confront their abusers, and take care of their "inner child" by reenacting parts of their childhood. Repressed memories were pushed further into the public spotlight in 1991 when actor Roseanne Barr claimed that she had recovered memories of her parents abusing her as an infant and toddler.

> It is not clear how many people have claimed repressed memory, but a professor at Brown University keeps a list of court cases where it is mentioned. As of this writing, there are over fifty cases. Check it out at https://blogs.brown.edu/recoveredmemory/case-archive/legal-cases/.

Public attention to repressed memory began to slow after several influential psychologists published studies showing that adult memory is malleable, that people actually tend to remember trauma quite clearly, and that infants do not have the capacity to form memories (although seeing photos of an event that took place when someone was an infant can create the sensation of memory).[16] Criticism was leveled against therapists who suggested to clients that they might have repressed memories of abuse. For example, some therapists told clients that there was a high rate of child abuse in society, and that abuse was often linked with the particular mental health symptoms they reported. Because memory is malleable, these adults had the capacity to "remember" events that did not happen.[17]

Survivors of Child Sexual Abuse: Featuring "Honoring the Truth, a Response to the Backlash," 3rd ed., rev. up. (New York: Harper Perennial, 1994).

16. J. Laurence and C. Perry, "Hypnotically Created Memory among Highly Hypnotizable Subjects," *Science* 222, no. 4623 (1983): 523–24; Elizabeth F. Loftus and Edith Greene, "Warning: Even Memory for Faces May Be Contagious," *Law and Human Behavior* 4, no. 4 (1980): 323–34, https://link.springer.com/content/pdf/10.1007/BF01040624.pdf.

17. Shelley M. Park, "False Memory Syndrome: A Feminist Philosophical Approach," *Hypatia* 12, no. 2 (1997): 1–50, https://philpapers.org/archive/SHEFMS.pdf.

Figure 2. Roseanne Barr. "File:Roseanne Barr in 2010.jpg" by Leah Mark is licensed under CC BY-SA 2.0.

Another important force turning the public against the idea of repressed memory was the False Memory Syndrome Foundation (FMSF). This group was formed by family members who felt that they had been falsely accused through therapist-induced repressed memories. They engaged in public-information campaigns and paid for the legal defense of people accused of abuse through recovered memories.[18] Finally, the media began to run articles questioning the reliability of repressed memory. This was a significant turn in the framing of the story, with the accused people being quoted far more often than the people making the claims of abuse. The media began to highlight the emotions of accused parents as a way to illustrate their innocence, while coverage portrayed some of the accusers as "hysterical."[19]

> The False Memory Syndrome Foundation is still in existence. You can check them out at http://www.fmsonline.org/.

Five years after George Franklin was convicted, his sentence was overturned because of the lack of corroborating evidence and because so many doubts had been raised about the reliability of repressed memory. At the same time, many people continue to believe in the idea. In a set of surveys conducted in 2012, researchers found that over 80 percent of undergraduates agreed that "traumatic memories are often repressed." They also looked at the attitudes of PhD-trained therapists and were able to compare the results with survey data collected in 1990. They found that therapists became much more skeptical of repressed memory over the period. At the same time, in 2012, more than 9 percent reported that hypnosis could recover memories "back to birth."[20]

---

18. Richard Beck, *We Believe the Children: A Moral Panic in the 1980s*, 1st ed. (New York: PublicAffairs 2015).

19. Kitzinger, "Media Coverage of Sexual Violence against Women and Children."

20. Lawrence Patihis et al., "Are the 'Memory Wars' Over? A Scientist-Practitioner Gap in Beliefs about Repressed Memory," *Psychological Science* 25, no. 2 (2014): 519–30, https://escholarship.org/uc/item/8do226zh.

The repressed memory issue is complex and still highly controversial. Check out a recent *This American Life* radio broadcast about an adult woman trying to find out why her mother lost custody of her when she was young. The episode involves the work of Elizabeth Loftus. She is a well-known psychologist cited elsewhere in this chapter. The story is in act 2: https://www.thisamericanlife.org/676/heres-looking-at-you-kid.

Sparked by a spate of CSA cases that involved abductions, "stranger danger" emerged as a public concern in the late 1980s and early 1990s. In 1989, five boys were abducted in four separate incidents in Washington State. Two were sexually assaulted and a third was recovered before an assault could take place. Three of the boys were murdered. In one of the cases, the perpetrator had previously served time for sexually assaulting two teenage girls.[21] In 1993, Polly Klaas, a twelve-year-old living in California, was abducted from a slumber party and murdered and, in 1994, seven-year-old Megan Kanka was killed by a sex offender who lived in her New Jersey neighborhood. The fact that these terrible events were heavily reported over just a few years gave the impression of a wave of violence against children.

Heavy media coverage of CSA cases involving strangers, like those above, has been instrumental in forming public opinion and driving legislation to try and prevent it. In chapters 4 and 5, I will discuss the many laws that came out of this period, often pushed forward by activists. Marc Klaas (Polly's father) became a child advocate and appeared on many news stories. He also started a foundation to prevent and solve child abduction cases. It still exists today (check it out at https://klaaskids.org/ if you are interested in the work they do). There were at least three television shows about Polly Klaas's murder (including one on A&E and one on the

---

21. Daniel M. Filler, "Silence and the Racial Dimension of Megan's Law," *Iowa Law Review* 89 (2004): 1535-94, https://papers.ssrn.com/sol3/papers.cfm?abstract_id=648261.

Figure 3. John Walsh has hosted a number of shows about missing children. Most recently he hosted *In Pursuit with John Walsh*. Source: Everett Collection at Shutterstock.

Discovery Channel). Running for four seasons starting in 1995, a show called *Missing Children* reenacted child abductions with the goal of solving them. It is not surprising that, in line with this kind of media coverage, the public has come to overestimate the proportion of assaults on children that are committed by strangers and are violent.[22]

Abuse in organizations is the most recent wave of public attention to CSA. In 1985, a Roman Catholic priest in Louisiana was convicted on several hundred counts of child sexual abuse. The *National Catholic Reporter* (a major Catholic news outlet) subsequently published an article about his case and about child sex abuse in the Church more generally. The public did not seriously focus on the topic, however, until a 2002 *Boston Globe* series revealed widespread abuse of children by priests and seminarians. Vocal groups of victims began to press the Church for accountability (the most visible of these groups—still in existence today—is called the Survivors Network of those Abused by Priests, or SNAP). Since 2002, numerous domestic and international cases of abuse have been revealed. For example, between 1950 and 2002, at least 4,392 priests in the United States were accused of abusing 10,667

---

22. Jill S. Levenson et al., "Public Perceptions about Sex Offenders and Community Protection Policies," *Analyses of Social Issues and Public Policy* 7, no. 1 (2007): 137–61, https://scholar.google.com/scholar?hl=en&as_sdt=0%2C36&q=+Public+Perceptions+about+Sex+Offenders+and+Community+&btnG=; James F. Quinn, Craig J. Forsyth, and Carla Mullen-Quinn, "Societal Reaction to Sex Offenders: A Review of the Origins and Results of the Myths Surrounding Their Crimes and Treatment Amenability," *Deviant Behavior* 25, no. 3 (2004): 215–32, https://www.researchgate.net/publication/233453674_Societal_reaction_to_sex_offenders_A_review_of_the_origins_and_results_of_the_myths_surrounding_their_crimes_and_treatment_amenability; Daniel A. Fuselier, Robert L. Durham, and Sandy K. Wurtele, "The Child Sexual Abuser: Perceptions of College Students and Professionals," *Sexual Abuse: A Journal of Research and Treatment* 14, no. 3 (2002): 271–80, https://scholar.google.com/scholar?hl=en&as_sdt=0%2C36&q=The+Child+Sexual+Abuser%3A+Perceptions+of+College+&btnG=.

minors.[23] Media coverage of Catholic abuse cases hit a high in 2002, and then again in 2010 when there were accusations that then Pope Benedict had covered up cases of abuse when he was a bishop in Germany.[24] In 2018, the Diocese of Pittsburgh released the names of ninety-nine priests who had credible allegations made against them. Many other dioceses have followed suit, generating a great deal of publicity.

The media has covered many other large-scale cases of abuse in organizations. Notably, in 2012, the Boy Scouts of America (BSA) was forced to release the contents of 1,247 confidential files that contained information about CSA accusations against its employees and volunteers. The files, created between 1965 and 1985, showed that the Scouts often did not contact law enforcement and even allowed some accused molesters to continue within the organization.[25] Between 1985 and 1991 (when background checks became widely available), the BSA allowed two hundred and thirty adults with arrests or convictions to work with children.[26] The BSA has been particularly aggressive in its legal defense. In one notorious 2010 case of a repeat offender, the BSA lawyer argued that the parents of victims were at fault for not supervising their

---

23. Karen J. Terry et al., The Causes and Context of Sexual Abuse of Minors by Catholic Priests in the United States, 1950–2010: A Report Presented to the United States Conference of Catholic Bishops by the John Jay College Research Team (Washington, DC: United States Conference of Catholic Bishops Communications, 2011), http://www.bishop-accountability.org/reports/2011_05_18_John_Jay_Causes_and_Context_Report.pdf.

24. Pew Research Center, "The Pope Meets the Press: Media Coverage of the Clergy Abuse Scandal," June 11, 2010, http://www.pewforum.org/2010/06/11/the-pope-meets-the-press-media-coverage-of-the-clergy-abuse-scandal/.

25. Kim Christensen, "Scouts Employ Aggressive Tactics in Abuse Defense," Los Angeles Times, December 24, 2012, http://www.latimes.com/local/california/la-me-scouts-victims-2-story.html.

26. Robert McCoppin, "Boy Scouts to Expand Background Checks to All Adults Chaperoning 3-Day Events," Chicago Tribune, March 1, 2018, https://www.chicagotribune.com/news/breaking/ct-met-boy-scouts-background-checks-training-20180228-story.html.

children properly. In another case prosecuted in 2002, a different lawyer argued that a thirteen-year-old had sex "consensually" with a thirty-year-old leader.[27] In February of 2020, however, the BSA filed for bankruptcy, citing 275 pending lawsuits and fourteen hundred other potential lawsuits.[28]

USA Gymnastics and the US Olympic Committee are other groups that have come under intense scrutiny because they employed Dr. Larry Nassar to care for their athletes. An investigation by the *Indianapolis Star* in 2016 led to hundreds of women and girls coming forward and accusing Nassar of sexual abuse. Ultimately, he was arrested, and over one hundred women and girls gave televised victim-impact statements at his trial, mesmerizing the nation. It became clear that Nassar had been allowed to continue his work with the Olympics and with Michigan State, even though some top officials at both institutions were aware that there were allegations against him.[29]

IMAGES OF THE TYPICAL CHILD SEXUAL ABUSE CASE

Periods of attention to CSA, like those discussed above, are important because they help shape perceptions. But even when CSA is not a "hot topic," it does not disappear from view. What are some of the broader trends in how people talk about and understand CSA?

27. Christensen, "Scouts Employ Aggressive Tactics in Abuse Defense," http://www.latimes.com/local/california/la-me-scouts-victims-2-story.html.

28. Nathan Bomey, Lindsay Schnell, and Cara Kelly, "Boy Scouts Files Chapter 11 Bankruptcy in the Face of Thousands of Child Abuse Allegations," *USA Today*, February 18, 2020, https://www.usatoday.com/in-depth/news/investigations/2020/02/18/boy-scouts-bsa-chapter-11-bankruptcy-sexual-abuse-cases/1301187001/.

29. Christine Hauser and Karen Zraick, "Larry Nassar Sexual Abuse Scandal: Dozens of Officials Have Been Ousted or Charged," *New York Times*, October 22, 2018, https://www.nytimes.com/2018/10/22/sports/larry-nassar-case-scandal.html; Kim Kozlowski, "What MSU Knew: 14 Were Warned of Nassar Abuse," *Detroit News*, 2018, https://www.detroitnews.com/story/tech/2018/01/18/msu-president-told-nassar-complaint-2014/1042071001/.

I will start with messages about what the "typical" CSA case looks like. The media has a powerful role in defining our ideas about what is typical through their selection of stories. An example of this involves crime more generally. We know that crimes are more likely to receive media coverage when the perpetrator is a person of color. In turn, this has caused (or at least reinforced) the public's belief that people of color are the typical criminal.[30]

Perhaps not surprisingly, research finds that the majority of CSA cases never appear in the media.[31] Those cases that do, however, usually exhibit one or more of the following traits: the accused is somebody perceived to be an upstanding citizen, the case is particularly violent or bizarre, there are multiple victims, a celebrity is either accused or victimized, or there is a cover-up.[32] We also know that the media overrepresent cases where the perpetrator is a stranger or an authority figure and they underrepresent incest.[33] The media (and most of us) are drawn to stories where good and evil are clearly defined.[34] Finally, the media often run stories that resonate with viewers' cultural beliefs, fears, and attitudes.[35] This is related to confirmation bias (described in the preface) as people seek out stories that appear to correspond to their preexisting beliefs.

In addition to what the media choose to present, how they present

30. Roger D. Klein and Stacy Naccarato, "Broadcast News Portrayal of Minorities: Accuracy in Reporting," *American Behavioral Scientist* 46, no. 12 (2003): 1611–16.

31. Ross E. Cheit, "What Hysteria? A Systematic Study of Newspaper Coverage of Accused Child Molesters," *Child Abuse & Neglect* 27, no. 6 (2003): 607–23.

32. Cheit, "What Hysteria?"

33. Cheit; Jenny Kitzinger and Paula Skidmore, "Playing Safe: Media Coverage of Child Sexual Abuse Prevention Strategies," *Child Abuse Review* 4 (1995): 47–56, https://scholar.google.com/scholar?hl=en&as_sdt=0,36&q=playing+safe:+Media+coverage+of+child+sexual+abuse+prevention+strategies+kitzinger&btnG=.

34. Gray Cavender, "Media and Crime Policy: A Reconsideration of David Garland's the Culture of Control," *Punishment & Society* 6, no. 3 (2004): 335–48.

35. Beckett, "Culture and the Politics of Signification: The Case of Child Sexual Abuse," https://www.researchgate.net/publication/249985363_Culture_and_the_Politics_of_Signification_The_Case_of_Child_Sexual_Abuse.

that material matters. Most media coverage of CSA is through the lens of a particular case. In other words, they present the story of one crime (or one series of crimes perpetuated by the same person), rarely reporting on the topic of CSA more generally. In the language of media scholars, the coverage is "episodic" rather than "thematic."[36] The box below contains an example of each type of frame.

An Example of Episodic vs. Thematic Framing

Episodic Frame: A story about child sexual abuse that uses an episodic frame would focus on what happened in one individual case. An example can be found in the *New York Times*'s coverage of a 2013 retrial of a 2008 CSA case that involved multiple victims: https://www.nytimes.com/2013/08/14/nyre gion/judge-grants-new-trial-to-man-convicted-of-child-sexu al-abuse.html.

Thematic: A thematic frame would present CSA as a larger issue and looks at trends. An example of this type of frame appears in the *New York Times*'s 2012 coverage of decreasing rates of CSA: https://www.nytimes.com/2012/06/29/us/rate-of-child-sexual-abuse-on-the-decline.html.

Episodic framing is popular because it appeals to our emotions.[37] Most people like to read stories about other people's lives,

---

36. Kitzinger and Skidmore, "Playing Safe," https://scholar.google.com/scholar?hl=en&as_sdt=0,36&q=playing+safe:+Media+coverage+of+child+sexual+abuse+prevention+strategies+kitzinger&btnG=; Jenny Kitzinger, "The Ultimate Neighbor from Hell? Stranger Danger and the Media Framing of Paedophiles," in *Social Policy, the Media and Misrepresentation*, ed. Bob Franklin (New York: Routledge, 1999), 207–21, https://books.google.com/books?hl=en&lr=&id=uWbBNA-orCAC&oi=fnd&pg=PA145&dq=ultimate+neighbor+from+hell+kitzinger&ots=wzhW4dEOl2&sig=FVd9h-K3qQslpPsLu3nM_p3LC_k#v=onepage&q=ultimate%20neighbor%20from%20hell%20kitzinger&f=false.

37. Kimberly Gross, "Framing Persuasive Appeals: Episodic and Thematic

and our hearts go out to children who are victims. The problem, however, is that episodic framing does not give a representative picture of CSA. The public ends up knowing a lot about particular cases but very little about trends. When this is combined with the media's tendency to cover only severe cases and those that involve strangers, this skews the vision of what CSA most often looks like.

IMAGES OF VICTIMS

What images do the word *child* bring to mind? Perhaps you, like many people, think about innocence. Historians have found that people have long made this association.[38] Interestingly, you might also think about victimization. Sociologist Joel Best argues that, since the 1950s, repeated waves of media attention to crimes against children (like those described above) have made victimization a primary lens through which people view children.[39] A good example is local television news. A group of researchers examined the frames that were used in newscasters' coverage of children and found that the most dominant was the "imperiled child."[40] In other words, children appear as victims in television news more than they appear in any other role.

The idea of children as victims is easy to accept because it goes hand-in-glove with images of them as innocent, passive, and unable to protect themselves. These characteristics also make them what some scholars call the *ideal victim*. This term refers to the kind of

Framing, Emotional Response, and Policy Opinion," *Political Psychology* 29, no. 2 (2008): 169–92.

38. Estelle B. Freedman, "'Uncontrolled Desires': The Response to the Sexual Psychopath, 1920–1960," *Journal of American History* 74, no. 1 (1987): 83–106, https://pdfs.semanticscholar.org/4ef2/88e27c4a90b7f069735e193bee17c52809e4.pdf.

39. Joel Best, *Threatened Children: Rhetoric and Concern about Child-Victims* (Chicago: University of Chicago Press, 1990).

40. Franklin D. Gilliam, "A New Dominant Frame: 'The Imperiled Child,'" Frameworks Institute, 2003.

people who receive the most sympathy in the aftermath of a crime. Ideal victims have the following characteristics:[41]

1. They are weak in comparison to the offender.
2. They are not doing anything that could be seen as unordinary or of questionable morality at the time that they are victimized.
3. They bear no blame for the crime committed against them.
4. The person who harms them is clearly bad.

Women and children are particularly likely to be seen as ideal victims because they are assumed to be weak and unlikely to be engaged in immoral activities. This is why, when people are asked what image they associate with the word *victim*, most see a woman or child.[42]

Unfortunately, ideal-victim status is not equally granted to all children. Specifically, children of color are less likely to be seen as innocent victims and therefore are less often featured in media stories about abuse. One study of missing children's cases found that those involving children of color are less likely to receive attention from the media.[43] Ideal victim imagery also focuses on

41. Nils Christie, "The Ideal Victim," in *From Crime Policy to Victim Policy: Reorienting the Justice System*, ed. Ezzat A. Fattah (London: MacMillan, 1990), 17–30.

42. Best, Threatened Children.

43. Clara Simmons and Joshua Woods, "The Overrepresentation of White Missing Children in National Television News," *Communication Research Reports* 32, no. 3 (2015): 239–45; Zach Sommers, "Missing White Woman Syndrome: An Empirical Analysis of Race and Gender Disparities in Online News Coverage of Missing Persons," *Journal of Criminal Law and Criminology* 106, no. 2 (2017): 275–314, https://scholarlycommons.law.northwestern.edu/cgi/viewcontent. cgi?referer=https://scholar.google.com/scholar?hl=en&as_sdt=0,36&q=Missing+white+woman+syndrome&httpsredir=1&article=7586&context=jclc; Seong-Jae Min and John C. Feaster, "Missing Children in National News Coverage: Racial and Gender Representations of Missing Children Cases," *Communication Research Reports* 27, no. 3 (2010): 207–16, https://www. researchgate.net/profile/Seong_Jae_Min/publication/233010024_Missing_Children_in_National_News_Coverage_Racial_and_Gender_Representations_of_Missing_Children_Cases/links/5a25bec9a6fdcc8e866b9d5b/ Missing-Children-in-National-News-Coverage-Racia.

girls, hiding the reality that boys are victims too. Finally, envisioning ideal victims as innocent can overlook particular children. For example, the public tends to be less sympathetic to CSA victims who have engaged in other sexual activities or who seem to have a lot of sexual knowledge.[44]

IMAGES OF OFFENDERS

What are common images of offenders? In general, the media depicts them as evil and unlike "normal" people. Newspapers often run photos of offenders smirking. Terms like *animals* or *beasts* are used to describe them. The *pedophile* label also serves to separate people who sexually abuse children from other humans—and even from people who abuse adults.[45] One researcher describes media depictions of offenders as portraying "compulsive recidivist(s) whose behavior often escalates to lethal violent crime."[46]

---

44. Shafiqul Islam, "Ideal Victims of Sexualized Violence: Why Is It Always Female?," *European Journal of Research in Social Sciences* 4, no. 8 (2016): 82–92, https://www.researchgate.net/profile/Shafiqul_Islam26/publication/321267260_Ideal_Victims'_of_Sexualized_Violence_Why_is_it_always_Female_European_Journal_of_Research_in_Social_Sciences/links/5a17b1aba6fdcc5oade61a08/Ideal-Victims-of-Sexualized-Violence-W.

45. This paragraph has drawn from the following: Kitzinger and Skidmore, "Playing Safe," https://scholar.google.com/scholar?hl=en&as_sdt=0,36&q=playing+safe:+Media+coverage+of+child+sexual+abuse+prevention+strategies+kitzinger&btnG=; Kitzinger, "The Ultimate Neighbor from Hell?" https://books.google.com/books?hl=en&lr=&id=uWbBNA-orCAC&oi=fnd&pg=PA145&dq=ultimate+neighbor+from+hell+kitzinger&ots=wzhW4dEOl2&sig=FVd9h-K3qQslpPsLu3nM_p3LC_k#v=onepage&q=ultimate%20neighbor%20from%20hell%20kitzinger&f=false; Kitzinger, "Media Coverage of Sexual Violence against Women and Children"; Islam, "Ideal Victims of Sexualized Violence," https://www.researchgate.net/profile/Shafiqul_Islam26/publication/321267260_Ideal_Victims'_of_Sexualized_Violence_Why_is_it_always_Female_European_Journal_of_Research_in_Social_Sciences/links/5a17b1aba6fdcc5oade61a08/Ideal-Victims-of-Sexualized-Violence-W.

46. Lisa L. Sample, *The Social Construction of the Sex Offender* (St. Louis: University of Missouri-St. Louis, 2001).

The public's views about offenders tend to correspond with and be shaped by the media.[47] Thus, while we hold negative attitudes toward all types of criminals, feelings are especially hostile toward child sexual offenders. In one survey, for example, respondents were asked about their levels of fear of sex offenders. They reported the strongest fear of those who offend against children.[48] Mona Lynch's analysis of congressional debate about four proposed CSA prevention bills bears out these highly negative feelings. The politicians revealed feelings of disgust toward sex offenders, portraying them as contaminated and polluting.[49] Even other criminals view CSA offenders as different and more deviant.[50] This is why people who are convicted for CSA are routinely beaten up and harassed in prison.

It turns out that how we view offenders is linked to our explanations for why they abuse children. Psychologists call these explanations for behavior "attributions," and they distinguish between those that are external and internal. As the name implies, external attributions locate the reason for behavior somewhere outside the individual. For example, one might say that an offender abuses because he was beaten as a child. An internal attribution identifies some personality or other individual trait as responsible ("He's an evil person"). Interestingly, across many situations, people tend to use external attribution for

47. Katz-Schiavone, Levenson, and Ackerman, "Myths and Facts about Sexual Violence."

48. Poco D. Kernsmith, Sarah W. Craun, and Jonathan Foster, "Public Attitudes toward Sexual Offenders and Sex Offender Registration," *Journal of Child Sexual Abuse* 18, no. 3 (2009): 290–301.

49. Mona Lynch, "Pedophiles and Cyber-Predators as Contaminating Forces: The Language of Disgust, Pollution, and Boundary Invasions in Federal Debates on Sex Offender Legislation," *Law & Social Inquiry* 27, no. 3 (2002): 529–57.

50. James F. Quinn, Craig J. Forsyth, and Carla Mullen-Quinn, "Societal Reaction to Sex Offenders: A Review of the Origins and Results of the Myths Surrounding Their Crimes and Treatment Amenability," *Deviant Behavior* 25, no. 3 (2004): 215–32, https://www.researchgate.net/publication/233453674_Socie tal_reaction_to_sex_offenders_A_review_of_the_origins_and_results_of_the_ myths_surrounding_their_crimes_and_treatment_amenability.

their own actions and internal attributions for others. This is called the fundamental attribution error. For example, if a stranger is rude to us in a store, we are likely to think that they are a mean person. When we say something rude to someone else, however, we settle on external factors as the cause. We might think about how our car just broke down or how we lost our job.

> An interesting video about the fundamental attribution error can be found at https://www.khanacademy.org/test-prep/ mcat/individuals-and-society/perception-prejudice-and-bias/v/ attribution-theory-attribution-error-and-culture.

What are the most common attributions for CSA? One study found that there are four main categories—three internal and one external. In the first internal attribution, offenders are seen as having a particular sexual orientation (pedophilia) that makes them attracted to children. The second internal attribution sees CSA as caused by mental illness. In the third attribution, offenders are portrayed as making a choice to harm kids. The last attribution—and the only one that is external—assumes that offenders abuse children because of their own prior victimization.[51] In fact, this "cycle of abuse" explanation is so popular, it leads the public to overestimate the percentage of offenders who were victims.[52]

While pedophilia, mental illness, choice, and the cycle of violence are the most common attributions for CSA, they are not the

---

51. Kelly Richards, "Born This Way? A Qualitative Examination of Public Perceptions of the Causes of Pedophilia and Sexual Offending against Children," *Deviant Behavior* 39, no. 7 (2018): 835–51.

52. Timothy Fortney et al., "Myths and Facts about Sexual Offenders: Implications for Treatment and Public Policy," *Sexual Offender Treatment* 2, no. 1 (2007): 18, https://www.researchgate.net/profile/Jill_Levenson/publication/267256472_ Myths_and_Facts_About_Sexual_Violence_Public_Perceptions_and_Implica tions_for_Prevention/links/55af992308ae11d310384076.pdf; Katz-Schiavone, Levenson, and Ackerman, "Myths and Facts about Sexual Violence."

only ones present in public discourse. Emerging from some segments of the feminist movement in the 1970s, gender oppression is one important alternate explanation.[53] This view places CSA into the same category as other forms of violence against women and children, identifying men's disproportionate power and privilege in society as the cause.[54] The structure of the family, with the male head of household, leads men to feel entitled to sex and, in turn, their very sexuality comes to be defined by the ability to dominate less powerful others like women and children.[55] Obviously this attribution is external since it sees the cause of CSA as embedded in the very structure of society. Although it has not achieved much mainstream success, the gender attribution still appears today, particularly as an explanation for why the majority of CSA is committed by men against girls.[56]

Before leaving the topic of attribution and CSA, it is important to mention a persistent myth that links CSA with homosexuality. While research has thoroughly debunked it,[57] the myth gained traction in 1977, when the Miami city council passed an ordinance that prohibited discrimination in housing, employment, and public accommodation on the basis of sexual orientation. This might have attracted little attention except that a minister at a local church preached about the bill's passage. Anita Bryant (a popular actor and singer and the spokesperson for Florida orange juice) attended church that day and was very disturbed by what

53. Beckett, "Culture and the Politics of Signification," https://www.researchgate.net/profile/Katherine_Beckett/publication/249985363_Culture_and_the_Politics_of_Signification_The_Case_of_Child_Sexual_Abuse/links/596fc1a4a6fdccc6c96c1407/Culture-and-the-Politics-of-Signification-The-Case-of-Child-Sexual-Abuse.p.

54. Kitzinger, "Media Coverage of Sexual Violence against Women and Children."

55. Vikki Bell, *Interrogating Incest: Feminism, Foucault, and the Law* (London and New York: Routledge, 1993).

56. Anne Cossins, *Masculinities, Sexualities, and Child Sexual Abuse* (The Hague and Boston: Kluwer Law International, 2000).

57. For a good summary of the research, see Gregory Herek, "Facts About Homosexuality and Child Molestation," University of California, Davis, 2013, https://psychology.ucdavis.edu/rainbow/html/facts_molestation.html.

she heard. She felt that the ordinance infringed on her religious rights. She also believed (without any evidence) that homosexuals were disproportionately child molesters and that the bill would put children at risk. She was quoted as saying, "Some of the stories I could tell you of child recruitment and child abuse by homosexuals would turn your stomach."[58]

Bryant's outrage sparked a public campaign that came to be called Save Our Children. The group was ultimately successful in helping to convince voters to rescind the ordinance. Her organization also inspired groups in other areas of the country to overturn similar antidiscrimination legislation. At the same time, her actions had the unanticipated effect of prompting gay people and allies to action. Protestors began appearing at her events, and some places refused to host her shows. Some gay bars even refused to sell orange juice, replacing screwdrivers with an apple juice-based drink named after Bryant. Bryant has been credited with the rare feat of mobilizing both Christian fundamentalists and gay activists. More to the point here, however, Save Our Children helped link homosexuality and child sexual abuse in the public's mind. This was reinforced by the media. Sometimes a story would simply assert that gay people were more likely to abuse children; other times the supposed link was more nuanced. For example, the term *homosexual* was used to describe abuse when the offender was a man and the victim a boy, but the term *heterosexual* was never used to refer to abuse between a man and girl. This implicitly suggested that homosexuality is linked to abuse but that heterosexuality is not.[59]

The Catholic Church has also actively worked to place blame for CSA on gay people. In 2005, the Congregation for Catholic Education, the most important Catholic office prescribing educational standards, published a document with guidelines for admitting men to the priesthood. While the document had been

58. Morton Kondracke, "Anita Bryant Is Mad about Gays," *New Republic* 176, no. 19 (1977): 13–15.

59. Kitzinger, "Media Coverage of Sexual Violence against Women and Children."

in preparation for many years, its publication in the wake of the 2002 Boston priest abuse scandal made it appear to be a response. In it, the Church states that ordination should be denied to any man who exhibits "deep-seated homosexual tendencies." Critics charged that this implicitly placed the blame for CSA on gay men.[60] Additionally, in 2009, the Vatican released a statement that attributed CSA in the Church to homosexual priests.[61] Even today, high-ranking leaders in the Catholic Church continue to blame gay men for the Church's CSA crisis. For example, Bishop Robert Morlino of Madison, Wisconsin, wrote a letter in 2018 saying sexual abuse is "deviant sexual—almost exclusively homosexual—acts by clerics. It is time to admit that there is a homosexual subculture within the hierarchy of the Catholic Church that is wreaking great devastation in the vineyard of the Lord."[62]

MESSAGES ABOUT CHILD SEXUAL ABUSE PREVENTION

The way that we frame CSA sets the stage for our thinking about appropriate solutions. The gender-based frame described above, for example, leads to societal rather than individual solutions. In fact, many feminists argued that the solution was for women to have more power, both inside and outside of the home. But, as described, the gender-based frame has not been widely accepted, perhaps because it threatens traditional family structures. We much more commonly employ what could be called a "bad apples" frame. In this frame, CSA is attributed to individual bad guys:

---

60. See, for example, Mary E. Hunt, "American Catholics: Time for a Stonewall Moment," *Pride Source* (blog), December 22, 2005, https://pridesource.com/article/16979/.

61. Riazat Butt, "Sex Abuse Rife in Other Religions, Says Vatican," *Guardian*, September 28, 2009, https://www.theguardian.com/world/2009/sep/28/sex-abuse-religion-vatican.

62. Robert C. Morlino, "Bishop Robert C. Morlino's Letter to the Faithful Regarding the Ongoing Sexual Abuse Crisis in the Church," *Diocese of Madison Catholic Herald*, August 18, 2018, http://www.madisoncatholicherald.org/bishopsletters/7730-letter-scandal.html.

people who are aberrations from what is normal. The popularity of this kind of frame likely has something to do with the media's episodic approach and our tendency to attribute CSA to internal causes. When individuals are identified as the problem, this leads to solutions directed at those individuals. Thus, it should not be surprising that when the media reports on CSA prevention, the proposed solutions most often involve law enforcement (locking up the bad individuals) or education (helping individual parents or children prevent CSA).[63]

The focus on criminal justice solutions is enhanced by media attention to particular aspects of CSA. For example, most stories are about the crimes and the subsequent legal developments— with a particular emphasis on pretrial events (like arrest, bail, and indictment). This draws attention to the criminal justice process and away from alternatives. Interestingly, sentencing receives relatively little attention, although particularly long sentences are more likely to be covered.[64] This may be because the media rely heavily on government sources when choosing what to report (as opposed to asking advocacy groups, family members, or victims).[65] Prosecutors and the attorney general are elected positions, and incumbents may want to publicize long sentences to appear to be "tough on crime" to the electorate.[66]

Social movements have contributed to the definition of CSA as an issue for criminal justice. The victim's rights movement (VRM) began in the 1970s because of the perception that the few rights victims had in the criminal justice system were being eroded. To support their claims, some early VRM activists pointed to changes

---

63. Pamela Mejia, Andrew Cheyne, and Lori Dorfman, "News Coverage of Child Sexual Abuse and Prevention, 2007–2009," *Journal of Child Sexual Abuse* 21, no. 4 (2012): 470–87.

64. Mejia, Cheyne, and Dorfman, "News Coverage of Child Sexual Abuse and Prevention, 2007–2009."

65. Kitzinger and Skidmore, "Playing Safe," https://scholar.google.com/schol ar?hl=en&as_sdt=0,36&q=playing+safe:+Media+coverage+of+child+sexual+a buse+prevention+strategies+kitzinger&btnG=.

66. Cheit, "What Hysteria?"

during the 1960s that increased due-process rights for defendants. The US Supreme Court, for example, ruled that evidence taken without a search warrant could not be used in court. A group called Americans for Effective Law Enforcement was formed to push back against this and other new rights for criminal defendants. They seemed to see rights as a zero-sum game: that if defendants gained rights, victims lost theirs. In 1968, Richard Nixon ran for president on a "law and order" platform, stating that defendants had too many rights and that victims were going unheard.[67]

There is little question that, historically, victims have had very little control or say in the criminal justice process, especially when it came to sexual assault. They were often not informed about important hearings in their cases, nor were they told when their assailant was released from custody. They were not eligible for any sort of restitution for damages incurred in the crime. Lawyers for the defense routinely asked victims about their past sexual history, treating them as though they, rather than the defendant, were on trial. The odds were so stacked against sexual abuse victims that few were able to win their cases.[68] Outrage over these injustices led to an unusual alliance between some segments of the feminist movement and law-and-order conservatives.[69] The goal was to find criminal justice solutions to abuse issues.

Why haven't noncriminal justice solutions gained more traction with the public? One reason is that a large proportion of the public

---

67. Jill Lepore, "The Rise of the Victims'-Rights Movement," *New Yorker*, May 14, 2018, https://www.newyorker.com/magazine/2018/05/21/the-rise-of-the-victims-rights-movement.

68. Gary D Lafree, Barbara F. Reskin, and Christy A. Visher, "Jurors' Responses to Victims' Behavior and Legal Issues in Sexual Assault Trials," *Social Problems* 32, no. 4 (1985): 389–407, https://www.jstor.org/stable/pdf/800760.pdf?casa_token=kP_M5Z8oyfoAAAAA:MilCeZR1KvJK1Ay921l4IFpCvlFCMYZqM-3tl qUie9ULFBEnM64Gtlcv4y4EQc1w5Wrbjaa8SfY_YSLrqoBKwpttsjcAzGWctT wB5eEOo7N48byTvTl.

69. Lepore, "The Rise of the Victims'-Rights Movement," https://www.newyorker.com/magazine/2018/05/21/the-rise-of-the-victims-rights-movement.

believes that rehabilitation is ineffective.[70] It turns out that this belief has a long history. One of the first studies to look at the efficacy of treatment programs in reducing recidivism was conducted by Robert Martinson. The article that resulted from his study was published in 1974 and was called "What Works: Questions and Answers about Prison Reform."[71] It explored whether or not the rehabilitative programming provided in prison was effective at reducing recidivism. Importantly, the study looked at recidivism rates for people convicted for all types of crime, not just CSA. Martinson and his colleagues did not conduct any program evaluations themselves, but instead reviewed 231 published studies that had been conducted around the world between 1945 and 1967. All of these studies evaluated various types of rehabilitative prison programming (like educational programs, vocational training, and therapy).

Martinson's review led him to conclude that rehabilitative programs are not effective in reducing recidivism. At the same time, however, he strongly cautioned that the methods of the studies he used to draw this conclusion were weak. He also pointed out that many of the rehabilitative programs were underfunded and not implemented properly. In other words, it might have been the delivery of the program that was the problem, not the program itself. Finally, Martinson pointed out that incarcerated people live in a dangerous and isolating environment, raising the risk of long-term mental-health issues. Perhaps the programs were helpful but simply not strong enough to overcome the negative impact of having been in prison.

While the Martinson article was careful about drawing strong conclusions about the efficacy of prison programming, the public

---

70. Katz-Schiavone, Levenson, and Ackerman, "Myths and Facts about Sexual Violence," https://www.researchgate.net/profile/Jill_Levenson/publica tion/267256472_Myths_and_Facts_About_Sexual_Violence_Public_Percep tions_and_Implications_for_Prevention/links/5592face08ae5af2b0eb6774.pdf.

71. Robert Martinson, "What Works? Questions and Answers about Prison Reform," *The Public Interest* 44 (Spring 1974): 22–54, https://www.nationalaffairs.com/ public_interest/detail/what-works-questions-and-answers-about-prison-reform.

did not receive that message. The study was widely described in the popular press as proof that rehabilitation does not work. Its findings came to be summarized by "nothing works," a play on its title. It was an important factor leading the public to lose faith in society's ability to rehabilitate.

In the years following the publication of "What Works," a number of well-designed studies showed that rehabilitation can be effective in reducing recidivism, but few of those studies received public attention. In 1989, however, researchers published another review of previous studies that appeared to support Martinson's findings.[72] It included forty-two studies of male sex offenders. Only some of the studies, however, focused on the effects of treatment. Like Martinson, the authors were extremely critical of the studies that they reviewed. They noted significant methodological problems and a lack of comparability due to the use of different populations, time periods, and definitions. At least in part because of these problems, the researchers were not able to conclude that clinical treatment is effective—although they could not conclude that it was ineffective either. Once again, the media did not provide the public with the details of the findings, instead choosing to simply report that treatment does not work.[73] The study was so influential, Senator Orrin Hatch used it to argue in favor of the Lifetime Sentences for Sex Offenders Act of 2003. Of course, Hatch did not mention the methodological flaws or limitations of the study but simply cited it to show that rehabilitation does not work.

---

72. Lita Furby, Mark R Weinrott, and Lyn Blackshaw, "Sex Offender Recidivism: A Review," *Psychological Bulletin* 105, no. 1 (1989): 3–30, https://pdfs.semanticscholar.org/d6b8/b92a9cb322ee664f5148fe3cfc0030fa840f.pdf.

73. Quinn, Forsyth, and Mullen-Quinn, "Societal Reaction to Sex Offenders," 2004, https://www.researchgate.net/publication/233453674_Societal_reaction_to_sex_offenders_A_review_of_the_origins_and_results_of_the_myths_surrounding_their_crimes_and_treatment_amenability.

CONCLUSION

This chapter has examined how knowledge and attitudes about CSA emerge in a social context. The media is clearly important, although its attention tends to come in waves after a tragedy or in response to a social movement. Most often, media coverage is episodic and is focused on extreme cases involving white victims. Frames used tend to emphasize individualistic explanations for CSA, ignoring possible social causes (like the lack of treatment options).

Media coverage about CSA runs in parallel to public opinion, both reflecting it and helping to create it. The public tends to be very sympathetic toward child victims, at least those who fit the ideal-victim model. Offenders are viewed as monsters, even though many people attribute their actions to previous victimization. Some social movements have had success in promoting particular frames and policy solutions. The victim rights movement, for example, has been successful in emphasizing CSA as a criminal justice issue.

Now, returning to the quiz at the beginning of the chapter: Can you remember where you learned the information you used to answer the questions? Are your views generally congruent with public opinion? If not, why might that be? The next two chapters will give you an opportunity to compare your knowledge with the findings from a variety of research studies. You will see that some popular beliefs about CSA are borne out by the research, while others are not. These discrepancies, more often than not, are a result of the social processes outlined in this chapter.

FURTHER READING

Cheit, Ross E. *The Witch-Hunt Narrative: Politics, Psychology, and the Sexual Abuse of Children*. Oxford: Oxford University Press, 2016.

Kara, Siddarth. *Sex Trafficking: Inside the Business of Modern Slavery*. New York: Columbia University Press, 2017.

Kitzinger, Jenny. *Framing Abuse: Media Influence and Public Understanding of Sexual Violence Against Children*. London: Pluto Press, 2004.

Prendergrast, Mark. *The Repressed Memory Epidemic: How it Happened and What We Need to Learn from It*. New York: Springer, 2017.

Whittier, Nancy. *The Politics of Child Sexual Abuse: Emotion, Social Movements, and the State*. Oxford: Oxford University Press, 2009.

CHAPTER TWO

CHILD SEXUAL ABUSE DEFINITION, PREVALENCE, AND HARM

Prior to the 1970s, not much was known about child sexual abuse (CSA). It was seen as a taboo topic and virtually no research had been conducted.[1] In 1969, however, Vincent de Francis, director of the children's division of the Humane Association, published an influential study of two hundred and fifty cases of children who had been sexually abused in New York City.[2] He found that the majority suffered emotional damage as a result of the abuse. The data did not allow de Francis to estimate the prevalence of CSA, but he believed that rates were very high. His work sparked others to study the topic. In this chapter, I will talk about how these

---

1. John E. B. Myers, "A Short History of Child Protection in America," *Family Law Quarterly* 42, no. 3 (2008): 449–65, https://www.jstor.org/stable/25740668?read-now=1&refreqid=excelsior%3A58cod8880331e786dce7bad43e2bd130&seq=14#page_scan_tab_contents.

2. Vincent de Francis, *Protecting the Child Victim of Sex Crimes Committed by Adults: Final Report* (Denver, CO: American Humane Association, Children's Division, 1969).

researchers define CSA and what they estimate its prevalence to be. I also cover what has been learned about the effects of abuse on victims and on society.

It turns out that CSA is difficult to study, but research methods have become increasingly sophisticated over time. It's important to recognize, however, that research is similar to media coverage in that it is not conducted in a vacuum. The topics that researchers choose, the results that are published, and the findings that are ultimately publicized are the product of social forces. For example, grant agencies shape knowledge when they decide how to allocate money. Although academic journals use a blind peer review process, editors have considerable power to decide which studies go to review and which are ultimately published. Because grants and publications are what count for advancement in an academic career, researchers are incentivized to choose popular topics and to avoid those that might be highly controversial.[3]

Another way that social factors impact research is through limiting access to it. As discussed in the preface, most journals do not make their articles available to the public for free. While more open-access journals are appearing, the vast majority of academic research is housed behind paywalls (where articles can cost as much as fifty dollars each). Even people who are lucky enough to have free access to an academic database, however, may be put off by the academic jargon in articles. Even I, who have been an academic for over twenty years, am sometimes confused by the jargon and statistics. As a result of these kinds of barriers, most people find out about research from the media or from interest groups. This means that we only learn about the research these groups deem important, and our knowledge is shaped by their interpretation and framing of the studies.

---

3. Joseph R. Gusfield, "Constructing the Ownership of Social Problems: Fun and Profit in the Welfare State," *Social Problems* 36, no. 5 (1989): 431–41, https://www.jstor.org/stable/3096810?read-now=1&refreqid=excelsior:4ccf530163bf fa18d2820dea7c839161&seq=11#page_scan_tab_contents.

This chapter and the next present a lot of information about what researchers have learned about CSA, and along the way, I provide some social context for their studies and a discussion of the methodological difficulties they have faced. I'll start with what seems like a basic (and perhaps even obvious) question about CSA and see what the researchers have to say about it.

WHAT IS CHILD SEXUAL ABUSE?

In 1964, the US Supreme Court heard a case involving a movie theater in Ohio. Its owner had been convicted and fined for showing an "obscene" movie called *The Lovers* (or *Les Amants* in the original French). A number of lower courts upheld the initial ruling, but the Supreme Court overturned them, deciding that the film was not obscene. Judge Potter Stewart explained his opinion by saying, "I know it [obscenity] when I see it and the motion picture in this case is not that."[4] I suspect that most people feel the same way about CSA: They don't need to define it because they know it when they see it.

While the Judge Stewart test may work fairly well in most situations, researchers live by a higher standard. This is because a failure to define concepts makes it impossible to apply their findings in the real world. If, for example, a researcher says that offenders tend to commit less abuse as they age, we need to know what kinds of "offenders" were in their study. Was it just people who committed rape? Or did it solely include people who possessed child pornography? Effective policy making requires clear definitions.

Unfortunately, it is difficult to define CSA. Even a seemingly simple term, like *childhood*, can cause debate. Some argue that it should only include people under the age of sixteen, others think a cutoff of seventeen is appropriate, and some argue for eighteen

---

4. Jacobellis v Ohio, 378 US 184 (1964).

as the upper limit.[5] *Abuse* is an even trickier concept. Most would agree that a father bathing his fourteen-year-old daughter is CSA (with a possible exception if the child is severely disabled) but do not see the same father bathing his two-year-old in the same way. Where is the line? Is massaging a child's thigh sexual? What about sleeping in bed with a child? Does the child's age and gender matter? What about a child seeing a parent naked?[6] Another complicated definitional issue is whether to include consensual sexual activity between an adult and an adolescent. For example, deciding if an eighteen-year-old having sex with a seventeen-year-old is CSA.

As with so many policy issues, different constituencies advocate for different definitions of CSA. Therapists often argue for a broad definition that will allow them to offer help in more cases. The legal system is interested in a more concise definition to provide guidance on when to prosecute someone. What about researchers? Studies of CSA conducted in the 1960s and 1970s generally let the respondents define abuse for themselves. Researchers saw this as an important way to validate victims' experiences and feelings.[7] Not imposing a definition, however, resulted in people labeling a wide range of acts as abuse—many of which were quite minor. This has complicated efforts to assess CSA prevalence and harm. If incidents of minor abuse are counted as equal to serious abuse, the amount of harm that CSA causes is likely underestimated. In other words, the low level of harm caused by minor acts dilutes the high level of harm caused by serious acts. Some also argue that a broad definition overestimates the number of CSA victims.[8]

---

5. Juliette D. G. Goldman and Usha K. Padayachi, "Some Methodological Problems in Estimating Incidence and Prevalence in Child Sexual Abuse Research," *Journal of Sex Research* 37, no. 4 (2000): 305–14.

6. Jeffrey J. Haugaard, "The Challenge of Defining Child Sexual Abuse," *American Psychologist* 55, no. 9 (2000): 1036–39.

7. Haugaard, "The Challenge of Defining Child Sexual Abuse."

8. Haugaard.

A final definitional issue that researchers confront involves the survey questions they use to measure CSA. It turns out that question wording can impact responses.[9] For example, there is a difference between asking people if they have "ever been abused" and asking if they have "ever been touched on their private parts without permission." This is partly an issue of specificity versus generality, but it is also about the meaning that words carry. The word *abuse* elicits particular emotions and images, different from those evoked by the *private parts* question. In the sections that follow, there are several ways researchers have worded questions about CSA. One unfortunate consequence of this variation is that it makes it difficult to compare the findings across studies.

PREVALENCE OF CHILD SEXUAL ABUSE

I now turn to a key question: What percent of children are sexually abused? Unfortunately, the use of different definitions of abuse can result in widely varying estimates. For example, researchers reviewed 166 studies of CSA conducted between 1985 and 1997 with men from North America. The studies differed in their definitions, and—partly as a result—the prevalence estimates ranged from a low of 4 percent to a high of 76 percent![10] Prevalence estimates also vary by data-collection methods. One common methodology is to use official records of abuse, such as reports made to the police or to Child Protective Services. While these sources are highly likely to be accurate (it is known that most cases of CSA that are reported are true),[11] they also underrepresent the actual level

---

9. Pew Research Center, "Questionnaire Design," *Pew Research Center Methods* (blog), 2020, https://www.pewresearch.org/methods/u-s-survey-research/questionnaire-design/.

10. William C. Holmes and Gail B. Slap, "Sexual Abuse of Boys: Definition, Prevalence, Correlates, Sequelae, and Management," *JAMA* 280, no. 21 (1998): 1855–62, https://www.jimhopper.com/pdf/holmes_and_slap_1998.pdf.

11. Mark D. Everson and Barbara W. Boat, "False Allegations of Sexual Abuse by Children and Adolescents," *Journal of the American Academy of Child &*

of abuse. Many abused children, possibly up to two out of three, never tell anyone, and disclosure does not guarantee that a report will be filed.[12]

Research suggests that official records undercount some groups of people more than others. For example, there may be differences by race, ethnicity, and immigrant status. Asian immigrants who do not speak English may fear that they cannot make themselves understood and that translation services will not be available.[13] People who are in the country illegally are often unwilling to report crime to official agencies for fear of being deported.[14] Hispanics traditionally have a particularly strong sense of family loyalty that can discourage individuals from taking actions against other family members, although in cases of abuse, the more acculturated the child's family, the more likely they are to make a report.[15] Native American people sometimes resist reporting abuse to an official

Adolescent Psychiatry 28, no. 2 (1989): 230–35, https://scholar.google.com/schol ar?hl=en&as_sdt=0%2C36&q=False+Allegations+of+Sexual+Abuse+by+Chil dren+and+Adolescents&btnG=.

12. Kamala London et al., "Disclosure of Child Sexual Abuse: What Does the Research Tell Us about the Ways That Children Tell?" *Psychology, Public Policy, and Law* 11, no. 1 (2005): 194–226, http://www.wondercatdesign.com/mecasa/ images/pdfs/disclosure%20of%20child%20sa.pdf.

13. Maureen C. Kenny and Adriana G. McEachern, "Racial, Ethnic, and Cultural Factors of Childhood Sexual Abuse: A Selected Review of the Literature," *Clinical Psychology Review* 20, no. 7 (2000): 905–922, https://scholar.google.com/ scholar?hl=en&as_sdt=0%2C36&q=Racial%2C+Ethnic%2C+and+Cultural+Fac tors+of+Childhood&btnG=.

14. Leslye E. Orloff et al., "Battered Immigrant Women's Willingness to Call for Help and Police Response," *UCLA Women's Law Journal* 13 (2003): 43, https:// escholarship.org/uc/item/07q5k83p.

15. Lisa Aronson Fontes, "Sin Vergüenza: Addressing Shame with Latino Victims of Child Sexual Abuse and Their Families," *Journal of Child Sexual Abuse* 16, no. 1 (2007): 61–83, https://www.researchgate.net/profile/Lisa_Fontes/publica tion/6549237_Sin_Verguenza_Addressing_Shame_with_Latino_Victims_of_ Child_Sexual_Abuse_and_Their_Families/links/0c9605269caf655ed8000000. pdf; David A. Katerndahl et al., "Differences in Childhood Sexual Abuse Experience between Adult Hispanic and Anglo Women in a Primary Care Setting," *Journal of Child Sexual Abuse* 14, no. 2 (2005): 85–95.

agency due to the long-standing discrimination they have faced from child welfare and social services.[16] There is also evidence to suggest that boys are less likely to report abuse than are girls, possibly because they fear being ridiculed or, if the offender was male, perceived as homosexual.[17]

Retrospective studies offer an alternative to the use of official records to estimate prevalence. These studies ask adults (ideally a randomly selected group) whether or not they were abused as children. This method is more accurate than the use of official records because people do not usually forget serious incidents of abuse. Additionally, when interviewed, few people report abuse that did not actually take place.[18] Unfortunately, research suggests that retrospective reports still suffer from underreporting. This is particularly true when respondents forget about more minor events, but underreporting can even occur with major traumatic incidents. About a third of adults who, as children, were victims of documented cases of sexual abuse choose not to acknowledge it when asked.[19] A final

16. Jeremy Braithwaite, "Colonized Silence: Confronting the Colonial Link in Rural Alaska Native Survivors' Non-Disclosure of Child Sexual Abuse," *Journal of Child Sexual Abuse* 27, no. 6 (2018): 589–611.

17. David Finkelhor et al., "Sexual Abuse in a National Survey of Adult Men and Women: Prevalence, Characteristics, and Risk Factors," *Child Abuse & Neglect* 14, no. 1 (1990): 19–28; Ramona Alaggia, Delphine Collin-Vézina, and Rusan Lateef, "Facilitators and Barriers to Child Sexual Abuse (CSA) Disclosures: A Research Update (2000–2016)," *Trauma, Violence, & Abuse* 20, no. 2 (2017): 260–83, https://journals.sagepub.com/doi/pdf/10.1177/1524838017697312.

18. Jochen Hardt and Michael Rutter, "Validity of Adult Retrospective Reports of Adverse Childhood Experiences: Review of the Evidence," *Journal of Child Psychology and Psychiatry* 45, no. 2 (2004): 260–73.

19. C. S. Widom and S. Morris, "Accuracy of Adult Recollections of Childhood Victimization," *Psychological Assessment* 9, no. 34–46 (1997): 34–46, https://pdfs.semanticscholar.org/bef8/86828da82e06fb4f41aeacaef44dd2dcc420.pdf; L. M. Williams, "Recall of Childhood Trauma: A Prospective Study of Women's Memories of Child Sexual Abuse," *Journal of Consulting and Clinical Psychology* 62 (1994): 1167–76, https://scholar.google.com/scholar?hl=en&as_sdt=0%2C36&q=Recall+of+Childhood+Trauma%3A+A+Prospective+Study+of+Women's+Memories+of+Child+Sexual+Abuse&btnG=.

problem with retrospective studies is that they can only tell us what happened in the past. This is because they ask adults about their childhood (which could have occurred over seventy years ago). If we are interested in current snapshot of CSA, a retrospective study is not an appropriate method to use.

The third way researchers estimate prevalence is by directly asking children or their caretakers about abuse. This method is powerful because it can potentially yield a current estimate of CSA that is not based on official records. Interviewing children, however, requires training, patience, and a deep understanding of their psychology. Some psychologists argue it is simply impossible to conduct any sort of meaningful interview with children under the age of four because they lack the language and conceptual skills to provide accurate information. It is even difficult to interview four- to eight-year-olds because they are suggestible and still learning language.[20] Interviewing children can also be impossible when parents refuse access because they worry that being asked about sexual abuse might upset or confuse them. For all of these reasons, most researchers interview the caretakers (usually the parent) of children under the age of ten. This, of course, raises the possibility of underreporting since some children may be abused without their parent's knowledge. Parents are also unlikely to report abuse in cases where they are the perpetrator.

A challenge for all of these kinds of prevalence studies is getting a large and representative group of respondents. For example, when a researcher wants to draw conclusions about the whole US population, they generally try to include over one thousand randomly selected respondents. This is expensive and time consuming. Further complicating matters, researchers need a high

---

20. Natacha Borgers, Edith de Leeuw, and Joop Hox, "Children as Respondents in Survey Research: Cognitive Development and Response Quality 1," *Bulletin of Sociological Methodology/Bulletin de Méthodologie Sociologique* 66, no. 1 (2000): 60–75, https://scholar.google.com/scholar?hl=en&as_sdt=0%2C36&q=Children+as+Respondents+in+Survey+Research%3A+&btnG=.

response rate. If a study has a lot of people who refuse to participate, we start worrying about inaccuracy. Here's an example. Imagine a CSA researcher calls three thousand parents and asks for an interview about their children. Only one thousand people say yes. This would be fine if there was no pattern to who said yes and who said no, but that's rarely the case. If I were the researcher, I would be concerned that people whose children have experienced abuse would be more likely to refuse. That would, obviously, completely distort the prevalence estimate and result in an undercount. This is why surveys of this type need a lot of respondents, as well as a high response rate.

Obtaining a high response rate for surveys has always been hard, but it appears to be getting even harder. Between 2002 and 2003, David Finkelhor and his colleagues at the University of New Hampshire conducted a national survey to determine rates of childhood victimization. They randomly selected home phone numbers (this was in the days before widespread use of cell phones) and called people to ask if they would participate. I should probably say, "they called and called" because they tried each number up to thirteen times and offered a ten-dollar reward for participation. Once they received a participant's consent, they sometimes had to call up to a total of twenty-five times to complete the survey![21] The study ended up with a response rate of 79 percent. While this may not sound very impressive, it is a remarkable number for a survey of this type and is high enough to make us confident that its findings are representative. Unfortunately, response rates tend to be much lower today. Cell phones have made it more complicated to reach potential respondents, and people are less willing to take the time to complete a survey than they were in the past, especially if they are not offered any compensation. Fortunately, there is evidence to suggest that most surveys continue to be fairly representative,

21. David Finkelhor et al., "The Victimization of Children and Youth: A Comprehensive National Survey," *Child Maltreatment* 10, no. 1 (2005): 5–25, http://takeroot.org/ee/pdf_files/library/Finkelhor_1994.pdf.

but the downward trend in the response rate is concerning.[22] I will say that this fact causes me to feel a little bit bad every time I hang up on a survey call on my cell phone.

Keeping in mind the methodological issues, I can now turn to the findings of the studies. One of the first prevalence estimates came from a retrospective study conducted in the 1970s. David Finkelhor (who is mentioned above and who many consider to be the preeminent researcher studying CSA) surveyed college students and found that 19.2 percent of the women and 8.6 percent of the men reported experiencing childhood sexual abuse.[23] Diana Russell found even higher rates in her retrospective study of women living in San Francisco. A full 38 percent reported having experienced at least one incident of sexual abuse before the age of eighteen.[24] These numbers were shocking and garnered public attention.

How to Read Prevalence Estimates

Past Year: Some researchers report abuse that happened to children in the year preceding the study. This gives a good snapshot of the current moment. A past year estimate of 1 percent would mean that 1 percent of the respondents reported being the victim of sexual abuse in the last year.

Lifetime: This statistic tells us the percent of people who became a victim before they turned eighteen. These are the rates we usually get from retrospective studies since they are conducted with adults. They can also be based on surveys with current children, but that underestimates the true lifetime

---

22. Scott Keeter et al., "Gauging the Impact of Growing Nonresponse on Estimates from a National RDD Telephone Survey," *Public Opinion Quarterly* 70, no. 5 (2006): 759-79, http://citeseerx.ist.psu.edu/viewdoc/download?doi=10.1.1.550.1100&rep=rep1&type=pdf.

23. David Finkelhor, *Sexually Victimized Children* (New York: Free Press, 1979).

24. Diana E. H. Russell, "The Incidence and Prevalence of Intrafamilial and Extrafamilial Sexual Abuse of Female Children," *Child Abuse & Neglect* 7, no. 2 (1983): 133-46.

rate since the children in the study have not yet turned eighteen. A lifetime rate of 15 percent would mean that 15 percent of children either in the past (in a retrospective study) or currently are victims. The media usually reports lifetime rates.

Since the 1980s, researchers have worked hard to obtain current estimates for CSA. I focus here on nonretrospective data collected since 2010 since readers are probably most interested in what is happening today. While reading about the studies, remember to note how the researchers define CSA because it affects their estimates of prevalence. Note also the sample sizes and response rates.

In 2011, Finkelhor and colleagues were interested in estimating the prevalence of all kinds of child abuse (not just CSA).[25] They conducted a residential telephone survey of US households with at least one child under the age of eighteen. They were worried about excluding households without landlines, so they also tried to contact a random group of cell phone numbers. Not surprisingly, this turned out to be ineffective, and this method was dropped. Finally, the researchers contacted a randomly selected group of households by mail and called those who responded to the mailing. Contacting by mail turned out to be useful because it reached a lot of people who did not have landlines. The study ended up including over 4500 children with a response rate of 60 percent for the telephone-contact sample and 40 percent for the mail-contact sample.

When the researchers contacted a home where more than one child lived, they just asked questions about the child with the closest birthday (this is essentially a way of randomly selecting among all the children in the house). Researchers interviewed the caretakers of children who were under the age of ten, but they talked directly with older children. This study asked a number of questions about sexual abuse. The primary ones included:

25. David Finkelhor et al., "The Lifetime Prevalence of Child Sexual Abuse and Sexual Assault Assessed in Late Adolescence," *Journal of Adolescent Health* 55, no. 3 (2014): 329–33, http://www.sciencedirect.com/science/article/pii/S1054139X13008549.

1. Did a grown-up in your/your child's life touch your/their private parts when they shouldn't have or make you/this child touch their private parts?
2. Did a grown-up in your/your child's life force you/this child to have sex?
3. Now think about other kids, like from school, a boyfriend or girlfriend, or even a brother or sister. At any time in your/their life, did another child or teen make you/this child do sexual things?
4. At any time in your/their life, did anyone TRY to force you/this child to have sex, that is sexual intercourse of any kind, even if it didn't happen?

The answers Finkelhor obtained led him to conclude that, in the past year, the lifetime prevalence rate for seventeen-year-old girls was 26.6 percent and the comparable rate for boys was 5.1 percent. Although those rates may be a slight undercount because they do not include any abuse that occurred between the time of the interview and the participants' eighteenth birthdays, they still provide a highly accurate estimate of true lifetime prevalence.

Although rates of CSA continue to be high, there has been a strong and consistent decline in CSA since 1990, although there was a worrisome 6 percent uptick in cases from 2017 to 2018.[26] The overall downward trend, however, has been confirmed by multiple sources—from reports made to Child Protective Services (down 62 percent from 1990 to 2010), to a well-respected national survey of victims (finding CSA involving teenage victims to have decreased 69 percent from 1993 to 2008), to rapes known to police (50 percent of which involve a victim under the age of eighteen, down 35 percent from 1992 to 2010).[27] It is pretty much indisputable that CSA has decreased dramatically.

---

26. Finkelhor, Saito, and Jones, "Updated Trends in Child Maltreatment, 2018."

27. David Finkelhor and Lisa M. Jones, *Have Sexual Abuse and Physical Abuse Declined Since the 1990s?* (Durham, NH: Crimes against Children Research Center, 2012), http://scholars.unh.edu/ccrc/61/.

U.S. Maltreatment Trends: 1990-2018

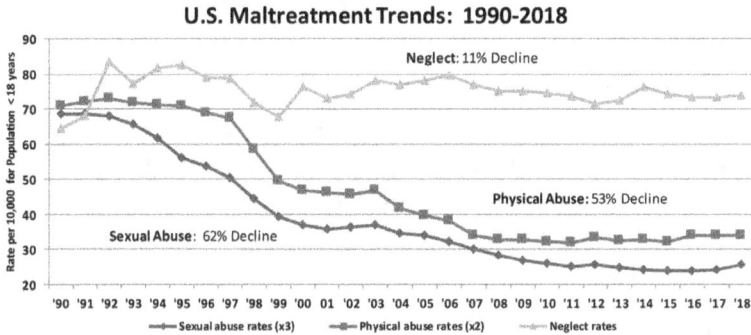

Note: Trend estimates represent total change from 1992 to 2018. Annual rates for physical abuse and sexual abuse have been multiplied by 2 and 3 respectively in Figure 1 so that trend comparisons can be highlighted.

Figure 4. U.S. Maltreatment Trends 1990-2018. Source: Crimes Against Children Research Lab. University of New Hampshire. February 2020. Updated Trends in Child Maltreatment, 2018.

So, why is CSA declining? That is the million-dollar question. One important clue is that CSA is not the only crime that has decreased. In fact, the rate of almost every type of crime has shown similarly dramatic declines starting in the 1990s. Violent crime rates today, for example, are at historic lows.[28] This suggests that there might have been some sort of large-scale societal shift that affected criminal behavior more generally. Nobody knows for sure what that shift is, but researchers have come up with a number of hypotheses. While these hypotheses have varying levels of empirical support, none perfectly explains the phenomena. I found a succinct description of these hypotheses in one of Finkelhor's books. If you are interested in a more detailed discussion of this topic than I can provide here, I encourage you to check out his work.[29]

The first hypothesis that explains decreases in crime involves economic prosperity during the 1990s. Times were simply getting better—more people had jobs, and there was more money to go

---

28. John Gramlich, "5 Facts about Crime in the U.S.," *Pew Research Center* (blog), October 17, 2019, https://www.pewresearch.org/fact-tank/2019/10/17/facts-about-crime-in-the-u-s/.

29. David Finkelhor, Childhood Victimization: Violence, Crime and Abuse in the Lives of Young People (New York: Oxford University Press, 2008).

around. We know that employment makes people less likely to engage in crime.[30] This hypothesis is much less convincing when applied to the 2000s, however, since the decline appears to have continued through the Great Recession of 2008–2010. Another hypothesis is that the increasing availability of contraception and abortion during the 1970s and 1980s ensured that more children were born to adults who were prepared to take care of them. This, at least in theory, would decrease both the children's chances of being abused and their likelihood of engaging in later criminality. A third hypothesis posits that the crime decrease is related to increasing incarceration rates. These rates started to climb in the 1960s, jumped dramatically in the 1980s, and have only recently flattened out (many people refer to the increase as a period of "mass incarceration"). Locking up a lot of people for a long period of time may have exerted a deterrent effect and/or simply taken enough criminals off the streets to drive down crime rates. Most research, however, concludes that this hypothesis has some support but can only explain a small percentage of the decrease.[31]

The hypothesis that I personally find the most compelling involves the societal climate. It posits that the decline in crime was the result of society shifting back to a more "normal" state after the tumultuous 1960s and 1970s. Those years saw tremendous

---

30. Stephen J. Tripodi, Johnny S. Kim, and Kimberly Bender, "Is Employment Associated with Reduced Recidivism? The Complex Relationship Between Employment and Crime," *International Journal of Offender Therapy and Comparative Criminology* 54, no. 5 (2010): 706–20, https://diginole.lib.fsu.edu/islandora/object/fsu%3A253662/datastream/PDF/view; Megan Denver, Garima Siwach, and Shawn D. Bushway, "A New Look at the Employment and Recidivism Relationship through the Lens of a Criminal Background Check," *Criminology* 55, no. 1 (2017): 174–204, https://onlinelibrary.wiley.com/doi/pdf/10.1111/1745-9125.12130?casa_token=r352aQCd7kwAAAAA:SfCgNNlwll7oCf5O2DEhcLipvtzHB2KwByQXx4XlVX1mSqrEtCfWFUGMFoZkLGiM1x7jcVFBVQ4HvA.

31. Christy A. Visher, "Incapacitation and Crime Control: Does a 'Lock 'Em up' Strategy Reduce Crime?," *Justice Quarterly* 4, no. 4 (1987): 513–43, https://scholar.google.com/scholar?hl=en&as_sdt=0%2C36&q=Incapacitation+and+Crime+Control%3A+Does+a+'Lock+%27Em+up'+&btnG=.

questioning of sexual and other kinds of behavioral rules. It is possible that people simply became more lawless as the hold of traditional restrictions loosened. In support of this idea, virtually all crimes increased during this period. Specific to CSA, Finkelhor suggests that maybe the relaxation of norms about premarital and gay sex led some people to believe that all the sexual rules were off. There is some compelling evidence for this position. For example, looking at the incidence of CSA in the Catholic Church, the rate started to pick up in the early 1950s but jumped substantially during the 1960s and 1970s before its downturn in the 1980s.[32]

Before walking away from this topic, I should mention that one of the more perplexing aspects of the decline in CSA is that it preceded the drop in other crimes by a couple of years. Why would that be? Finkelhor suggests several possibilities, although nobody has the definitive explanation. One possibility is that the media attention to CSA during the late 1980s might have increased awareness, improved parental and child-prevention skills, and made offenders less willing to risk abusing children. Many social workers and counselors were also hired during the 1970s and 1980s. This could have boosted the rate of reported CSA initially (because the workers identified and reported more cases), but then their prevention work could have caused the rate to decline. A final interesting possibility involves the increasing availability of effective psychotropic drugs. When people became less depressed, they may also be more able to control their behavior and less likely to abuse children.

ABUSE IN INSTITUTIONS

As described in the last chapter, the abuse of children in institutional contexts like schools and churches is a significant problem. It is difficult to estimate exactly how common this kind of abuse is overall,

---

32. Terry et al., *The Causes and Context of Sexual Abuse of Minors*, http://www. bishop-accountability.org/reports/2011_05_18_John_Jay_Causes_and_Context_Report.pdf.

but research gives us some clues as to its prevalence in particular institutions. For example, over the last twenty years, there have been many allegations in youth sports. This may be because of the way sports is organized, providing a lot of opportunity because coaches have a great deal of power, spend a lot of time with kids, and sometimes touch them as part of the training process. Abuse can go on for a long time when child athletes fear reporting because they do not want to harm their future in sports or they fear the reaction of the rest of the team—especially if the coach is well loved.[33]

Estimates from Europe suggest that about 3 percent of child athletes are the victims of abuse in sports contexts.[34] Data about children in the United States are harder to come by, but a survey of young women who were college athletes found that 20 percent reported being "subjected to potentially threatening behaviors" by their coach. Using a narrower definition of abuse, just under 2 percent reported that a coach had kissed them, stared at their breasts, or proposed a sexual encounter. [35] In another study with two hundred college athletes at three US universities, just under 2 percent reported coaches making verbal or physical advances toward them.[36]

33. Marianne Cense and Celia H. Brackenridge, "Temporal and Developmental Risk Factors for Sexual Harassment and Abuse in Sport," *European Physical Education Review* 7, no. 1 (2001): 61–79, https://journals.sagepub.com/doi/pdf/10.1177/1356336X010071006?casa_token=oaqFStQFP5QAAAAA:x HD69thmshUAtGxwrarZMWla5UGNJGco_GCEOLOfQDaM7d18oX3chqom VTWvcV6xyh9w8oWr6O4.

34. Toomas Timpka et al., "Lifetime History of Sexual and Physical Abuse among Competitive Athletics (Track and Field) Athletes: Cross Sectional Study of Associations with Sports and Non-Sports Injury," *British Journal of Sports Medicine* 53, no. 22 (2018): 1–7, https://scholar.google.com/scholar?hl=en&as_sdt=0%2C36&q=lifetime+history+of+sexual+and+physical+abuse+timp ka&btnG=; Jan Toftegaard Nielsen, "The Forbidden Zone: Intimacy, Sexual Relations and Misconduct in the Relationship between Coaches and Athletes," *International Review for the Sociology of Sport* 36, no. 2 (2001): 165–82.

35. Karin A. E. Volkwein et al., "Sexual Harassment in Sport: Perceptions and Experiences of American Female Student-Athletes," *International Review for the Sociology of Sport* 32, no. 3 (1997): 283–95.

36. Karin Volkwein-Caplan et al., "Sexual Harassment of Women in Athletics

Researchers have also tried to assess abuse prevalence in the US Catholic Church. John Jay College conducted a large-scale study of abuse claims against priests between 1950 and 2002. They found that about 4 percent of all priests (4,392 in total) were accused of abuse by 10,667 children over the period. This, of course, does not include unreported incidents.[37] Because priests are seen by Catholics as representatives of God, they have a great deal of power and trust placed in them. This gives them opportunities for abuse and makes victims hesitant to come forward.[38]

Abuse in a Boarding School

Here is a podcast about one boy's abuse at a boarding school: https://thisiscriminal.com/episode-82-the-choir-01-12-2018/.

One institution that is hidden from public view but that has a particularly high rate of CSA is juvenile prison. In 2018, the United States incarcerated about 12,750 children and adolescents. The federal government conducted a study and found that just over 7 percent reported having been sexually abused while in custody during the prior year. About a third of these incidents were perpetrated by other youth while the remainder involved staff.[39] Unlike

---

vs. Academia," in *Sexual Harassment and Abuse in Sport: International Research and Policy Perspectives*, ed. Celia H. Brackenridge and Kari Fasting (Chicago: Whiting & Birch, 2002), 91–110.

37. John Jay College of Criminal Justice, The Nature and Scope of Sexual Abuse of Minors by Catholic Priests and Deacons in the United States, 1950–2002: A Research Study Conducted by the John Jay College of Criminal Justice, the City University of New York: For the United States Conference of Catholic Bishops (Washington, DC: United States Conference of Catholic Bishops, 2004, http://www.bishop-accountability.org/reports/2011_05_18_John_Jay_Causes_and_Context_Report.pdf.

38. Carolyn M. Warner, "The Politics of Sex Abuse in Sacred Hierarchies: A Comparative Study of the Catholic Church and the Military in the United States," *Religions* 10, no. 4 (2019): 281–309.

39. Erica L. Smith and Jessica Stroop, *Sexual Victimization Reported by Youth in Juvenile Facilities, 2018* (Washington, DC: US Department of Justice, Office of Justice Programs, 2018), https://www.bjs.gov/content/pub/pdf/svryjf18.pdf.

in other institutions, the majority of accusations involved women staff members abusing boys.[40] While many of the youth reported the contact to be consensual, the power imbalance and age difference between staff and youth mark it as abusive.[41]

Research indicates that staff members hold a lot of power in juvenile prisons, enabling abuse. For example, they often control access to valued resources, and they also have input into decisions about when youth should be released. In chapter 6, I will discuss recently implemented policies to decrease sexual abuse in prison but, until recently, there was little focus on investigating or prosecuting prison assault.[42] It is known that more sexual abuse by staff occurs when facilities are understaffed, when staff members are not well trained, and when institutions are unable to weed out applicants who may be applying to work in juvenile prisons for the wrong reasons.[43]

Finally, at the time of this writing, there has been increasing coverage of CSA in immigrant detention centers. There is not yet a prevalence study, but the Department of Health and Human Services reports that, between October of 2014 and July of 2018, the Office of Refugee Resettlement received over forty-five hundred reports of child sexual abuse in immigration detention. The Department of Justice (DOJ) also received 1,303 reports. Of these reports, 178 involved staff at the facilities (the others involved other children or adults who were nonstaff members, and over two hundred of the reports had no perpetrator information).[44]

40. Allen Beck et al., *Sexual Victimization in Juvenile Facilities Reported by Youth, 2012* (Washington DC: Bureau of Justice Statistics, 2012).

41. Allen J. Beck and Romana R. Rantala, *Sexual Victimization Reported by Juvenile Correctional Authorities, 2007–12* (Washington DC: US Department of Justice, 2016), https://www.hivlawandpolicy.org/sites/default/files/Sexual%20Victimization%20Reported%20by%20Juvenile%20Correctional%20Authorities,%202007-12.pdf.

42. Natasha Lennard, "Will the Prison Rape Epidemic Ever Have Its Weinstein Moment?" *The Intercept* (blog), November 21, 2017, https://theintercept.com/2017/11/21/prison-rape-sexual-assault-violence/.

43. David W. Roush, "Staff Sexual Misconduct in Juvenile Justice Facilities: Implications for Work Force Training," *Corrections Today*, February 2008, 32–52.

44. Caitlin Owens, Stef W. Kight, and Harry Stevens, "Thousands of Migrant Youth Allegedly Suffered Sexual Abuse in U.S. Custody," Axios, February 26, 2019,

EFFECTS OF CHILD SEXUAL ABUSE

Today, there is little debate about whether CSA is harmful. Even the term *child sexual abuse* implies harm, otherwise we might call it something like child/adult sexual contact. But what is known about the nature and extent of the harm?

Research indicates that adult survivors of CSA struggle with a variety of mental-health issues.[45] For example, a longitudinal study found that CSA is associated with higher rates of mental illness among sixteen- to twenty-five-year-old survivors than among similar people with no history of CSA. These conditions include depression, anxiety, substance disorder, and suicide attempts.[46] Another study found increased rates of suicide and unstable marriages.[47] CSA appears to disrupt some victims' "body boundaries," making it difficult for them to feel comfortable when they are in close proximity to other people.[48] Stereotypes suggest that boys, particularly if they are victimized by women, suffer less harm than

---

https://www.axios.com/immigration-unaccompanied-minors-sexual-assault-32 22e230-29e1-430f-a361-d959c88c5d8c.html.

45. Shanta Dube et al., "Long-Term Consequences of Childhood Sexual Abuse by Gender of Victim," *American Journal of Preventive Medicine* 28, no. 5 (2005): 430–38; Natacha Godbout et al., "Child Sexual Abuse and Subsequent Relational and Personal Functioning: The Role of Parental Support," *Child Abuse & Neglect* 38, no. 2 (2014): 317–25, https://scholar.google.com/scholar?hl=en&as_sdt=0%2C36&q=Child+sexual+abuse+and+subsequent+relational+and+person al+functioning%3A+The+role+of+parental+support&btnG=; Elizabeth Oddone Paolucci, Mark L. Genuis, and Claudio Violato, "A Meta-Analysis of the Published Research on the Effects of Child Sexual Abuse," *Journal of Psychology* 135, no. 1 (2001): 17.

46. David M. Fergusson, Joseph M. Boden, and L. John Horwood, "Exposure to Childhood Sexual and Physical Abuse and Adjustment in Early Adulthood," *Child Abuse & Neglect* 32, no. 6 (2008): 607–19, http://citeseerx.ist.psu.edu/viewdoc/download?doi=10.1.1.413.2974&rep=rep1&type=pdf.

47. Dube et al., "Long-Term Consequences." https://scholar.google.com/scholar?hl=en&as_sdt=0%2C36&q=Child+sexual+abuse+and+subsequent+rela tional+and+personal+functioning%3A+The+role+of+parental+support&btnG=.

48. Anat Talmon and Karni Ginzburg, "'Body Self' in the Shadow of Childhood Sexual Abuse: The Long-Term Implications of Sexual Abuse for Male and Female Adult Survivors," *Child Abuse & Neglect* 76 (2018): 416–25.

do girls. The research findings, however, while somewhat mixed on this question, generally suggest that both groups report negative outcomes.[49] One study did find gender differences in responses with boys more likely to engage in substance abuse and girls more likely to become depressed and/or suicidal. No differences were found by racial/ethnic group.[50]

The Truth Project in the United Kingdom collects stories from victims and survivors. You can read some of these accounts at https://www.truthproject.org.uk/i-will-be-heard.

One of the effects of childhood victimization is a somewhat increased risk of engaging in abuse as an adult.[51] I talk about this at length in the next chapter. It also appears that CSA is related to the likelihood of engaging in other criminal behaviors. For example, a study that tracked women CSA victims from childhood into adulthood found that they were more likely than nonabused girls to run away from home and to be arrested for drug and violent offenses as adults. The authors point out that both running away and drug use are "escape" crimes that may be used to try and relieve the pain of abuse. Acting out violently may also be a way to reassert control after CSA.[52]

Incest appears to result in the same kinds of psychological damage as nonfamily abuse. People used to believe that abuse

49. Dube et al., "Long-Term Consequences," https://scholar.google.com/schol ar?hl=en&as_sdt=0%2C5&q=%22long+term+consequences%22+dube&btnG=.

50. Sandra Gray and Susan Rarick, "Exploring Gender and Racial/Ethnic Differences in the Effects of Child Sexual Abuse," *Journal of Child Sexual Abuse* 27, no. 5 (2018): 570–87.

51. Jill S. Levenson, Gwenda M. Willis, and David S. Prescott, "Adverse Childhood Experiences in the Lives of Male Sex Offenders: Implications for Trauma-Informed Care," *Sexual Abuse: A Journal of Research and Treatment* 28, no. 4 (2016): 340–59.

52. Jane A. Siegel and Linda M. Williams, "The Relationship between Child Sexual Abuse and Female Delinquency and Crime: A Prospective Study," *Journal of Research in Crime and Delinquency* 40, no. 1 (2003): 71–94, http://citeseerx.ist. psu.edu/viewdoc/download?doi=10.1.1.531.921&rep=rep1&type=pdf.

that involved a sibling was less damaging than parental abuse. It appears, however, that this is not the case. A study of incest survivors found that about 90 percent of victims of both sibling and parent offenders suffered "clinically significant distress on at least one (psychological) measure."[53]

When most people think about the impact of CSA, they think about mental health. But there is evidence that it can affect other areas of life as well. For example, one study looked at how being a victim of CSA affects Catholics' attitudes toward the church, priests, and God. The study included three groups of people: those who had been the victim of CSA by a priest, those whose abusers were nonclergy, and a group who had not been victimized at all. The results showed that victims of priests were less likely to trust both the Church and priests than were respondents from the other two groups. Women victims of priests felt a less close relationship to God than did women in the other two groups, although the same was not true of men.[54] It should be noted, however, that the study is dated (1995) and the response rate was very low (25 percent).

CSA does not appear to have any impact on victim's sexual orientation. While some research finds elevated rates of child sexual abuse in the histories of gay men, none can prove that the link is causal.[55] From a reading of the literature, I think the best answer to this question comes from Richard Gartner. He is a well-known psychologist who researches and treats boys and men who have been abused. He comments:[56]

---

53. Mireille Cyr et al., "Intrafamilial Sexual Abuse: Brother–Sister Incest Does Not Differ from Father–Daughter and Stepfather–Stepdaughter Incest," *Child Abuse & Neglect* 26, no. 9 (2002): 957–73, http://citeseerx.ist.psu.edu/viewdoc/download?doi=10.1.1.464.885&rep=rep1&type=pdf.

54. Stephen J. Rossetti, "The Impact of Child Sexual Abuse on Attitudes toward God and the Catholic Church," *Child Abuse & Neglect* 19, no. 12 (1995): 1469–81.

55. Helen W. Wilson and Cathy Spatz Widom, "Does Physical Abuse, Sexual Abuse, or Neglect in Childhood Increase the Likelihood of Same-Sex Sexual Relationships and Cohabitation? A Prospective 30-Year Follow-Up," *Archives of Sexual Behavior* 39, no. 1 (2010): 63–74.

56. Richard B. Gartner, "Talking about Sexually Abused Boys, and

When the abuser is male (and even sometimes when she is female), many boys—whether straight or gay—develop fears and concerns about sexual orientation. Conventional wisdom says sexual abuse turns boys gay, although there's no persuasive evidence that premature sexual activity fundamentally changes sexual orientation. Nevertheless, a heterosexual boy is likely to doubt himself, wondering why he was chosen by a man for sex. A homosexual boy may feel rushed into considering himself gay, or may hate his homosexuality because he believes it was caused by his abuse.

As Gartner suggests, while CSA does not cause homosexuality, it can have a significant effect on a victim's views about their own sexuality.

In sum, the research indicates that CSA is linked to many negative outcomes—but it also suggests that the level of harm on individuals varies widely. Some victims and survivors deal with significant mental-health issues, others experience few repercussions. One extremely controversial study even found that CSA caused very little harm at all.[57] Bruce Rind and his colleagues conducted a meta-analysis (see the box below for a definition of this term) of retrospective studies conducted with college students. The results suggested that people who have experienced CSA are just as well adjusted as their nonabused counterparts once family environment is statistically controlled. In other words, the students who were abused were much more likely to come from families with high levels of conflict and neglect, and it was this overall negative environment that caused maladjustment rather than CSA per se. Students who had been abused but who came from well-adjusted families did not report levels of psychological distress higher than students who had not been abused at all.

the Men They Become," *Psychology Today* (blog), January 30, 2011, http://www.psychologytoday.com/blog/psychoanalysis-30/201101/talking-about-sexually-abused-boys-and-the-men-they-become.

57. Bruce Rind, Philip Tromovitch, and Robert Bauserman, "A Meta-Analytic Examination of Assumed Properties of Child Sexual Abuse Using College Samples," *Psychological Bulletin* 124, no. 1 (1998): 22–53.

What Is a Meta-Analysis?

This research method combines the data from many different studies together and reanalyzes it with the much larger sample size. It is a potentially very powerful method, but it is challenging to conduct because studies often include different kinds of respondents (college students vs. the general population, for example) or are conducted at different points in time. Studies also define CSA differently. When done well, however, a meta-analysis can increase confidence in research findings.

Perhaps you are wondering how Rind could possibly reach the conclusion that CSA is not linked to serious harm. Well, you are not alone in questioning his study. In fact, its publication unleashed unprecedented public outrage. Talk show hosts criticized the study on television. The US Congress ultimately condemned it (this is the first and only time Congress has ever taken an action like this with an academic study). [58] I think it is important to mention, however, that the study went through a peer review process, and that it is problematic to dismiss it out of hand. At the same time, there have been a number of methodological critiques. Interested readers can check out a summary of these issues in the *American Psychologist* in 2002.[59]

Before I leave the topic of harm and CSA, I should note that harm is not only experienced by victims and their families. CSA also has societal costs. A recent study looked at the cost of all investigated nonfatal child maltreatment (including physical abuse and neglect as well as CSA) and found that the lifetime average cost per victim is over $830,000 (in 2015 dollars). This includes health care,

---

58. Richard Beck, *We Believe the Children: A Moral Panic in the 1980s*, 1st ed. (New York: PublicAffairs, 2015).

59. Scott O. Lilienfeld, "When Worlds Collide: Social Science, Politics, and the Rind et al. (1998) Child Sexual Abuse Meta-Analysis," *American Psychologist* 57, no. 3 (2002): 176–88, https://www.researchgate.net/publication/11459260_When_worlds_collide_Social_science_politics_and_the_Rind_et_al_1998_Child_sexual_abuse_meta-analysis.

psychological care, criminal justice, and child-welfare costs, as well as productivity losses.[60]

CONCLUSION

Research has come a long way from de Francis's 1969 study of CSA. Today, there are fairly solid data about prevalence, with the best estimates suggesting that between 10 and 15 percent of children experience sexual abuse. While unacceptably high, these numbers are a considerable improvement from thirty years ago. It is not entirely clear why CSA rates have declined, but there are a number of intriguing hypotheses involving economic and social conditions. Current research indicates that, while many abuse victims go on to lead happy and productive lives, some also struggle with mental-health issues, including depression and anxiety. In the next chapter, I look at what research says about the characteristics of victims and offenders.

FURTHER READING

Finkelhor, David. *Childhood Victimization: Violence, Crime, and Abuse in the Lives of Young People*. Oxford: Oxford University Press, 2014.

Sacco, Linda. *Unspeakable: Father-Daughter Incest in American History*. Johns Hopkins University Press, 2009.

Terry, Karen J. *The Causes and Context of Sexual Abuse of Minors by Catholic Priests in the United States, 1950–2010: A Report Presented to the United States Conference of Catholic Bishops by the John Jay College Research Team*. Washington, DC: United States Conference of Catholic Bishops, n.d. http://www.bishop-accountability.org/reports/2011_05_18_John_Jay_Causes_and_Context_Report.pdf.

Whitehead, Colson. *The Nickel Boys: A Novel*. New York: Doubleday, 2019.

---

60. Cora Peterson, Curtis Florence, and Joanne Klevens, "The Economic Burden of Child Maltreatment in the United States, 2015," *Child Abuse & Neglect* 86 (2018): 178–83, https://www.ncbi.nlm.nih.gov/pmc/articles/PMC6289633/pdf/nihms-992095.pdf.

CHAPTER THREE

VICTIMS AND OFFENDERS

He always came and helped my mom with me and my siblings so she could rest or helped her make arrangements.

He remembered I was so sad for not having these jeans like my other friends, and then he came over with these jeans as a present.

He gave me this doll and asked me to go to his room and take off my shirt, but I told him no, so he pushed me into his room and took the doll away.[1]

These quotes were drawn from interviews with children who had been abused. Each child is talking about the tactics that were used to initiate the abuse. In this chapter, I look at a number of issues raised by these quotes. Who are victims and offenders? Why do some people sexually abuse children? Can offenders stop abusing? As I was writing this chapter, I kept thinking about how the media coverage discussed in chapter 1 compares with the research findings. While there are certainly areas in which the media has done a

---

1. Carmit Katz and Zion Barnetz, "Children's Narratives of Alleged Child Sexual Abuse Offender Behaviors and the Manipulation Process," *Psychology of Violence* 6, no. 2 (2016): 223–32.

good job reflecting current knowledge, there are other areas where their coverage diverges substantially from the research.

CHARACTERISTICS OF VICTIMS

The easiest place to start talking about the characteristics of child sexual abuse (CSA) victims involves gender. All data sources (from official records to retrospective studies to surveys conducted with kids and caretakers) reveal that the majority of victims are girls. As described in the last chapter, the lifetime CSA prevalence rates estimated from reports of seventeen-year-olds suggests that, while girls have a lifetime prevalence rate of 26.6 percent, the comparable rate for boys is only 5.1 percent.[2] It is clear that, at all ages, girls are much more likely to become victims.

Stereotypes suggest that CSA victims are disproportionately poor, but research findings on this question are quite mixed, and caution should be taken in interpreting those studies that do show an association. There are biases that increase the chances that poor people are reported for abuse suspicions.[3] In other words, if a parent is poor, their behavior is more likely to be scrutinized and reported than if they are rich. It should also be noted that there are conditions associated with poverty that increase the risk of abuse. Single motherhood is a good example. Single mothers are disproportionately poor, and their children are at increased risk of CSA. This risk is not because of poverty, however. Instead, single mothers sometimes date or marry a new man, and these stepfathers (or

---

2. David Finkelhor et al., "The Lifetime Prevalence of Child Sexual Abuse and Sexual Assault Assessed in Late Adolescence," *Journal of Adolescent Health* 55, no. 3 (2014): 329–33, http://www.sciencedirect.com/science/article/pii/S1054139X13008549..

3. Jocelyn Brown et al., "A Longitudinal Analysis of Risk Factors for Child Maltreatment: Findings of a 17-Year Prospective Study of Officially Recorded and Self-Reported Child Abuse and Neglect," *Child Abuse & Neglect* 22, no. 11 (1998): 1065–78.

stepfather figures) abuse more often than do biological fathers.[4] Children of single parents are also more likely to live in severely disadvantaged neighborhoods with many other single-parent families, leading to less supervision.[5]

Children of single parents are not the only group who experience higher-than-average rates of CSA. Sadly, disabled children and children under the age of thirteen are also disproportionately at risk.[6] There is mixed evidence about a possible link between race and CSA, with some studies finding Black people to be more at risk than white people[7] while others find the opposite.[8] While Asians are underrepresented in child sexual abuse statistics, this may be the result of low levels of reporting.[9] It should be noted, however, that some very well-respected studies find no association

4. David Finkelhor et al., "Sexual Abuse in a National Survey of Adult Men and Women: Prevalence, Characteristics, and Risk Factors," *Child Abuse & Neglect* 14, no. 1 (1990): 19–28.

5. Janet L Lauritsen, "How Families and Communities Influence Youth Victimization," *Juvenile Justice Bulletin* (Washington DC: Office of Juvenile Justice and Delinquency Prevention, November 2003), https://www.ncjrs.gov/pdffiles1/ojjdp/201629.pdf.

6. Brown et al., "A Longitudinal Analysis of Risk Factors for Child Maltreatment"; William C. Holmes and Gail B. Slap, "Sexual Abuse of Boys: Definition, Prevalence, Correlates, Sequelae, and Management," https://www.jimhopper.com/pdf/holmes_and_slap_1998.pdf.

7. Andrea J. Sedlak et al., *Fourth National Incidence Study of Child Abuse and Neglect (NIS-4)* (Washington, DC: US Department of Health and Human Services, Administration for Children and Families, and Office of Planning, Research, and Evaluation, and the Children's Bureau, 2010), http://cap.law.harvard.edu/wp-content/uploads/2015/07/sedlaknis.pdf.

8. C. Brendan Clark et al., "Characteristics of Victims of Sexual Abuse by Gender and Race in a Community Corrections Population," *Journal of Interpersonal Violence* 27, no. 9 (2012): 1844–61, http://citeseerx.ist.psu.edu/viewdoc/download?doi=10.1.1.921.2464&rep=rep1&type=pdf.

9. Maureen C. Kenny and Adriana G. McEachern, "Racial, Ethnic, and Cultural Factors of Childhood Sexual Abuse: A Selected Review of the Literature," *Clinical Psychology Review* 20, no. 7 (2000): 905–922, https://scholar.google.com/scholar?hl=en&as_sdt=0%2C36&q=Racial%2C+Ethnic%2C+and+Cultural+Factors+of+Childhood&btnG=.

at all between CSA and race.[10] Finally, lesbian, gay, and bisexual youth, as well as those who are gender nonconforming, experience higher levels of abuse.[11]

A recent meta-analysis of seventy-two studies found that there are a number of factors associated with CSA victimization. For example, a child is at increased risk if they, or someone in their home, has been abused before. Parental problems, such as domestic abuse or drug/alcohol abuse, also predict CSA. Girls and disabled children are at greater risk, as are those who live with a stepfather. The study also found higher rates of abuse in socially isolated families.[12]

As discussed in the last chapter, abuse in institutional contexts is a significant problem. In general, risk factors in these contexts mirror those in the general population. For example, in sports, girls are more likely to be abused than are boys. Offenders often choose victims because they have low self-esteem, weak family connections, or few friends.[13] One study found that offenders choose

10. David Finkelhor et al., "The Victimization of Children and Youth: A Comprehensive National Survey," *Child Maltreatment* 10, no. 1 (2005): 5–25, http://takeroot.org/ee/pdf_files/library/Finkelhor_1994.pdf.

11. Sandra L. Kirby, Guylaine Demers, and Sylvie Parent, "Vulnerability/Prevention: Considering the Needs of Disabled and Gay Athletes in the Context of Sexual Harassment and Abuse," *International Journal of Sport and Exercise Psychology* 6, no. 4 (2008): 407–26, https://scholar.google.com/scholar?hl=en&as_sdt=0%2C36&q=Vulnerability%2FPrevention%3A+Considering+the+Needs+of+&btnG=; Andrea L. Roberts et al., "Childhood Gender Nonconformity: A Risk Indicator for Childhood Abuse and Posttraumatic Stress in Youth," *Pediatrics* 129, no. 3 (2012): 410–17, https://pediatrics.aappublications.org/content/pediatrics/129/3/410.full.pdf; Emily F. Rothman, Deinera Exner, and Allyson L. Baughman, "The Prevalence of Sexual Assault against People Who Identify as Gay, Lesbian, or Bisexual in the United States: A Systematic Review," *Trauma, Violence & Abuse* 12, no. 2 (2011): 55–66, https://www.ncbi.nlm.nih.gov/pmc/articles/PMC3118668.

12. Mark Assink et al., "Risk Factors for Child Sexual Abuse Victimization: A Meta-Analytic Review," *Psychological Bulletin* 145, no. 5 (2019): 459–89.

13. Celia H. Brackenridge, "'He Owned Me Basically . . .' Women's Experience of Sexual Abuse in Sport," *International Review for the Sociology of Sport* 32, no.

athletes who have been abused before (often in nonsports contexts).[14] Athletes who compete as high levels while young are also at increased risk.[15]

CSA in the Catholic Church and in juvenile prisons is associated with slightly different patterns of victimization. The large-scale John Jay College study of abuse in the Catholic Church between 1950 and 2010 found that more boys than girls were abused, and that most of the victims were adolescents rather than young children.[16] It appears that this is the case largely because priests were choosing victims based on availability, not preference. For example, priests spend a lot of time with the children and teenagers who serve as altar servers. While some dioceses began allowing girls in this role in the 1980s, the Vatican did not officially endorse the practice until 1993.

As in the Catholic Church, abuse victims in juvenile prisons are overwhelmingly boys and young men, but this is largely because the vast majority of youth in prison (over 90 percent) are male.

---

2 (1997): 115–30; Karin A. E. Volkwein et al., "Sexual Harassment in Sport: Perceptions and Experiences of American Female Student-Athletes," *International Review for the Sociology of Sport* 32, no. 3 (1997): 283–95.

14. Marianne Cense and Celia H. Brackenridge, "Temporal and Developmental Risk Factors for Sexual Harassment and Abuse in Sport," *European Physical Education Review* 7, no. 1 (2001): 61–79, https://bura.brunel.ac.uk/bit |stream/2438/547/3/EPER+&+Cense+(2001)-1.pdf.

15. Kate Alexander, Anne Stafford, and Ruth Lewis, *The Experiences of Children Participating in Organised Sport in the UK* (London: National Society for the Prevention of Cruelty to Children, 2011), https://www.research.ed.ac.uk/portal/ files/7971883/experiences_children_sport_main_report_wdf85014.pdf; Sandra L. Kirby, Lorraine Greaves, and Olena Hankivsky, *The Dome of Silence: Sexual Harassment and Abuse in Sport* (Halifax, Nova Scotia: Zed Books, 2008).

16. John Jay College of Criminal Justice, The Nature and Scope of Sexual Abuse of Minors by Catholic Priests and Deacons in the United States, 1950–2002: A Research Study Conducted by the John Jay College of Criminal Justice, the City University of New York: For the United States Conference of Catholic Bishops (Washington, DC: United States Conference of Catholic Bishops, 2004, http://www.bishop-accountability.org/reports/2004_02_27_JohnJay_ revised/2004_02_27_John_Jay_Main_Report_Optimized.pdf.

At the same time, incarcerated boys are somewhat more likely to report sexual abuse (7.1 percent) compared to girls (6.6 percent).[17] It also appears that incarcerated LBGTQ+ youths are much more likely than are those who are heterosexual and gender conforming to be abused by other youth, but they are less likely to be abused by a staff member.[18]

CHILD VICTIMS, MEMORY, AND FALSE ACCUSATIONS

In chapter 1, I talked about the McMartin preschool case. In hindsight, it is quite clear that the investigators used problematic techniques to elicit evidence from children. The social worker hired to investigate spoke with hundreds of former and current students of the McMartin preschool, many of whom told stories of abuse. Fortunately, those sessions were tape-recorded so we now know exactly how the evidence was elicited. The social worker interviewed most children multiple times and was extremely persistent in asking them about abuse. In more extreme cases, she accused children of lying if they denied being abused (and even called them names like "scaredy-cat"). She also suggested that good and honest children provide stories of abuse, pointing out that other children had already made reports. Children were observed as they played with anatomically correct dolls and any sexually suggestive behavior was assumed to be a result of abuse.

So, what has been learned about children and memory since the McMartin case? First, that children's memories are malleable. For example, when subjected to repeated interviews, their descriptions become less reflective of reality.[19] Children are also highly

---

17. Erica L. Smith and Jessica Stroop, *Sexual Victimization Reported by Youth in Juvenile Facilities, 2018* (Washington, DC: US Department of Justice, Office of Justice Programs, 2018), https://www.bjs.gov/content/pub/pdf/svryjf18.pdf.

18. Allen Beck et al., *Sexual Victimization in Juvenile Facilities Reported by Youth, 2012* (Washington DC: Bureau of Justice Statistics, 2012).

19. Stephen J. Ceci and Maggie Bruck, *Jeopardy in the Courtroom: A Scientific*

influenced by their peers and by a desire to please adults. To test this, researchers sent a character named Manny Morales to tell a story in five different day-care centers. Manny wore a silly hat and was warm and friendly with the kids. Before he left, he gave them cupcakes and a sticker. One week later, the researchers interviewed the children. They asked about what had actually happened ("Did Manny give you a sticker?"), but they also asked about made-up bad events ("Did Manny tear the book he was reading?"). The children agreed with the false statements 17 percent of the time. But this number increased dramatically (to 58 percent) when the researchers prefaced their questions by saying, "Well, I already talked to the big kids and they said that Manny did some bad things. I want to see if you have a good memory like they did. Are you smart enough to remember?"[20] These findings strongly suggest that children's memories are influenced by social pressure.

Today, investigators are very careful about how they interview children. For example, they ask open-ended questions such as, "Tell me about why you came to see me today," rather than suggestive questions like, "Did the teacher tell you to take off your clothes?" Investigators also now recognize that very young children are more suggestible than older children and that their memories are less reliable. That is why prosecutors rarely prosecute a CSA case based on the uncorroborated testimony of a child younger than three.[21] This does not mean that young children's allegations are ignored; it simply means that investigators make sure to find another source of evidence of abuse before prosecuting.

Analysis of Children's Testimony (Washington, DC: American Psychological Association, 1996).

20. Sena Garven et al., "More Than Suggestion: The Effect of Interviewing Techniques from the McMartin Preschool Case," *Journal of Applied Psychology* 83, no. 3 (1998): 347–59, http://eyewitness.utep.edu/Documents/Garven&98More ThanSuggestion.pdf.

21. Emily Bazelon, "Abuse Cases, and a Legacy of Skepticism," *New York Times*, June 9, 2014, https://www.nytimes.com/2014/06/10/science/the-witch-hunt-narrative-are-we-dismissing-real-victims.html.

Research about the accuracy of children's reports suggest that, if they are not subjected to manipulative interview techniques, they very rarely lie about (or make up) incidents of CSA. In general, researchers have settled on a rate of about 5 percent false allegations, although two summaries of the literature suggest that it is more accurate to say that the range is between 4.5 and 7.5 percent or an even more cautious 2 to 10 percent.[22] There is not a lot of research on the false-accusation rates of teenagers because most studies look at children and teenagers together. A review of Child Protective Services cases, however, found that if teenagers do have a higher rate of false reporting than younger children, it is only by a couple of percentage points.[23] An analysis of sexual assault cases at a large university found that only 5.9 percent of allegations by college women (many of whom were still teenagers) involved false accusations.[24]

CHARACTERISTICS OF OFFENDERS

Who are offenders? Unfortunately, as with many aspects of CSA, it is only possible to tentatively answer this question. This is because there is not a list of everyone who has abused a child. Thus, conclusions are drawn based on samples of incarcerated offenders or people who are on the nation's sexual-offender registries. It is also

22. Mark D. Everson and Barbara W. Boat, "False Allegations of Sexual Abuse by Children and Adolescents," *Journal of the American Academy of Child & Adolescent Psychiatry* 28, no. 2 (1989): 230–35, https://scholar.google.com/scholar?hl=en&as_sdt=0%2C36&q=False+Allegations+of+Sexual+Abuse+by+Children+and+Adolescents&btnG=; Edwin J. Mikkelsen, Thomas G. Gutheil, and Margaret Emens, "False Sexual-Abuse Allegations by Children and Adolescents: Contextual Factors and Clinical Subtypes," *American Journal of Psychotherapy* 46, no. 4 (1992): 556–70.

23. Everson and Boat, "False Allegations of Sexual Abuse by Children and Adolescents," https://scholar.google.com/scholar?hl=en&as_sdt=0,36&q=False+Allegations+of+Sexual+Abuse+by+Children+and+Adolescents&btnG=.

24. David Lisak et al., "False Allegations of Sexual Assault: An Analysis of Ten Years of Reported Cases," *Violence Against Women* 16, no. 12 (2010): 1318–34, https://www.falserapetimeline.org/false-rape-4937.pdf.

possible to survey people in the general population, but even this method misses people who are unwilling to report that they have engaged in abuse.

With all those caveats, research does provide some information about the people who commit CSA. First is that most offenders are men. In one of the studies I discussed in the last chapter, for example, David Finkelhor and his colleagues surveyed children and their caretakers and found that a full 96 percent of CSA perpetrators were male.[25] Using data from the sexual-offender registries in forty-nine states plus Washington, DC, Guam, and Puerto Rico, another study concluded that 98 percent were male.[26] The percentage of women perpetrators was higher in a study conducted using official criminal records in Canada. It found that women made up 10.7 percent of all CSA offenders.[27] A recent study of all substantiated cases that went through Child Protective Services (rather than through law enforcement) came up with an even higher number: a full 20 percent of the perpetrators were women.[28] Because the study did not include law enforcement cases, however, it likely significantly underestimates the proportion of men. What all of these studies indicate is that that there are women offenders but that they are very much in the minority.

25. Finkelhor et al., "Child Maltreatment Rates Assessed in a National Household Survey of Caregivers and Youth," http://unh.edu/ccrc/pdf/CV316.pdf

26. Alissa R. Ackerman et al., "Who Are the People in Your Neighborhood? A Descriptive Analysis of Individuals on Public Sex Offender Registries," *International Journal of Law and Psychiatry* 34, no. 3 (2011): 149–59, https://scholar.google.com/scholar?hl=en&as_sdt=0%2C36&q=Who+Are+the+People+in+Your+Neighborhood%3F+A+Descriptive+&btnG=.

27. Tracey Peter, "Exploring Taboos: Comparing Male- and Female-Perpetrated Child Sexual Abuse," *Journal of Interpersonal Violence* 24, no. 7 (2009): 1111–28, http://citeseerx.ist.psu.edu/viewdoc/download?doi=10.1.1.894.3891&rep=rep1&type=pdf.

28. David Axlyn McLeod, "Female Offenders in Child Sexual Abuse Cases: A National Picture," *Journal of Child Sexual Abuse* 24, no. 1 (2015): 97–114, https://scholar.google.com/scholar?hl=en&as_sdt=0%2C36&q=Female+Offenders+in+Child+Sexual+Abuse+Cases%3A&btnG=.

Delving a little more deeply into the data on gender and CSA offending, there is evidence to suggest that men and women offenders differ in some key ways. For example, women much more often co-offend and their co-offenders are often men.[29] In the Canadian study cited above, researchers also found that women were more likely than men to abuse their own biological children. Both men and women tend to choose a victim of the other gender, although this is more the case for men than women. Specifically, about 54 percent of women abuse a boy, while almost 90 percent of men abuse girls. There is also a very small percentage of both groups who victimize children of both genders.[30] Some research suggests that women who engage in CSA have more significant psychological problems than do male offenders.[31]

Researchers have not yet clarified whether there is a relationship between race and CSA. This is partly because studies often draw on data for all sexual offenses, rather than separating CSA into a separate category. One of these studies showed that, in 2010, about 66 percent of the people on sex-offender registries were white. This means that they were slightly underrepresented (whites made up just under 72 percent of the population that year). Blacks, however, were overrepresented (they were about 22 percent of registrants but only 12 percent of the US population). In contrast, Asians and

---

29. Katria S. Williams and David M. Bierie, "An Incident-Based Comparison of Female and Male Sexual Offenders," *Sexual Abuse: A Journal of Research and Treatment* 27, no. 3 (2015): 235–57, http://citeseerx.ist.psu.edu/viewdoc/download?doi=10.1.1.918.1750&rep=rep1&type=pdf.

30. Williams and Bierie, "An Incident-Based Comparison of Female and Male Sexual Offenders," http://citeseerx.ist.psu.edu/viewdoc/download?doi=10.1.1.918.1750&rep=rep1&type=pdf.

31. Rebecca Williams et al., "Characteristics of Female Solo and Female Co-Offenders and Male Solo Sexual Offenders against Children," *Sexual Abuse* 31, no. 2 (2019): 151–72, https://scholar.google.com/scholar?hl=en&as_sdt=0%2C36&q=Characteristics+of+Female+Solo+and+Female+Co-Offenders+&btnG=; Marie-Hélène Colson et al., "Female Sex Offenders: A Challenge to Certain Paradigms," *Sexologies* 22, no. 4 (2013): 109–17.

Hispanics were underrepresented.[32] Let me, however, urge caution in the interpretation of any racial criminal justice data. There is substantial evidence that racial disproportionality in official crime statistics is largely tied to discrimination in the criminal justice system, not to levels of criminality. For example, Blacks are arrested considerably more often than whites who commit similar crimes.[33]

One little-discussed fact about people who commit CSA is that about a third are children themselves. In fact, juvenile offenders are responsible for about 35 percent of all sexual crime against children. They are more likely than adult offenders to victimize children under the age of twelve and they are more likely to offend in groups. Most juvenile offenders are teenagers—because it appears that offending, especially among boys, increases dramatically around age twelve. Most of the time, juveniles abuse children in homes, but about 12 percent of the time, the abuse occurs in schools. This percentage is higher than the 2 percent of adult offenses that occur in schools.[34]

People who abuse children come from a wide range of backgrounds. One study looked at nonincarcerated people who had voluntarily requested treatment for sex offending. The majority sought help for CSA, but some had committed other types of sexual offenses like the rape of an adult. None, however, had been officially charged by law enforcement. As an inducement to

---

32. Ackerman et al., "Who Are the People in Your Neighborhood?" https://scholar.google.com/scholar?hl=en&as_sdt=0%2C36&q=Who+Are+the+People+in+Your+Neighborhood%3F+A+Descriptive+&btnG=; US Census Bureau, *Overview of Race and Hispanic Origin: 2010* (Washington, DC: US Department of Commerce Economics and Statistics Administration, 2011), https://www.census.gov/prod/cen2010/briefs/c2010br-02.pdf.

33. Tammy Rinehart Kochel, David B. Wilson, and Stephen D. Mastrofski, "Effect of Suspect Race on Officers' Arrest Decisions," *Criminology* 49, no. 2 (2011): 473–512.

34. David Finkelhor, Richard Ormrod, and Mark Chaffin, "Juveniles Who Commit Sex Offenses against Minors," *Juvenile Justice Bulletin* (Washington, DC: US Government Printing Office, 2009), http://scholars.unh.edu/ccrc/15/.

participate, free treatment was offered upon the completion of the study. There was remarkable diversity in the group in terms of education, income, race, and religion. [35]

DOES PEDOPHILIA CAUSE CHILD SEXUAL ABUSE?

When we talk about people who sexually abuse children, we often refer to them as *pedophiles*. But what does this term mean? Many psychologists say an adult has pedophilia if they show consistent and strong sexual attraction to children who are under the age of thirteen.[36] Psychologist Michael Seto more specifically defines the term as a group of people who, prior to reaching puberty, discover that they are attracted to children and who, into adulthood, continue to experience an exclusive sexual and romantic interest in them.[37] He also finds that pedophilia appears to be stable over time, although it is more amenable to change than heterosexual or homosexual orientation. People with pedophilia appear to be less discriminating about the gender of those they are attracted to than are nonpedophiles.

But does pedophilia cause CSA? It certainly plays a role in some cases, but research shows that a large percentage of CSA offenders do not meet the clinical definition of pedophilia because they actually prefer sex with adults.[38] This finding is supported by a unique study that assessed how aroused different groups of men were by children. They compared men who had been caught for three different types of offenses: CSA, possession of child pornography, and sexual crimes involving adults. The group who consumed child

---

35. Gene G. Abel et al., "Self-Reported Sex Crimes of Nonincarcerated Paraphiliacs," *Journal of Interpersonal Violence* 2, no. 1 (1987): 3–25.

36. Michael C. Seto, "Pedophilia," *Annual Review of Clinical Psychology* 5 (2009): 391–407, https://www.annualreviews.org/doi/10.1146/annurev.clinpsy.032408.153618.

37. Michael C. Seto, "Is Pedophilia a Sexual Orientation?" *Archives of Sexual Behavior* 41, no. 1 (2012): 231–36.

38. Seto, "Pedophilia," https://www.annualreviews.org/doi/10.1146/annurev.clinpsy.032408.153618.

pornography was the most aroused by children. This is a surprising finding since common sense suggests it would be the CSA offenders. The researchers speculate that pornography consumption is the best indicator of pedophilia because people can get any kind of images they want on the internet, so they tend to only look at what most interests them. In contrast, it is not always possible to have sex with the people we find attractive, so people sometimes choose based on availability.

It appears that many of the people who abuse children do so simply because that is who is available, not because they prefer them.[39] This is likely the case with many priests. As described, John Jay College's study of sexual abuse in the Catholic Church estimated that less than 5 percent of abusing priests could be considered pedophiles.[40] It is also important to note that there are people who meet the clinical definition of pedophilia but never act on their desires.[41] David Feige, a documentary filmmaker who specializes in policy issues related to CSA, compares the group of people with pedophilia who do not abuse children to faithfully married people. Most married people do not stop being attracted to people other than their spouses, but they simply stop acting on that attraction.[42] In chapter 8, I will talk more about programs that have been shown to be successful in helping people with pedophilia control their behavior.

39. Michael C. Seto, James M. Cantor, and Ray Blanchard, "Child Pornography Offenses Are a Valid Diagnostic Indicator of Pedophilia," *Journal of Abnormal Psychology* 115, no. 3 (2006): 610–15, https://psycnet.apa.org/full text/2006-09167-022.pdf.

40. John Jay College of Criminal Justice, "The Nature and Scope of Sexual Abuse of Minors," http://www.bishop-accountability.org/reports/2004_02_27_ JohnJay_revised/2004_02_27_John_Jay_Main_Report_Optimized.pdf.

41. James M. Cantor and Ian V. McPhail, "Non-Offending Pedophiles," *Current Sexual Health Reports* 8, no. 3 (2016): 121–28, https:// scholar.google.com/scholar?hl=en&as_sdt=0%2C36&q=James+M.+Can tor+and+Ian+V.+McPhail%2C+"Non-Offending+Pedophiles%2C"&btnG=.

42. Feige made these comments in a talk at the NARSOL conference in Cleveland on June 9, 2018.

OTHER POSSIBLE CAUSES OF OFFENDING

It is unfortunate that there is not a clear understanding of the causes of CSA. There are, however, known factors that are associated with it. Perhaps not surprisingly, people who sexually abuse children disproportionately abuse alcohol and drugs.[43] Additionally, an extensive study of 679 men who were sex offenders found that 38 percent reported having been sexually abused themselves as children. This is about three times the rate of men in the general population. The offenders in the study also reported high rates of neglect as well as physical and verbal abuse in their childhood homes.[44]

These statistics about prior victimization often lead people to worry that anyone who experiences abuse as a child will grow up to repeat the cycle. In truth, however, the vast majority of children who suffer abuse do *not* grow up to be offenders (see box below). Children who have supportive families are even less likely to go on to offend against others.[45] A large-scale study, this one conducted in Australia, found that only 5 percent of men who were abused as children were later charged with a sexual offense of any type. While they did offend at about 8 times the rate of the general population, the vast majority did not abuse children.[46] Further evi-

---

43. Roy R. Frenzel, Reuben A. Lang, and Pierre Flor-Henry, "Sex Hormone Profiles in Pedophilic and Incestuous Men," *Annals of Sex Research* 3 (1990): 59–74.

44. Jill S. Levenson, Gwenda M. Willis, and David S. Prescott, "Adverse Childhood Experiences in the Lives of Male Sex Offenders: Implications for Trauma-Informed Care," *Sexual Abuse: A Journal of Research and Treatment* 28, no. 4 (2016): 340–59.

45. Natacha Godbout et al., "Child Sexual Abuse and Subsequent Relational and Personal Functioning: The Role of Parental Support," *Child Abuse & Neglect* 38, no. 2 (2014): 317–25, https://scholar.google.com/scholar?hl=en&as_sdt=0%2C36&q=Child+sexual+abuse+and+subsequent+relational+and+personal+functioning%3A+The+role+of+parental+support&btnG=.

46. Margaret C. Cutajar, James R. P. Ogloff, and Paul E. Mullen, *Child Sexual Abuse and Subsequent Offending and Victimisation: A 45-Year Follow-up Study* (Canberra, Australia: Criminology Research Council, 2011), http://citeseerx.ist.psu.edu/viewdoc/download?doi=10.1.1.421.9799&rep=rep1&type=pdf.

dence that victimization does not automatically lead to offending is provided by the fact that most victims of CSA are girls, but most offenders are male.[47]

Thinking Error: Backward Reasoning

Backward reasoning is a common—but flawed—thought process that involves starting with a fact and then trying to infer back in time to understand what caused it. Here are two examples involving CSA: First, we know that it is the case that many adult sexual offenders began offending when they were children or adolescents. It is very tempting to reason backward from this fact and conclude that all young offenders continue to offend into adulthood. If you think about this a second, it should be clear why this reasoning is faulty. There might be a thousand juveniles who abuse children but only twenty continue to offend as adults. If ten of these adults were arrested and interviewed, it would appear that all adult offenders start their careers early in life. The problem, of course, is that there would be no awareness of the 980 young offenders who stopped their behavior. Since they were never arrested, they would never be counted. It becomes clear, later in this chapter, that while my made-up numbers do not reflect reality, the rate of recidivism for juveniles is notably low.[48]

A second common use of backward reasoning involves the relationship between prior victimization and later abuse offenses. While it is true that many CSA offenders were victims themselves, this in no way means that abuse inevitably leads to offending. When reasoning correctly, one can recognize that looking just at the pool of offenders blinds us to the

---

47. Anne Cossins, *Masculinities, Sexualities, and Child Sexual Abuse* (The Hague and Boston: Kluwer Law International, 2000).

48. Michael F. Caldwell, "Quantifying the Decline in Juvenile Sexual Recidivism Rates," *Psychology, Public Policy, and Law* 22, no. 4 (2016): 414–26.

many abused children who grow up to be law-abiding citizens. As the studies described above suggest, researchers have found that this is a large number.[49]

Another way that CSA offenders who are caught appear to stand out from the general population is that they have a high rate of *intimacy deficits*. This means that they are less connected to others, more fearful of intimacy, and lonelier than people who have not been convicted of CSA.[50] Sociologist Anne Cossins, however, argues that we should be cautious about jumping to the conclusion that intimacy deficits cause CSA.[51] Perhaps the offenders with intimacy deficits are simply more likely to get caught than those with closer social circles. It makes sense that loners are more likely to be suspected of abuse than people with a lot of friends and strong intimate relationships. A second possibility is that arrest and incarceration cause intimacy difficulties—not the other way around. People with strong social networks may discover that their friends and families start to shun them once they are arrested. It is also hard for people with CSA convictions to make friends in prison because they are socially ostracized by both correctional staff and other inmates.[52]

49. Mark Chaffin, "Our Minds Are Made Up—Don't Confuse Us with the Facts: Commentary on Policies Concerning Children with Sexual Behavior Problems and Juvenile Sex Offenders," *Child Maltreatment* 13, no. 2 (2008): 110–21, https://ok-rsol.org/resources/Documents/Chaffin%20-%20Policies%20Concerning%20JSOs%20%28May%202008%29%20-%20Child%20Maltreatment.pdf.

50. Kurt M. Bumby and David J. Hansen, "Intimacy Deficits, Fear of Intimacy, and Loneliness among Sexual Offenders," *Criminal Justice and Behavior* 24, no. 3 (1997): 315–31, https://scholar.google.com/scholar?hl=en&as_sdt=0%2C36&q=Intimacy+Deficits%2C+Fear+of+Intimacy%2C+and+Loneliness+&btnG=.

51. Cossins, Masculinities, Sexualities, and Child Sexual Abuse.

52. Chantal van den Berg et al., "Sex Offenders in Prison: Are They Socially Isolated?" *Sexual Abuse: A Journal of Research and Treatment* 30, no. 7 (2017): 828–45, https://journals.sagepub.com/doi/pdf/10.1177/1079063217700884.

A Note on Causation and Correlation

Readers are likely familiar with the expression "correlation does not equal causation." It means that just because two events occur together, one does not necessarily cause the other. A classic example of the correlation/causation problem involves the proven fact that the more firefighters respond to a fire, the more property damage results. This could lead to the conclusion that firefighters cause property damage, but that clearly does not make a lot of sense. Instead, there is a third factor involved. The size of the fire determines both how many firefighters respond and how much property damage there is. Big fires cause the dispatcher to send a lot of firefighters. Big fires also lead to a lot of property damage. In other words, the number of firefighters is correlated with property damage, but it does not cause it.

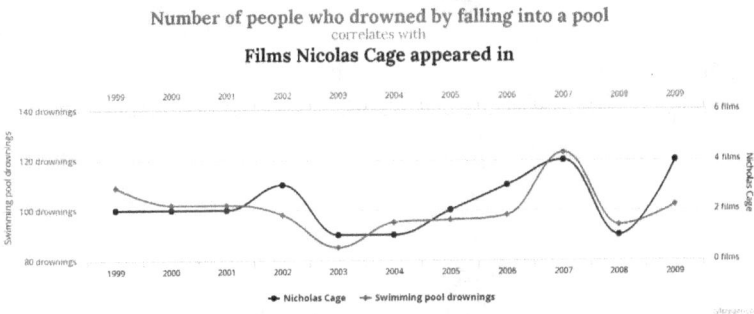

Number of people who drowned by falling into a pool
correlates with
Films Nicolas Cage appeared in

Figure 5. Number of people who drowned by falling into a pool, correlated with films Nicolas Cage appeared in. Source: Tyler Vigen at tylervigen.com

Researchers have uncovered a lot of factors that correlate with CSA, but it is important to not jump too quickly to conclude causality. For example, there is a correlation between exposure to pornography at a young age and later CSA offending.[53] While it is certainly possible that pornography causes

---

53. Dominique A. Simons, Sandy K. Wurtele, and Robert L. Durham, "Developmental Experiences of Child Sexual Abusers and Rapists," *Child Abuse &*

people to offend later in life, it is more likely that a third factor is involved. As described, many adult offenders grew up in disorganized homes where there was very little supervision and a lot of chaos and violence. The household disorganization could have enabled them to obtain pornography as children and—quite separately—it could also be linked to their later offending.

One of the more controversial explanations for why people commit CSA involves gender. As discussed in the last chapter, the vast majority of offenders are men. Cossins argues that this fact may be key to understanding CSA. In fact, she believes that societal definitions of masculinity are a direct cause. [54] Men are expected to be strong, sexually potent, and in control at all times. When they believe that they have failed to meet these expectations, they feel powerless and emasculated (even if, in reality, they have a great deal of power). In order to restore their masculine image, some sexually exploit weaker people through pornography, rape, sex with prostitutes, child sexual abuse, or intimate partner violence. This is a compelling argument, but it is also incomplete since it does not do a good job explaining why many men do not sexually exploit others, even when they feel powerless. Nor does it explain why some women commit CSA.

In sum, it is impossible to pin down one cause of CSA. It is multicausal and may vary across groups of offenders. While there does appear to be a small subgroup of offenders who are exclusively attracted to children ("pedophiles"), most offenders do not fit into this category. Most are opportunistic offenders—engaging in a wide variety of crimes when the opportunity arises. In a study of incarcerated child sexual offenders in Australia, for example,

---

Neglect 32, no. 5 (2008): 549–60, https://scholar.google.com/scholar?hl=en&as_sdt=0%2C36&q=Developmental+Experiences+of+Child+Sexual+Abusers+&btnG=.

54. Cossins, Masculinities, Sexualities, and Child Sexual Abuse.

researchers found that 59 percent were involved in nonsexual as well as sexual criminal behavior.[55] This suggests that, in most cases, CSA is just one part of a package of problematic behaviors.

THE CONTEXT OF ABUSE

Now that I have discussed some of the characteristics of people who abuse children, I can look at their methods and how they gain access to children. First, most victims of CSA are not abused by strangers; much more often the abuser is someone known and trusted. Pulling together data from surveys conducted in 2003, 2008, and 2011, researchers found that 5.5 percent of all seventeen-year-old girls reported being sexually abused by a family member during their lifetime, 19.6 percent by an acquaintance, and just 3 percent by a stranger. The equivalent numbers for seventeen-year-old boys were 0.6, 3.1, and 1.4, respectively.[56] Over half of all family abuse is perpetrated by fathers and another 20 percent by male live-in relatives.[57]

Offenders usually engage in a process of "grooming" potential victims. This means that they employ tactics designed to ensure that the child (and their family) trust and like them. Grooming can include gift giving, fun trips, or helping the family with child-care or other needs. In a study conducted with ninety-one sex offenders, the most common grooming strategies were playing or teaching the children, bribing them, showing them affection and

---

55. Richard Wortley and Stephen Smallbone, "A Criminal Careers Typology of Child Sexual Abusers," *Sexual Abuse: A Journal of Research and Treatment* 26, no. 6 (2014): 569–85, https://scholar.google.com/schol ar?hl=en&as_sdt=0%2C36&q=A+Criminal+Careers+Typology+of+Child+Sexu al+Abusers&btnG=.

56. David Finkelhor et al., "The Lifetime Prevalence of Child Sexual Abuse and Sexual Assault Assessed in Late Adolescence," *Journal of Adolescent Health* 55, no. 3 (2014): 329–33.

57. Finkelhor et al., "Child Maltreatment Rates Assessed in a National House hold Survey of Caregivers and Youth." http://unh.edu/ccrc/pdf/CV316.pdf

love, isolating them through babysitting, and gaining the trust of their family. Physical force was less common, but 19 percent of the offenders reported using it during their first encounter with a child.[58]

As I talked about in chapter 1, the media is more likely to publicize CSA cases when they involve many victims. But is it common for offenders to abuse many children? One study conducted with 248 incarcerated CSA offenders in Austria found that the average number of victims varied by how the offender gained access. The offenders were asked how many people they had victimized sexually over their lifetime (whether or not they were caught for these crimes). For those who abused their own family members, the average number of victims was 1.66; the comparable number for those who abused children through their work in child-serving organizations was 5.87. Finally, the offenders who neither worked with children nor abused their own family members abused an average of 3.52 children.[59] This study suggests that, while there are certainly offenders with many victims, these cases are extreme; most offenders victimize one or a few children.

Many parents worry about their children's online activities because they fear that offenders commonly lurk in chat rooms, video games, or other online forums. Their fears are not irrational—there are documented cases of offenders who have met children online and arranged to meet them in real life. Adults also sometimes use the internet to solicit sexual pictures of children or engage in sexual talk with them.[60] It is difficult to know how

---

58. Michele Elliot, Kevin Browne, and Jennifer Kilcoyne, "Child Sexual Abuse Prevention: What Offenders Tell Us," *Child Abuse and Neglect* 19, no. 5 (1995): 579–94.

59. Daniel Turner et al., "Pedophilic Sexual Interests and Psychopathy in Child Sexual Abusers Working with Children," *Child Abuse & Neglect* 38, no. 2 (2014): 326–35, https://scholar.google.com/scholar?hl=en&as_sdt=0%2C36&q=Pedo philic+Sexual+Interests+and+Psychopathy&btnG=.

60. L. Alvin Malesky, "Predatory Online Behavior: Modus Operandi of Convicted Sex Offenders Identifying Potential Victims and Contacting Minors over the Internet," *Journal of Child Sexual Abuse* 16, no. 2 (2007): 23–32.

common these crimes are because there is no national database that pulls together data collected at the state level. Additionally, some data sources do not separate out the crimes of accessing and distributing child pornography from actual solicitation crimes.[61]

The best-known information is drawn from three national surveys of children ages ten to seventeen conducted by the Crimes Against Children Lab at the University of New Hampshire. They asked children if they had ever received an unwanted internet-based request to talk about sex or engage in sexual activities. The children were also asked if any adult had ever made these requests (regardless of whether they were unwanted). The results of the survey indicated that internet solicitation decreased 53 percent between 2000 and 2010. While this decrease is good, solicitation is still a problem. In 2010, 9 percent of children reported having experienced it. Only 3 percent of the respondents, however, reported experiencing solicitation that involved offline contact such as telephone calls or arrangements to meet. It is also important to note that in 38 percent of all solicitation cases, the victim knew the offender offline before the online contact.[62]

> If you are a parent worried about keeping your child safe on the internet, *Parenting Magazine* provides some good suggestions: https://www.parenting.com/child/keeping-your-child-safe-on-the-internet/.

The focus of this book is on sexual contact, not the distribution of child pornography. This should not be taken to mean that child pornography is not a problem. In fact, it makes up the vast majority

61. Michael Seto, *Internet-Facilitated Sexual Offending* (Washington, DC: Sex Offender Management Assessment and Planning Initiative, 2015).

62. Kimberly J. Mitchell et al., *Trends in Unwanted Sexual Solicitations: Findings from the Youth Internet Safety Studies* (Durham, NH: Crimes against Children Research Center, 2014), http://www.unh.edu/ccrc/pdf/Sexual%20Solicitation%201%20of%204%20YISS%20Bulletins%20Feb%202014.pdf.

of internet sexual crime against children.[63] If you are interested in reading about the problem of child pornography, I include a suggestion at the end of the chapter. The *New York Times* also ran a well-researched (and deeply upsetting) article about the availability of child pornography on the web. It can be found at https://www.nytimes.com/interactive/2019/09/28/us/child-sex-abuse.html.

Thinking Error: Overestimating Victims from Official Records

In the last chapter, we learned that most estimates of CSA prevalence are from official law enforcement or Child Protective Services reports. This leads to underestimates because many victims never report their abuse. Here, I cover a second problem with the use of official records: the overestimation of serial offenders (those who have multiple victims or who abuse one victim multiple times). Mark Chaffin does a good job explaining this problem. He says that serial offenders are simply more likely to be caught than are people who offend only once. This is because when there are multiple victims, it is likely that at least one of them will eventually report the abuse. Repeat abuse of one child also increases the chances of detection because it gives the adults in the child's life more opportunities to notice suspicious patterns or behavioral signals in the child. Serial offenders may also get caught more because they become careless over time. At any rate, the fact that *many* serial offenders end up in prison cannot be used to assume that *most* offenders are serial offenders.[64]

---

63. Seto, Internet-Facilitated Sexual Offending.

64. Chaffin, "Our Minds Are Made Up," https://ok-rsol.org/resources/Documents/Chaffin%20-%20Policies%20Concerning%20JSOs%20%28May%202008%29%20-%20Child%20Maltreatment.pdf.

RECIDIVISM AND TREATMENT

Stereotypes suggest that CSA offenders have very high recidivism rates. In common usage, the term *recidivism* refers to the commission of a new crime after one or more past convictions. It turns out that it is a myth that that CSA offenders are more likely to recidivate than other types of criminals. Where did the myth come from? It has a long history, but it received official sanction in a famous Supreme Court case decided in 2002. I describe *McCune v. Lyle* in the box below.

The *McCune v. Lile* Supreme Court Case

In 2002, the Supreme Court heard the case *McCune vs. Lile*. Robert Lile was an inmate in Kansas, serving a prison sentence for a sexual offense. As part of his mandated treatment, he was told that he would need to detail his entire previous sexual history. This would be followed by a lie detector test. Lile felt that he was in a catch-22: if he listed illegal sexual contact that had not previously come to the attention of law enforcement, he could be prosecuted for those crimes. Not listing it, however, was likely to cause him to fail the lie detector test. He finally refused to fill out the sexual history form and the prison punished him by sending him to a higher security prison where he lost many privileges (including the ability to send home the money he earned at his prison job). He claimed that the prison's actions violated his Fifth Amendment rights (which include freedom from self-incrimination). Lile won in two lower court cases before his case was appealed to the Supreme Court.

In his Supreme Court decision, Justice Anthony Kennedy wrote that the state had a compelling interest in lowering sexual offense recidivism by forcing people into treatment. Therefore, the state could legally require inmates to comply with treatment or risk sanctions. Most relevant to our discussion

---

> here, Kennedy supported his assertion of compelling state
> interest by claiming that there was an 80 percent recidivism
> rate among untreated sexual offenders.

Justice Kennedy's argument certainly sounds compelling. Eighty percent is a big number. But where did that figure come from? It appears that Kennedy found it in a publication put out by the National Institute of Justice (NIJ), which is generally considered to be a reputable source. Unfortunately, the NIJ must not have been at the top of their game that day because they pulled the 80 percent number from a 1986 *Psychology Today* article. *Psychology Today* is a popular, nonacademic magazine for people interested in learning about psychological issues. It's fun to read. The article in question, however, interviewed a counselor at a prison-treatment program for very serious sexual offenders. With no research or statistics to back him up, the counselor said that in his experience, 80 percent of untreated sex offenders who left prison recidivated. Even at that time, most research suggested that the actual recidivism rate was lower, but once the 80 percent number appeared in a Supreme Court decision, it became part of the canon for future decisions. It has been cited in other court cases across the nation and has been repeated multiple times in the popular press.[65]

What is the real rate of recidivism? One of the major studies of sexual offender recidivism drew on data from ten jurisdictions in Canada, the United States, and Britain between 1970 and the early 1990s. The study included 4,724 convicted rapists and CSA offenders. Recidivism was counted somewhat differently in each jurisdiction but always involved a new sexual crime charge. The study, commissioned by the Canadian government, found that five years after release from prison, 13 percent of the CSA offenders had been arrested for a new crime. Within fifteen years, a total of 23 percent

65. Ira Mark Ellman and Tara Ellman, "'Frightening and High': The Supreme Court's Crucial Mistake about Sex Crime Statistics," *Constitutional Commentary* 30 (2015): 495–508.

of the group had been rearrested.[66] While this number is not good news, it is substantially less than the 80 percent figure published in the *Psychology Today* article. Additionally, the researchers argued that the current recidivism rate is likely to be even lower than 23 percent because treatment is more widely available in prisons than it was when they collected their data.

The fact that the Canadian study had an extremely large sample size enabled the researchers to arrive at very detailed conclusions about recidivism. For example, they found that the risk of recidivism decreases each year a person has been out of prison. This means that by the time someone has been conviction free for fifteen years, their recidivism rate is only 4 percent. The study also found that people with multiple convictions for sexual offenses had higher recidivism rates than those who had only one. Finally, older adults were less likely to recidivate than younger adults. This last finding was not a surprise, as people tend to age out of most types of crime (see the further reading section if you are interested in this phenomenon). It should be noted, however, that juveniles have a particularly low rate of recidivism. In a recent study that looked at data collected over many years, it appears that the rate of juvenile recidivism between 2010 and 2015 was about 2.5 percent. Like adult recidivism, this rate decreased substantially between 1980 and 1995.[67]

Chapter 2 discussed research showing that women are underrepresented in the group of people who sexually abuse children. This leads to the question of whether their recidivism rates are different as well. Researchers reviewed studies of people who had been convicted of any type of sexual crimes in the United States, Canada, the United Kingdom, Australia, and New Zealand. Only

---

66. Andrew John Rawson Harris and Robert Karl Hanson, *Sex Offender Recidivism: A Simple Question* (Ottawa: Minister of Public Safety and Emergency Preparedness, 2004), 3, https://www.publicsafety.gc.ca/cnt/rsrcs/pblctns/sx-ffndr-rc-dvsm/index-en.aspx?wbdisable=true.

67. Caldwell, "Quantifying the Decline in Juvenile Sexual Recidivism Rates."

1 percent of the women committed another sexual offense after being released. This compared to 13 to 14 percent for men. Interestingly, most recidivism involved nonsexual crimes. Overall, 20 percent of women and 36 percent of men were later convicted of any type of crime.[68] In other words, when sexual offenders—both men and women—recidivate, it is more often for a nonsexual than sexual crime.

It appears that certain conditions help people refrain from sexual reoffending. For example, people who prefer to have sexual relationships with adults, who do not have a high sexual drive, and who are able to form emotional bonds with other adults are better able to resist having sex with children. Supportive networks are key: when people have strong relationships with law-abiding others, it helps them refrain from illegal activities. Employment, sobriety, and an ability to problem solve also help.[69] A meta-analysis of eighty-two studies that included almost thirty thousand sexual offenders found generally low rates of recidivism among sexual offenders (13.7 percent of them committed another sexual crime within five to six years). Rates were higher, however, for people who were very preoccupied with sex, especially if their thoughts involved "deviant sexual interests" (like having sex with children or rape). High levels of criminal involvement, drug use, and antisocial personality disorder are also associated with recidivism.[70]

Factors that have been linked to serial abuse and recidivism are "cognitive distortions" that enable offenders to preserve their positive self-image even as they engage in behavior that is societally

68. Franca Cortoni and R. Karl Hanson, *A Review of the Recidivism Rates of Adult Female Sexual Offenders* (Ottawa: Correctional Service of Canada, 2005), http://saratso.org/pdf/Corton_and_Hanson-2005.pdf.

69. Michiel de Vries Robbé et al., "An Exploration of Protective Factors Supporting Desistance from Sexual Offending," *Sexual Abuse* 27, no. 1 (2015): 16–33.

70. R. Karl Hanson and Kelly E. Morton-Bourgon, "The Characteristics of Persistent Sexual Offenders: A Meta-Analysis of Recidivism Studies," *Journal of Consulting and Clinical Psychology* 73, no. 6 (2005): 1154–63, https://www.icmec.org/wp-content/uploads/2015/10/Characteristics-of-Persistent-Sex-Offenders-Meta-Analysis-of-Recidivism-2005.pdf.

shunned. Researchers have identified a large number of distortions that can serve this purpose. For example, some offenders believe that children have sexual desires and want to have sex with adults. Others find ways to shift the blame for their act onto others ("the child's parent should have supervised them better") or they say that the abuse was a result of their uncontrollable sexual urges.[71] It should be noted that cognitive distortions are not specific to CSA—we all find ways to excuse or justify our bad behavior to make ourselves look better. Distortions around CSA, however, are much more harmful than those that many of us use to justify speeding or overeating. Some researchers believe that helping CSA offenders deconstruct their particularly harmful distortions can prevent recidivism.

Recent work indicates that treatment is effective in lowering rates of recidivism, particularly for juveniles.[72] One of the more effective types of treatment is called multisystemic therapy (MST). MST is offered to juveniles in their homes and involves their whole family. In terms of the efficacy of treatment with adults, the findings are more mixed, with some studies finding treatment does not reduce recidivism and others (including two large meta-analyses) showing it to be effective. For example, R. Karl Hanson and Kelly E. Morton-Bourgon found that treatment programs reduced sexual recidivism by about four percentage points and recidivism for all crime types by nine percentage points. It is important to note, however, that their study included all sexual offenders, not just those who were convicted of CSA.[73]

---

71. Tony Ward and Thomas Keenan, "Child Molesters' Implicit Theories," *Journal of Interpersonal Violence* 14, no. 8 (1999): 821–38, https://scholar.google.com/scholar?hl=en&as_sdt=0%2C36&q=Tony+Ward+and+Thomas+Keenan%2C+"Child+Molesters'+Implicit+Theories%2C"+&btnG=; Jason D. Spraitz and Kendra N. Bowen, "Techniques of Neutralization and Persistent Sexual Abuse by Clergy: A Content Analysis of Priest Personnel Files from the Archdiocese of Milwaukee," *Journal of Interpersonal Violence* 31, no. 15 (2016): 2515–38.

72. Tamar Mendelson and Elizabeth J. Letourneau, "Parent-Focused Prevention of Child Sexual Abuse," *Prevention Science* 16, no. 6 (2015): 844–52.

73. R. Karl Hanson et al., "First Report of the Collaborative Outcome Data Project on the Effectiveness of Psychological Treatment for Sex Offenders,"

CONCLUSION

I started this chapter with the voices of children talking about their experiences with abuse. I selected the quotes because they contained representative elements. While victims are a diverse group, girls, disabled children, and children growing up in a single-parent home are particularly at risk. Offenders are disproportionately male, often have a childhood history of abuse, and have difficulties with intimacy. Children usually know the person who abuses them, and that person often leads up to abuse with gifts and favors. Called *grooming*, this process decreases the chance that a child will disclose the abuse and, when they do tell someone, families are often skeptical because of the high level of trust that has been developed with the offender.

Why do some adults sexually abuse children? Only a small percentage of offenders meet the criteria to be considered pedophiles. More often, CSA is one part of a package of criminal behaviors that also includes drug and alcohol abuse. Interfamily abuse is common, and a substantial proportion of abuse also occurs in child-serving organizations. While recidivism is a real concern, it is much lower than popular stereotypes suggest. Treatment can be effective in reducing reoffense rates, especially for juvenile offenders.

In the next chapter, I am going to shift gears to look at CSA prevention efforts. While reading, think about the material covered in the last two chapters. Do these prevention efforts make sense in light of what is now known about the dynamics of child sexual abuse?

Sexual Abuse: A Journal of Research and Treatment 14, no. 2 (2002): 169–94, https://www.researchgate.net/publication/11405528_First_Report_of_the_Collaborative_Outcome_Data_Project_on_the_Effectiveness_of_Psychological_Treatment_for_Sex_Offenders.

FURTHER READING

Sales, Nancy Jo. *American Girls: Social Media and the Secret Lives of Teenagers*. New York: Vintage Press, 2017.

Seto, Michael C. *Internet Sex Offenders*. Worcester, MA: American Psychological Association, 2017.

Wortley, Richard. *Psychological Criminology*. New York: Routledge, 2010.

SECTION TWO

ACTION

CHAPTER FOUR

LEGAL RESPONSES IN THE WAKE OF AN ALLEGATION

> Natalie was eight when she was molested by her older cousin. The cousin was babysitting Natalie and her sister while their parents were out for the evening. When the parents returned, the sister made an offhand comment that set off their alarm bells. They questioned Natalie and she disclosed the abuse. Her parents filed a police report, launching an inquiry that included an investigator coming to Natalie's school to interview her. Ultimately, the parents decided to spare her the trauma of further investigation and courtroom testimony. The cousin is now married with children. Natalie wrote movingly about these events in an article in the *Atlantic*.[1]

Natalie's story illustrates how the disclosure of abuse is only the beginning of a long and difficult process. Sometimes families do not contact authorities, choosing to ignore the issue or to deal with it on their own. Other families, like Natalie's, turn to either child-protective agencies or to the police. This leads to an investigation

1. Natalie Shure, "Why Young Sexual Assault Victims Tell Incoherent Stories," *Atlantic*, February 5, 2014, https://www.theatlantic.com/national/archive/2014/02/why-young-sexual-assault-victims-tell-incoherent-stories/283613/.

and, in some cases, a court trial. In this chapter, I look at this official process and the issues it raises for both child victims and accused offenders. Along the way, I discuss plea bargains, sentencing, victim impact statements, risk assessment, and failure-to-protect laws.

To understand legal responses to child sexual abuse (CSA), it is important to consider the purpose of punishment. Many social scientists identify four different rationales. First, punishment is used to incapacitate an offender, ensuring that they are unable to commit a new crime. Incarceration works to achieve this goal, as does capital punishment. In the case of CSA, an offender might be incapacitated by giving them drugs to make them impotent. A second rationale for punishment sees it as a warning to the offender and to others in the community. The hope is that they will see the punishment and decide that the crime is not worth the risk. This is called *deterrence*. A third rationale is rehabilitation, enabling the offender to return to society as a better-behaving citizen. Finally, many people cite retribution as a reason for punishment. This is represented by the expression "an eye for an eye."

US attitudes toward punishment have shifted over time. During the 1960s and 1970s, there was fairly widespread support for rehabilitation as a goal of prisons. The other three rationales were present as well, but the public placed relatively more emphasis on rehabilitation. That orientation began to shift toward retribution by the 1980s.[2] Some trace the shift to the publication of Robert Martinson's article "What Works? Questions and Answers about Prison Reform."[3] Regardless of its origin, the increased focus on retribution has led to a host of new public policies about CSA. I should note, however, that it is overly simplistic to say that Americans

---

2. Jody L. Sundt et al., "The Tenacity of the Rehabilitative Ideal: Have Attitudes Toward Offender Treatment Changed?" *Criminal Justice and Behavior* 25, no. 4 (1998): 426–42.

3. Robert Martinson, "What Works? Questions and Answers about Prison Reform," *The Public Interest* 44 (Spring 1974): 22–54, https://www.nationalaffairs.com/public_interest/detail/what-works-questions-and-answers-about-prison-reform.

are retributive. Research suggests that attitudes are actually more nuanced. While Americans tend to be retributive when asked general questions about what penalty criminals should receive, they are much less so when asked about specific cases.[4]

One of the factors that drives feelings about punishment involves the assessment of blame. The sociologist Charles Tilly argues that when something good happens, humans look for someone to credit, and when something bad happens, they look to assign blame.[5] He identifies a number of factors used to assign blame for bad events. These include how much harm is associated with the event, the assessment of the degree to which a particular person's (or group's) actions caused it, and judgement of the degree to which a person was aware that their action would cause a bad outcome and whether or not they intended that outcome. Applying these criteria to CSA, one can generally assume that offenders intended the abuse and were aware that it would cause harm. This leads people to assign a lot of blame to them. Tilly's work also suggests that more blame would be assigned to an offender with multiple victims and a particularly high level of harm.

Unfortunately, offenders are not the only people to whom blame is assigned in CSA cases. Victims are also blamed. This has been a problem historically, but it still happens today. Which victims are blamed most? Perhaps not surprisingly, it's usually the people who are seen as the least like us. When victims seem similar to us, more empathy than blame is expressed. As an example of this, men are more likely than women to blame women victims of sexual assault. They see themselves as different from the victim

---

4. Brandon K. Applegate et al., "Assessing Public Support for Three-Strikes-and-You're out Laws: Global versus Specific Attitudes," *Crime & Delinquency* 42, no. 4 (1996): 517–34, https://scholar.google.com/scholar?hl=en&as_sdt=0%2C36&q=Assessing+Public+Support+for+Three-Strikes-and-&btnG=.

5. Charles Tilly, *Credit and Blame* (Princeton, NJ: Princeton University Press, 2008), http://repository.umpwr.ac.id:8080/bitstream/handle/123456789/301/Credit%20and%20Blame.pdf?sequence=1&isAllowed=y.

and identify, at least to some degree, with the male offender.[6] Similarly, when white people see a victim who is a person of color, they disassociate themselves, doubting that they can relate to them.[7] The blame placed on victims is important because, among other things, it affects views of appropriate punishments for offenders.

INVESTIGATION THROUGH CHARGES

I turn now look at the beginning of the criminal justice process. What happens when a report of CSA suspicions is filed with the police or the local Child Protective Services (CPS)? In most states, CPS investigates all CSA claims—although the investigation can also be conducted by the police or by both agencies together. Policies vary widely across the country, and there continue to be many unresolved issues with interagency cooperation, communication, and agreement. For example, it is sometimes hard for the police and CPS to work together because the police are most interested in investigating the crime and CPS is most interested in protecting the child.[8]

In 2016, CPS agencies received 4.1 million referrals and found

---

6. Sudie Back and Hilary M. Lips, "Child Sexual Abuse: Victim Age, Victim Gender, and Observer Gender as Factors Contributing to Attributions of Responsibility," *Child Abuse & Neglect* 22, no. 12 (1998): 1239–52, https://scholar. google.com/scholar?hl=en&as_sdt=0%2C36&q=Child+Sexual+Abuse%3A+Vic tim+Age%2C+Victim+Gender%2C+and+&btnG=; Lisa Graham, Paul Rogers, and Michelle Davies, "Attributions in a Hypothetical Child Sexual Abuse Case: Roles of Abuse Type, Family Response and Respondent Gender," *Journal of Family Violence* 22, no. 8 (2007): 733–45.

7. Eduardo Bonilla-Silva, "The Invisible Weight of Whiteness: The Racial Grammar of Everyday Life in Contemporary America," *Ethnic and Racial Studies* 35, no. 2 (2012): 173–94, https://www.jstor.org/stable/23292648?seq=1.

8. For a review of this literature, see Andrea J. Sedlak et al., "Child Protection and Justice Systems Processing of Serious Child Abuse and Neglect Cases," *Child Abuse & Neglect* 30, no. 6 (2006): 657–77, https://scholar.google.com/schol ar?hl=en&as_sdt=0%2C36&q=Child+Protection+and+Justice+Systems+Process ing+&btnG=.

that 2.1 million of them met their criteria for investigation. Of those, 8.5 percent involved sexual abuse.[9] An investigation does not, however, ensure that a criminal prosecution will occur. Sometimes CPS decides that an accusation is unfounded or that the issue is minor and can be dealt with through offender counseling or other noncriminal justice means. Research has found that CPS concludes investigations without law enforcement involvement more often when cases involve younger children, first-time and less-serious offenders, and intrafamilial abuse. The chance of law enforcement involvement is also lowered if a person other than the victim makes the report. Not surprisingly, when the accused has a previous CSA conviction, the case is more likely to lead to further legal action.[10] A study of police sexual abuse investigators found that they are less likely to believe children when there is no physical evidence (like abrasions) or when a child does not show stereotyped emotional responses (like bedwetting).[11] It is not clear what percent of cases end up being sent on for prosecution; one meta-analysis of referrals from both CPS and law enforcement found tremendous variation across place and time. Rates ranged from 40 to 85 percent.[12]

The next stop in the criminal justice process is the prosecutor's office. Prosecutors file charges in about two-thirds of the CSA cases

9. Children's Bureau/ Administration on Children, Youth and Families/Administration for Children and Families/Health and Human Services, *Child Maltreatment 2016: Summary of Key Findings* (Washington, DC: Child Welfare Information Gateway, 2018), https://www.acf.hhs.gov/sites/default/files/cb/cm2016.pdf.

10. Delores D. Stroud, Sonja L. Martens, and Julia Barker, "Criminal Investigation of Child Sexual Abuse: A Comparison of Cases Referred to the Prosecutor to Those Not Referred," *Child Abuse & Neglect* 24, no. 5 (2000): 689–700.

11. Bradley A. Campbell, Tasha A. Menaker, and William R. King, "The Determination of Victim Credibility by Adult and Juvenile Sexual Assault Investigators," *Journal of Criminal Justice* 43, no. 1 (2015): 29–39.

12. Theodore P. Cross et al., "Prosecution of Child Abuse: A Meta-Analysis of Rates of Criminal Justice Decisions," *Trauma, Violence, & Abuse* 4, no. 4 (2003): 323–40, https://scholar.google.com/scholar?hl=en&as_sdt=0%2C36&q=Prosecution+of+Child+Abuse%3A+A+Meta-Analysis+of+&btnG=.

Figure 6. In the United States, prosecutors hold a lot of power because they decide when to file charges. Copyright [2020] American Civil Liberties Union. Originally posted by the ACLU at https://www.aclu.org/blog/smart-justice/across-america-single-most-powerful-person-local-criminal-justice-systems

that are referred to them, a number that has increased substantially from the 1990s.[13] Charges are more likely when at least two of the following conditions are met: the child victim reports the abuse themselves, there is a corroborating witness, the accused has a previous CSA conviction, or the accused confesses. There is a particularly low likelihood of charges when the only evidence is a victim disclosure.[14] It is important to note, however, that prosecutors do not just consider the strength of the evidence when they make decisions about charges. For example, they also consider the

13. Cross et al., "Prosecution of Child Abuse," https://scholar.google.com/scholar?hl=en&as_sdt=0%2C36&q=Prosecution+of+Child+Abuse%3A+A+Meta-Analysis+of+&btnG=.

14. Wendy A. Walsh et al., "Prosecuting Child Sexual Abuse: The Importance of Evidence Type," *Crime & Delinquency* 56, no. 3 (2010): 436–54, https://scholar.google.com/scholar?hl=en&as_sdt=0%2C36&q=Prosecuting+Child+Sexual+Abuse%3A+The+Importance+&btnG=.

potential impact of a prosecution on the child victim and their family.[15] In the United States, prosecutors may also consider public opinion because, unlike most other Western countries, their position is elected.[16]

Once charges are filed, defendants choose whether to plead guilty. A guilty plea causes the case to move directly to the sentencing phase, while a not guilty plea triggers a "preliminary hearing" or, depending on the state, a grand jury hearing. The purpose of this hearing is to determine if there is enough evidence to move forward to trial. State laws vary in terms of a child's participation in the preliminary hearing. In some states, a police officer can testify in a child's place, but in others, a child must testify in person or via closed-circuit television. If the judge finds that there is insufficient evidence presented at the hearing, they will dismiss the case. In cases where the evidence is deemed to be sufficient, a trial date is set, and the judge can decide whether to offer bail to the defendant. Having a trial date, however, does not ensure that a trial will actually happen. In some districts, cases can still be dropped if a defendant agrees to plead guilty and participate in a diversion program.[17] Victims or their parents can also stop cooperating in a case if they decide that it would be too emotionally difficult to go through a trial. This decreases the chance a prosecutor will go to trial.[18]

A common complaint about the court system is that it takes a very long time to resolve cases. For example, while the stated goal

15. Cross et al., "Prosecution of Child Abuse," https://scholar.google.com/scholar?hl=en&as_sdt=0%2C36&q=Prosecution+of+Child+Abuse%3A+A+Meta-Analysis+of+&btnG=.

16. Michael Tonry, "Prosecutors and Politics in Comparative Perspective," *Crime and Justice* 41, no. 1 (2012): 1–33.

17. Cross et al., "Prosecution of Child Abuse," https://scholar.google.com/scholar?hl=en&as_sdt=0%2C36&q=Prosecution+of+Child+Abuse%3A+A+Meta-Analysis+of+&btnG=.

18. Isabelle V. Daugnault, Mireille Cyr, and Martine Hébert, "Working with Non-Offending Parents in Cases of Child Sexual Abuse," in *The Wiley Handbook of What Works in Child Maltreatment: An Evidence-Based Approach to Assessment and Intervention in Child Protection*, ed. Louise Dixon et al. (Hoboken, NJ: John Wiley & Sons, 2017), 415–32.

of the Oregon criminal justice system is to resolve CSA cases in under four months, researchers studied three counties and found that only a minority of cases made that deadline (from 18 percent in one county to 37 and 47 percent in the other two). At the same time, few cases lasted longer than a year (11, 7, and 3 percent, respectively). A lengthy process can be frustrating and upsetting to victims, especially if hearings and trials are frequently rescheduled. In one county in the Oregon study, trials were rescheduled a full 98 percent of the time. The other counties rescheduled 33 and 75 percent of the time.[19]

PLEA BARGAINS

A plea bargain is an offer that a prosecutor makes to a person charged with a crime. If they agree to plead guilty, the prosecutor promises to lower the charge to something less serious. There are advantages and disadvantages to plea bargains. The state relies on them because they decrease the number of trials in an already-overwhelmed legal system. Guilty people often see plea bargains as advantageous because they result in a lighter sentence. Unfortunately, however, plea bargains can have unintended consequences. For example, innocent people sometimes take plea bargains when they lack a strong alibi or fear that a jury will be biased against them. Both innocent and guilty people can feel pressure to take plea bargains if they need to get out of jail to keep their jobs or care for their kids.[20]

CSA cases raise a number of unique issues in terms of plea bargains. For example, a plea bargain can result in charges that

---

19. Wendy A. Walsh et al., "Length of Time to Resolve Criminal Charges of Child Sexual Abuse: A Three-County Case Study," *Behavioral Sciences & the Law* 33, no. 4 (2015): 528–45.

20. Jed S. Rakoff, "Why Innocent People Plead Guilty," *New York Review of Books*, November 20, 2014, https://www.nacdl.org/getattachment/8e5437e4-79b2-4535-b26c-9fa266de7de8/why-innocent-people-plead-guilty-_-jrakoff_ny-review-of-books-2014.pdf.

do not accurately reflect the seriousness of a crime. This is worrisome when an offender pleads a sexual crime down to a nonsexual charge and avoids some of the consequences that are unique to sex crimes (like counseling). I discuss this problem at some length in the next chapter. At the other end of the spectrum, when innocent people plead guilty to a sexual crime in order to take advantage of a plea bargain, they may not fully understand or appreciate the lifelong consequences that are attached to that decision.

The vast majority of criminal charges in the United States end in a plea bargain. In fact, across the federal and state court systems, 97 percent of cases do not go to trial, largely because defendants plead guilty.[21] While this percentage is lower in CSA cases, it is still significant. In a study in Outagamie County, Wisconsin, for example, half the CSA charges between 2009 and 2014 were reduced, mostly through plea bargains.[22] In three counties in Oregon between 2007 and 2008, the percentages of plea bargains in felony CSA cases were 63, 77, and 79.[23]

THE CRIMINAL JUSTICE EXPERIENCE FOR CHILDREN

Over one hundred thousand children testify in various kinds of legal trials in the United States each year. In order to be allowed to testify, a child victim must be mature enough to accurately recall events and to understand the seriousness of an oath. They must also be able to understand that telling the truth is required.[24] If the

---

21. National Association of Criminal Defense Lawyers, "The Trial Penalty: The Sixth Amendment Right to Trial on the Verge of Extinction and How to Save It," *Federal Sentencing Reporter* 31, no. 4–5 (2018): 331–68.

22. Ariel Cheung, "Reduced Charges Common for Child Sex Assault," *Post Crescent*, January 25, 2015, https://www.postcrescent.com/story/news/local/2015/01/25/outagamie-county-child-sex-assaults-part-two/22179753/.

23. Walsh et al., "Length of Time to Resolve Criminal Charges of Child Sexual Abuse."

24. Robert H. Pantell, "The Child Witness in the Courtroom," *Pediatrics* 139, no. 3 (2017): 1–9, https://pediatrics.aappublications.org/content/139/3/e20164008.

court determines that a child meets these criteria, they can decide whether or not to testify. This decision can be highly stressful, particularly when adults have a stake in the decision. For example, a prosecutor might pressure a child to testify to increase the chance of a conviction. Pressure can also come from a child's relatives in intrafamilial cases—either because the relatives really want a conviction or because they do not.

Alternatives to Child Testimony

When children are unwilling or unable to testify in CSA cases, it can be very difficult for a prosecutor to secure a conviction. This has led to a search for alternatives. For example, an adult could testify about what a child victim told them, or a prosecutor could show a videotape of an investigative interview conducted with the child. While these solutions may sound promising, many are also illegal. This is because the Confrontation Clause of the US Constitution gives defendants the right to cross-examine all witnesses in person.

This issue of out-of-court statements being admissible as evidence was litigated in 2004 in the Supreme Court case *Crawford v. Washington*. The court found that defendants must be given an opportunity to confront accusers. An exception was made, however, for out-of-court statements that were "not testimonial," meaning that they were not gathered as part of an attempt to build a case against a defendant. For example, if a child spontaneously tells her teacher that her stepfather abused her, the teacher can recount that in court. If, however, a child tells a police officer that they have been abused in response to a direct question, that is not admissible. Video recordings taken as part of an investigation are also prohibited. The *Crawford* decision means that today, many victims of CSA are forced to testify in court

since most evidence is gathered as part of investigations.[25]

25. Thomas D. Lyon and Julia A. Dente, "Child Witnesses and the Confrontation Clause," *Journal of Criminal Law and Criminology* 102, no. 4 (2012):

Interviews with abuse victims reveal that they often experience the legal process as frustrating, intrusive, and terrifying. Courthouses are scary places, with rules that are difficult for children to understand.[26] While some courts allow children to testify over closed-circuit television, others force them to appear in the courtroom with the person who abused them.[27] Research suggests that long-term psychological distress and distrust of the legal system sometimes result when children testify in CSA cases. This is particularly true when they have to testify multiple times or when the perpetrator is acquitted.[28] At the same time, children who do not testify can also experience psychological distress, especially when their abusers are acquitted or end up with minimal sentences.[29]

Courthouse Dogs

Dogs can be very comforting to children who have to testify in legal hearings and trials. Courthouses are increasingly allowing these support animals to accompany child victims. There is an organization that provides therapy dogs to courthouses. Check them out at https://courthousedogs.org/.

1181–1232, https://www.ncbi.nlm.nih.gov/pmc/articles/PMC4212261/.

26. Jennifer M. Foster and W. Bryce Hagedorn, "Through the Eyes of the Wounded: A Narrative Analysis of Children's Sexual Abuse Experiences and Recovery Process," *Journal of Child Sexual Abuse* 23, no. 5 (2014): 538–57, https://www.researchgate.net/publication/262268905_Through_the_Eyes_of_the_Wounded_A_Narrative_Analysis_of_Children's_Sexual_Abuse_Experiences_and_Recovery_Process.

27. Jodi A. Quas and Gail S. Goodman, "Consequences of Criminal Court Involvement for Child Victims," *Psychology, Public Policy, and Law* 18, no. 3 (2012): 392–414.

28. Foster and Hagedorn, "Through the Eyes of the Wounded," https://www.researchgate.net/publication/262268905_Through_the_Eyes_of_the_Wounded_A_Narrative_Analysis_of_Children's_Sexual_Abuse_Experiences_and_Recovery_Process.

29. Jodi A. Quas et al., Childhood Sexual Assault Victims: Long-Term Outcomes after Testifying in Criminal Court, vol. 70, Monographs of the Society for Research in Child Development (Washington, DC: Society for Research in Child Development, 2005), https://www.jstor.org/stable/3701439?seq=1.

Figure 7. Dogs can be comforting for kids at the courthouse. Source: Caleb Fisher on Unsplash.

CONVICTION OR ACQUITTAL?

Many factors go into whether a defendant in a CSA trial is convicted or acquitted. Clearly, the strength of the evidence matters, but what about the characteristics of offenders or victims? It turns out that the research findings on this question are not entirely clear, although most studies find no link between convictions and victim characteristics such as age.[30] At the same time, a recent study of child stranger rape in the United Kingdom found that when a weapon was used or when the assault occurred outside, it dramatically increased the chances of conviction. This is probably because weapons and the outside setting conform to images of what a "real" rape looks like.[31] When

---

30. Stacia N. Stolzenberg and Thomas D. Lyon, "Evidence Summarized in Attorneys' Closing Arguments Predicts Acquittals in Criminal Trials of Child Sexual Abuse," *Child Maltreatment* 19, no. 2 (2014): 119–29, https://www.ncbi.nlm.nih.gov/pmc/articles/PMC4263691/; Samantha Lundrigan, Mandeep K. Dhami, and Kelly Agudelo, "Factors Predicting Conviction in Child Stranger Rape," *Child Abuse & Neglect* 101 (2020): 1–9.

31. Lundrigan, Dhami, and Agudelo, "Factors Predicting Conviction in Child Stranger Rape."

medical evidence (like DNA or abrasions) is submitted as evidence, it also increases the chances of conviction in CSA cases.[32] A study with mock jurors found that gay men who abused children were more likely to be convicted than either women or heterosexual men.[33]

At several points in this book, I have talked about common misperceptions of CSA. These are of particular concern in a court context because they can lead to mistaken assumptions about guilt and innocence. For example, if members of a jury believe that all abused children act out sexually, they may be disinclined to believe a child who does not. In a study of jurors and jury-eligible college students, researchers found that knowledge about CSA is extremely variable and frequently incorrect.[34] A recent study with undergraduate students also uncovered significant misperceptions about CSA. For example, a full 71 percent agreed that medical evidence exists in most CSA cases.[35] This belief is actually wildly inaccurate, with less than 1 percent of cases involving this kind of evidence.[36] The college students also held

---

32. Suzanne Blackwell and Fred Seymour, "Prediction of Jury Verdicts in Child Sexual Assault Trials," *Psychiatry, Psychology and Law* 21, no. 4 (2014): 567–76.

33. Tisha R. A. Wiley and Bette L. Bottoms, "Effects of Defendant Sexual Orientation on Jurors' Perceptions of Child Sexual Assault," *Law and Human Behavior* 33, no. 1 (2009): 46–60, https://scholar.google.com/scholar?hl=en&as_sdt=0%2C36&q=Effects+of+Defendant+Sexual+Orientation+on+Jurors'+&btnG=.

34. Jodi A. Quas, William C. Thompson, and K. Alison Clarke-Stewart, "Do Jurors 'Know' What Isn't So about Child Witnesses?" *Law and Human Behavior* 29, no. 4 (2005): 425–56, https://www.researchgate.net/profile/William_Thompson14/publication/7627081_Do_jurors_Know_what_isn%27t_so_about_child_witnesses/links/569567f808aeab58a9a4e7db.pdf.

35. Katherine McGuire and Kamala London, "Common Beliefs about Child Sexual Abuse and Disclosure: A College Sample," *Journal of Child Sexual Abuse* 26, no. 2 (2017): 175–94, https://www.nationalcac.org/wp-content/uploads/2018/01/Common-Beliefs-About-Child-Sexual-Abuse-and-Disclosure-A-College-Sample.pdf.

36. Nancy D. Kellogg, Juan M. Parra, and Shirley Menard, "Children with Anogenital Symptoms and Signs Referred for Sexual Abuse Evaluations," *Archives of Pediatrics & Adolescent Medicine* 152, no. 7 (1998), https://jamanetwork.com/journals/jamapediatrics/article-abstract/189669.

significant misperceptions of behavioral signs of abuse as well as likelihood of disclosure.

Given that a significant percentage of the population believes myths about CSA, it would make sense to educate juries. This has proven to be difficult, however, because there are limits on what experts are allowed to say in court. In most cases, they must confine their testimony to explaining child behavior in general terms. For example, an expert would be allowed to tell a jury that many child victims delay the disclosure of abuse. The expert could not, however, suggest that a particular defendant is guilty because the child victim delayed disclosure. Additionally, in most jurisdictions, experts are barred from providing juries with statistics because of concerns about bias. To understand this, imagine being on a jury in a CSA case and an expert says that less than 5 percent of abuse claims are false. This might make it hard to consider the possibility that a particular claim might be untrue.[37]

Expert testimony that relies on "syndromes" is also problematic in court. In the 1980s, a psychologist named Roland Summit proposed the existence of child sexual abuse accommodation syndrome (CSAAS). Summit did not systematically collect data, but rather based the syndrome on his clinical experiences with abused children. He found that abused children often react in five ways: with secrecy, helplessness, entrapment/accommodation, delayed and unconvincing disclosure, and recantation.[38] Summit's work appeared at a time when syndromes, like battered-women syndrome, were popular in legal cases. Even though Summit clearly stated that CSAAS was not to be used to substantiate claims of

---

37. Kenneth J. Weiss and Julia Curcio Alexander, "Sex, Lies, and Statistics: Inferences from the Child Sexual Abuse Accommodation Syndrome," *Journal of the American Academy of Psychiatry and the Law* 41, no. 3 (2013): 412–20, https://www.nationalcac.org/wp-content/uploads/2016/10/Sex-lies-and-statistics-Inferences-from-the-child-sexual-abuse-accommodation-syndrome.pdf.

38. Roland C. Summit, "The Child Sexual Abuse Accommodation Syndrome," *Child Abuse & Neglect* 7 (1983): 177–93, https://www.abusewatch.net/Child%20Sexual%20Abuse%20Accommodation%20Syndrome.pdf.

CSA, it began to appear in court cases as evidence to bolster child credibility.[39] Some courts, however, disallowed prosecutors from arguing CSAAS because it is difficult to falsify. If a child is unconvincing, for example, the prosecutor can simply say it's a result of CSAAS. Additionally, research has only found empirical support for some of the reactions Summit identified. This is one of the reasons that CSAAS is not listed in the American Psychological Association's *Diagnostic and Statistical Manual*—the book that is essentially the bible for establishing scientific credibility in psychology. Nonetheless, the use of CSAAS by lawyers for the prosecution continues in some courts even today.[40]

It is clear that CSA trials are difficult to navigate—for both the defense and the prosecution. What is the rate of convictions versus acquittals? Pulling together data from twenty-four studies on child abuse conducted in the United States (five of these studies included physical as well as sexual abuse), researchers found that 66 percent of cases that went to trial resulted in convictions. It is important to note, however, that 82 percent of the people who had originally been charged with abuse ended up pleading guilty and not going to trial at all. This means that 94 percent of all the cases in which charges were filed resulted in conviction.[41]

THE ROLE OF RISK ASSESSMENT IN SENTENCING

Risk assessment has played a role in criminal justice decision-making for many years. Sometimes risk assessment is used to determine what type of treatment offenders should receive. Other

---

39. Roland C. Summit, "Abuse of the Child Sexual Abuse Accommodation Syndrome," *Journal of Child Sexual Abuse* 1, no. 4 (1992): 153–64.

40. Weiss and Alexander, "Sex, Lies, and Statistics," https://www.nation alcac.org/wp-content/uploads/2016/10/Sex-lies-and-statistics-Inferences-from-the-child-sexual-abuse-accommodation-syndrome.pdf.

41. Cross et al., "Prosecution of Child Abuse," https://scholar.google.com/ scholar?hl=en&as_sdt=0%2C36&q=Prosecution+of+Child+Abuse%3A+A+ Meta-Analysis+of+&btnG=.

times, judges use risk assessment as part of sentencing itself.[42] Here, I'll focus on its role in sentencing.

Prior to the 1960s, clinical psychologists commonly interviewed offenders and deemed them either "dangerous" or "not dangerous." Today, courts tend to rely on actuarial tools developed to estimate the probability that a person will reoffend. These tools are basically checklists with factors, like drug addiction or a previous conviction, associated with recidivism. Sometimes the checklists also include factors that are associated with desistence from crime. These are called *promotive* factors because rather than increasing risk, they lower it. For example, it is known that people with supportive family systems are less likely to engage in crime than are people who do not have such support.[43] The checklists are scored by adding points for risk factors and subtracting them for promotive factors. The higher the score, the greater a person's chance of recidivism is estimated to be.[44]

Some of the factors on risk assessment inventories are *fixed*, meaning that they do not change over time. Gender is an example of a fixed factor because the majority of people do not change their gender. Men automatically receive more risk points because they are more likely than women to engage in crime. Another fixed factor is crime type. Particular crimes are associated with elevated reoffense risk and receive more points. Risk factors that have the potential to change over time are called *variable*. For example, people are categorized as being lower risk if they have skills that make them employable. This means it is possible to get training

42. John Monahan and Jennifer L. Skeem, "Risk Assessment in Criminal Sentencing," *Annual Review of Clinical Psychology* 12, no. 1 (2016): 489–513, http://www.annualreviews.org/doi/10.1146/annurev-clinpsy-021815-092945.

43. Monahan and Skeem, "Risk Assessment in Criminal Sentencing," http://www.annualreviews.org/doi/10.1146/annurev-clinpsy-021815-092945.

44. R. Karl Hanson and Kelly E. Morton-Bourgon, "The Accuracy of Recidivism Risk Assessments for Sexual Offenders: A Meta-Analysis of 118 Prediction Studies," *Psychological Assessment* 21, no. 1 (2009): 1–21, http://static99.org/pdfdocs/hansonandm-b2009riskassessment.pdf.

and reduce one's risk score. Some variable factors, however, simply change at their own pace. Age is one of these—the older you are, the less likely you are to commit a crime, but no amount of effort on your part will make you age faster.

There are many different risk-assessment tools available today. Some have been created by private companies and others by academics or nonprofits. There is wide variation in the factors that are included, but a study found that most contain measurements of criminal history, criminal lifestyle (like being friends with other people who are engaged in criminal activities), mental health, and drug/alcohol use. Many assessments also use personality traits that are associated with crime, such as being manipulative or lacking self-control.[45] It is important to note that none of these commonly used measures is promotive—they all represent negative risk factors.

The goal of risk assessment is fairly obvious: to predict whether people will engage in criminal behavior in the future. Unfortunately, it is very difficult to determine which (if any) of the available tools actually meet this goal. Researchers are an intrepid bunch, however, and have tried various tactics. One method involves administering the tool to incarcerated people, calculating a risk score for them, and then monitoring them postrelease. An effective risk-assessment tool would assign higher risk scores to the people who end up being rearrested. Another methodology is to apply the tool to cases from the past using prison records. Scores for former inmates are calculated and compared with official records of rearrests. This methodology is challenging because prison records are not very detailed. For example, as described above, family support helps people desist from crime, but few criminal justice systems keep records about the strength of people's family ties.

---

45. Daryl G. Kroner, Jeremy F. Mills, and John R. Reddon, "A Coffee Can, Factor Analysis, and Prediction of Antisocial Behavior: The Structure of Criminal Risk," *International Journal of Law and Psychiatry* 28, no. 4 (2005): 360–74, https://www.researchgate.net/publication/7806392_A_Coffee_Can_factor_analysis_and_prediction_of_antisocial_behavior_The_structure_of_criminal_risk.

Using a combination of different methodologies, researchers have found that actuarial tools are much better at predicting the recidivism of sexual offenders than are the unstructured psychological interviews used in the past.[46] Interestingly, it also appears that actuarial tools are more effective when used alone than when combined with the judgement of psychologists.[47] In terms of determining which tool is best, one meta-analysis found that commonly used risk-assessment techniques have somewhat different levels of success in predicting recidivism but that the differences are extremely small. In general, the tools accurately predict sexual recidivism in about 70 percent of cases.[48] Unfortunately, however, the tests provide quite different results on individual cases. While 55 percent of the offenders were identified as being at high risk on at least one of the tests, only 3 percent of the sample were identified as high risk by all of the assessments.[49]

Are Brain Scans the Future of Risk Assessment?

Imagine if a simple brain scan could predict which CSA offenders were at high risk of reoffending. While it sounds more like science fiction than reality, scientists at the University of New Mexico are experimenting with just this technique. They believe that brain scans, in combination with standard assessment tools, will provide better accuracy. These

---

46. D. A. Andrews, James Bonta, and J. Stephen Wormith, "The Recent Past and near Future of Risk and/or Need Assessment," *Crime & Delinquency* 52, no. 1 (2006): 7–27, https://scholar.google.com/scholar?hl=en&as_sdt=0%2C36&q=The+Recent+Past+and+near+Future+of+Risk+and%2For+Need+Assessment&btnG=.

47. Hanson and Morton-Bourgon, "The Accuracy of Recidivism Risk Assessments for Sexual Offenders," http://static99.org/pdfdocs/hansonandm-b2009riskassessment.pdf.

48. Hanson and Morton-Bourgon, http://static99.org/pdfdocs/hansonandm-b2009riskassessment.pdf.

49. Howard E. Barbaree, Calvin M. Langton, and Edward J. Peacock, "Different Actuarial Risk Measures Produce Different Risk Rankings for Sexual Offenders," *Sexual Abuse: A Journal of Research and Treatment* 18, no. 4 (2006): 423–40.

brain scans, however, are controversial because they raise many ethical issues. You can read about them here: https://www.themarshallproject.org/2018/08/14/a-dangerous-brain.

Risk assessment has received a lot of criticism, particularly when it is used in the sentencing phase of a trial. It's easy to see why. Imagine that a fifty-year-old employed married mother with no prior criminal history beats up and paralyzes a stranger in a bar. If risk assessment is allowed to influence sentencing, it is likely that the woman will receive a relatively short sentence because her age, gender, employment, marriage, and lack of prior criminal behavior/drug addiction mark her as low risk. Now imagine an unemployed young man who has a past drug offense commits exactly the same act. He will receive a longer sentence because he will be deemed at greater risk of reoffense. Many people think that is not fair—the older woman and the young man committed exactly the same act but are punished differently because of unchangeable characteristics and factors from their pasts. This criticism really boils down to a debate about the purpose of punishment. People who think that the point of punishment is retribution tend to be critical of using risk assessment in sentencing, but those who think that the purpose of punishment is rehabilitation might see it as being smart policy. Regardless, the fact that risk assessment is only correct about 70 percent of the time concerns people across punishment ideologies. Imagine that the young man in the bar happened to be in the group of people who are mistakenly identified as high risk by the assessment—would it be fair to sentence him to extra time?

Another criticism of risk assessment is that it reinforces biases already present in the criminal justice system. For example, racial minorities are more likely to be arrested, convicted, and receive a long sentence than are equivalent white people.[50] When past con-

---

50. Tammy Rinehart Kochel, David B. Wilson, and Stephen D. Mastrofski,

victions (or past sentence length) are used in risk assessment, it is essentially reinforcing prior racial discrimination. A similar argument can be made about assessment tools that include unemployment as a risk factor. While it is true that employed people are less likely to recidivate, we also know that discrimination, lack of transportation, and lack of skills keep many poor people from being able to get or keep a job. When unemployment is used as a risk factor, it effectively penalizes people for being poor.[51] Unfortunately, it is difficult to evaluate risk-assessment tools for bias because some of the most popular tools were created by private companies. These companies are unwilling to reveal their proprietary risk formulas.

VICTIM IMPACT STATEMENTS AT SENTENCING

The victim's rights movement mentioned in chapter 1 has been remarkably successful in passing legislation. For example, its work led to the 2004 federal Crime Victims' Rights Act that guaranteed eight different rights to victims, including notification about hearings and protection from the accused. The act also gave victims a greater role in sentencing outcomes. This led many states to allow victims to either submit a written statement or speak in front of the judge during sentencing or parole hearings. This is called a victim impact statement.

The admissibility of victim impact statements has been repeatedly contested in the courts. In the 1987 Supreme Court case *Booth*

"Effect of Suspect Race on Officers' Arrest Decisions," *Criminology* 49, no. 2 (May 1, 2011): 473–512; Jeffrey H. Reiman and Paul Leighton, *The Rich Get Richer and the Poor Get Prison: Ideology, Class, and Criminal Justice*, 10th ed. (New York: Routledge, 2012); Traci Burch, "Skin Color and the Criminal Justice System: Beyond Black-White Disparities in Sentencing," *Journal of Empirical Legal Studies* 12, no. 3 (2015): 395–420; William D. Bales and Alex R. Piquero, "Racial/Ethnic Differentials in Sentencing to Incarceration," *Justice Quarterly* 29, no. 5 (2012): 742–73.

51. Monahan and Skeem, "Risk Assessment in Criminal Sentencing," https://www.annualreviews.org/doi/10.1146/annurev-clinpsy-021815-092945.

v. Maryland, the justices ruled that family members of a homicide victim could not speak during sentencing because it would focus attention on the victim rather than on the crime itself. They also worried that it would encourage the judge to make decisions based on emotion instead of facts.[52] In other words, victim impact statements introduce the possibility that sentences are set based on how articulately and emotionally grief is expressed by victims rather than on the culpability of the defendant.[53] In 1991, however, the Supreme Court reversed its prior decision, ruling in *Payne v. Tennessee* that families could speak during the sentencing phase of capital trials.

Victim impact statements are designed to compensate for some of the unique ways the US criminal justice system excludes victims. Unlike in many other countries, US victims cannot directly bring a case against the person who harmed them—they have to go through the prosecutor. Criminal cases are between the accused and the state, and the victim's role is solely as a witness.[54] This leads to a situation where victims have very little control in the process and are not given an opportunity to speak freely. Victim impact statements are a way to rectify this situation. Anecdotal evidence suggests that giving a statement can be cathartic and meaningful for victims.[55] This is not always the case, however. There are

---

52. Janice Nadler and Mary R. Rose, "Victim Impact Testimony and the Psychology of Punishment," *Cornell Law Review* 88 (2003): 419–56; *Northwestern Public Law Research Paper*, no. 3–2; *University of Texas Law, Public Law Research Paper*, no. 47, https://papers.ssrn.com/sol3/papers.cfm?abstract_id=377521.

53. Susan A. Bandes, "What Are Victim-Impact Statements For?" *Atlantic*, July 23, 2016, https://www.theatlantic.com/politics/archive/2016/07/what-are-victim-impact-statements-for/492443/.

54. Jonathan Simon, Governing through Crime: How the War on Crime Transformed American Democracy and Created a Culture of Fear (Oxford: Oxford University Press, 2009).

55. Alan Hayakawa, "'Wound Is So Deep': Kin of Victims Speak," Penn Live, December 16, 2007, https://www.pennlive.com/midstate/2007/12/alone_in_the_harrisburg_apartm.html; National Center for Victims of Crime, "Victim Impact Statements," https://members.victimsofcrime.org/help-for-crime-victims/

victims who choose not to write an impact statement because they cannot stand to relive the crime.[56] Others find that reading the impact statement in court is distressing when the defendant smirks or appears not to care.[57]

One Survivor's Victim Impact Statement Experience

One CSA survivor wrote about her experience with creating and delivering a victim impact statement. It's a compelling and emotional piece:
https://www.newyorker.com/culture/culture-desk/
the-power-and-limitations-of-victim-impact-statements.

There have been a number of unintended consequences of victim impact statements. First, when victims express severe emotional harm, the crimes against them are seen as more serious and the criminal as deserving of harsher punishment.[58] Similarly, when juries in capital trials hear victim impact statements, they are more likely to feel sympathy toward the family and negative feelings toward the offender. Consequently, they are more likely to vote for the death penalty.[59] This scenario is exactly what the Supreme Court warned about in their ruling on the *Booth* case. A second problem with victim impact statements involves race. One study asked actual jurors about the decisions they had made

---

get-help-bulletins-for-crime-victims/victim-impact-statements.

56. Karen-Lee Miller, "Purposing and Repurposing Harms: The Victim Impact Statement and Sexual Assault," *Qualitative Health Research* 23, no. 11 (2013): 1445–58, https://scholar.google.com/scholar?hl=en&as_sdt=0%2C36&q=Purpos ing+and+Repurposing+Harms%3A+The+Victim+Impact+Statement+&btnG=.

57. Bandes, "What Are Victim-Impact Statements For?" https://www.theatlantic. com/politics/archive/2016/07/what-are-victim-impact-statements-for/492443/.

58. Nadler and Rose, "Victim Impact Testimony and the Psychology of Punishment," https://papers.ssrn.com/sol3/papers.cfm?abstract_id=377521.

59. Ray Paternoster and Jerome Deise, "A Heavy Thumb on the Scale: The Effect of Victim Impact Evidence on Capital Decision Making," *Criminology* 49, no. 1 (2011): 129–61.

in real-life murder cases. Specifically, they asked them about the factors that most influenced them to vote for or against the death penalty. The victim "having a loving family" and the grief and suffering of the family ranked lower in decisions made about Black defendants than white.[60]

Perhaps one of the biggest concerns about victim impact statements is that, in some cases, they are used as tools for prosecutors to impose maximum punishments. When a victim (or their family member) does not support severe sanctions, a prosecutor could discourage them from submitting a statement. There is only anecdotal evidence for this possibility. In one example, the husband and daughter of a murder victim in Nebraska were denied the right to speak at a commutation hearing because the prosecutor labeled them as "agents of the defendant" when they made known their opposition to the death penalty.[61] There are also examples of antideath penalty victims being denied services from victim advocacy agencies or not being told about hearings involving their case.[62]

SENTENCING

While the goal of this section of the book is to discuss average sentences for CSA offenses, I should warn that disappointment lies ahead. It is extremely difficult to summarize criminal sentences because most cases resolve in plea bargains—meaning that the sentences correspond to the reduced charge, not to the original

---

60. David Karp and Jarrett B. Warshaw, "Their Day in Court: The Role of Murder Victims in Decision Making," in *Wounds That Do Not Bind: Victim-Based Perspectives on the Death Penalty*, ed. James R. Acker and David R. Karp (Durham, NC: Carolina Academic Press, 2006), 275–95.

61. Judith Kay, "Murder Victims' Families for Reconciliation: Story-Telling for Healing, as Witness, and in Public Policy," in *Handbook of Restorative Justice: A Global Perspective*, ed. Dennis Sullivan and Larry Tifft (New York: Routledge, 2006), 230–45.

62. Randall T. Coyne, "Shooting the Wounded: First Degree Murder and Second Class Victims," *Oklahoma City University Law Review* 28 (2003): 93–117.

charge. It is also complicated by the fact that there are a lot of different CSA charges, ranging from minor to extremely serious. Averaging the sentences for such disparate violations does not make a lot of sense. Finally, the United States has multiple court systems. Most CSA cases are prosecuted through state courts, but the federal government can also take jurisdiction. These court systems have different sentencing structures. The situation on Native American lands is even more complex. While the federal government has jurisdiction there, tribes have concurrent jurisdiction and can also prosecute the case. This is important because federal prosecutors do not always agree to take on CSA cases that occur on reservations. By federal law, however, tribal justice systems only have the power to impose up to three years in prison and $15,000 in fines—regardless of the seriousness of the offense.[63] This lowers calculations of the "average" CSA sentence in the United States.

All across the United States, judges have the power to determine criminal sentences except in death penalty cases when juries have this responsibility. Judges, of course, are not allowed to set any sentence that they want. One of the factors that limits their discretion is mandatory minimum sentencing. As its name implies, mandatory minimums specify the lowest-level sentence that can be imposed. These minimums vary based on the severity of the offense and the offender's prior convictions. Sentencing guidelines are similar to mandatory minimums but are less deterministic. They provide judges with a range of suggested sanctions but allow them to choose a sentence that is shorter or longer than the recommendation.

---

63. Larry EchoHawk and Tessa Meyer Santiago, "What Indian Tribes Can Do to Combat Child Sexual Abuse," *Tribal Law Journal* 4 (2004): 1–14, https://lawschool.unm.edu/tlj/common/docs/volumes/vol-4-echohawk-and-santiago-issue-paper-what-indian-tribes-can-do-combat-child-sexual-abuse.pdf.

> **State-Level Sentencing Laws**
>
> If you are interested in state-level laws about CSA, check out the National Conference of State Legislatures website at http://www.ncsl.org/research/civil-and-criminal-justice/sex-offender-enactments-database.aspx.

Between the 1980s and 2010, rates of incarceration skyrocketed in the United States. This was not a result of more crime (in fact, the crime rate dropped to historic lows over the period) but instead was largely driven by increases in sentencing.[64] One example is the increase in the number of life sentences. In 1984, only thirty-four thousand people in the United States were sentenced to life. Today, that figure is over one hundred and sixty thousand—about one out of every nine incarcerated people.[65] Looking just at sexual abuse, between 1994 and 2006, the federal court system increased the median length of sentences from thirty-six to sixty-three months.[66] The 2003 federal passage of the Prosecutorial Remedies and Other Tools to End the Exploitation of Children Today (PROTECT) Act also boosted federal sentences because it allowed for life imprisonment for second-time offenses.

> **Some Examples of State Laws**
>
> Montana had a mandatory minimum sentence of twenty-five years for most sex crimes against children (rape, incest, and other types of assault). This was reduced to ten years in 2017 as part of a

---

64. Marc Mauer, "Long-Term Sentences: Time to Reconsider the Scale of Punishment," *UMKC Law Review* 87 (2018): 113–30, https://www.cmcainternational.org/wp-content/uploads/2019/05/UMKC-Law-Review-Scale-of-Punishment.pdf.

65. Ashley Nellis, "Still Life: America's Increasing Use of Life and Long-Term Sentences," The Sentencing Project, 2017, https://www.sentencingproject.org/publications/still-life-americas-increasing-use-life-long-term-sentences/.

66. Mark Motivans and Tracey Kychelhahn, "Federal Prosecution of Child Sex Exploitation Offenders, 2006," *Bureau of Justice Statistics Bulletin*, December 2007, https://www.bjs.gov/content/pub/pdf/fpcse006.pdf.

package of sentencing reforms. In 2019, however, the state legislature voted to go back to twenty-five years, with an exception for juvenile offenders that enables them to serve less time.[67]

Massachusetts has several laws governing different kinds of sexual abuse. In cases where an adult has sexual intercourse by force with a child under the age of sixteen, however, the offender can be subject to life imprisonment.[68]

California has legislation stating that sexual intercourse with a child under ten automatically triggers a sentence of at least twenty-five years. For other kinds of sexual acts (like oral copulation), the mandatory minimum is fifteen years.[69]

The imposition of increasingly long sentences for CSA has not been without controversy. There are concerns, for example, that high mandatory minimums encourage plea bargains, even among innocent people. Other people worry that the minimums increase the number of trials because people refuse to plead guilty to charges that bear very high penalties. As described above, this is problematic because the court system is already overwhelmed. More trials also mean more children needing to provide testimony. A final concern is that lengthy sentences might result in fewer reports of intrafamilial abuse. Family members may be unwilling to subject offenders to sentences that could involve incarceration for twenty-five years or more.[70]

67. Phoebe Tollefson, "Prosecutors Seek to Restore Stronger Penalties for Sex Crimes against Children in Montana," *Billings Gazette*, February 9, 2019, https://billingsgazette.com/news/state-and-regional/crime-and-courts/prosecutors-seek-to-restore-stronger-penalties-for-sex-crimes-against/article_578453ed-f51d-53be-8708-3636723a3c68.html.

68. State of Massachusetts, "Massachusetts Law about Child Sexual Abuse," Mass.gov, 2020, https://www.mass.gov/info-details/massachusetts-law-about-child-sexual-abuse.

69. State of California, "California Law," California Legislative Information, 2020, https://leginfo.legislature.ca.gov/faces/codes_displaySection.xhtml?sectionNum=288.7.&lawCode=PEN.

70. Robert Levy, "The Dynamics of Child Sexual Abuse Prosecution: Two

Figure 8. How Deterrence Works. © 2008 Ted Rall, all rights reserved, reprinted with permission, www.rall.com

It is clear that there are a number of risks associated with the imposition of long sentences. Perhaps these risks don't really matter, however, if long sentences effectively deter abuse. Deterrence could happen in one of two ways. First, convicted offenders could leave prison and choose not to reoffend because they are afraid of being caught and sentenced again. In this case, their experience of prison makes them less willing to engage in crime in the future. The other way deterrence might happen is that people in the general population decide not to abuse children because they fear heavy sanctions if caught.

Most of the research on the relationship between sentence length and deterrence does not focus on CSA, but rather looks at

Florida Case Studies," *Journal of Law and Family Studies* 7 (2005): 57–109, https://scholar.google.com/scholar?hl=en&as_sdt=0%2C36&q=Levy+The+Dynamics+of+Child+Sexual+&oq=Levy+The+Dynamics+of+Child+Se.

crime more generally. In a comprehensive review of this literature, two economists found that there are a number of conditions that must be met for a long sentence to deter crime.[71] First, the person considering crime needs to believe that there is a relatively high likelihood that they will be caught. In other words, if the person thinks they won't be caught, sentence length does not really matter. Unfortunately, many offenders underestimate the chance they will be arrested, especially if they have gotten away with crime in the past. A second condition necessary for long sentences to deter crime is that potential offenders need to be aware of the sentence. Many sentencing policies are not publicized or are only reported in select media outlets. As a result, most people don't know or can't remember what particular sentences are.

Ultimately, the economists' review found that, while there may be some deterrent effect of long sentences, it is very small, likely because the two conditions described above are rarely met. A study that looked specifically at the link between sentence length and recidivism in CSA cases came to essentially the same conclusion: sentence length does not affect the likelihood of a person committing a new crime.[72] Of course, deterrence is not the only goal of punishment. When offenders are in prison, they are also incapacitated and therefore unable to commit new crimes (except crimes against other incarcerated people or staff members). As discussed in chapter 3, however, as people age, they become far less likely to commit any type of crime. This means that the incapacitation effect of crime may be significant when people are young but that it likely fades over time.

---

71. Aaron Chalfin and Justin McCrary, "Criminal Deterrence: A Review of the Literature," *Journal of Economic Literature* 55, no. 1 (2017): 5–48, https://www.aeaweb.org/articles?id=10.1257/jel.20141147.

72. Kristen Budd and Scott A. Desmond, "Sex Offenders and Sex Crime Recidivism: Investigating the Role of Sentence Length and Time Served," *International Journal of Offender Therapy and Comparative Criminology* 58, no. 12 (2014): 1481–99.

FAILURE TO PROTECT

So far, this chapter has focused on the criminal justice experiences of victims and offenders. In some cases, however, it is not just the offender who is held responsible for abuse. Failure-to-protect laws are a type of mandatory reporting law (see chapter 6 for a more complete discussion of mandatory reporting laws). Failure-to-protect laws focus narrowly on caretakers' responsibility to report clear and dangerous situations of abuse to authorities. Specifically, these laws have been used to prosecute parents (usually mothers) who do not take action to prevent the abuse of their child by their spouse or romantic partner. Penalties associated with a failure to protect can involve prison time as well as a permanent child abuse record, making the offender ineligible for many jobs and for volunteering in schools.

There have been a number of successful prosecutions of people under failure-to-protect laws, and some of the resulting penalties have been quite harsh. [73] For example, a young woman named Tondalao Hall was sentenced to thirty years in prison in Oklahoma for failing to protect her children from abuse by her boyfriend. The boyfriend was sentenced to two years.[74] In 2019, after serving fifteen years, the governor finally commuted her sentence and she was released.

From a historical perspective, what happened to Hall is not terribly remarkable. The family has traditionally been seen as a "private" space mostly occupied by women and children. While men obviously live in homes too, most of their lives are conducted in the workplace—the "public" sphere. Women are seen as innate

---

73. Anne T. Johnson, "Criminal Liability for Parents Who Fail to Protect," *Law & Inequality: A Journal of Theory and Practice* 5 (1987): 359–92, https://scholar.google.com/scholar?hl=en&as_sdt=0%2C36&q=Criminal+Liability+for+Parents+Who+Fail+to+Protect&btnG=.

74. Tim Talley, "Group Takes Aim at Oklahoma's Failure-to-Protect Law," Associated Press, September 29, 2018, https://apnews.com/45a6f24af72c4750ac141f3fe10b3bc9.

caregivers, legitimizing and naturalizing their responsibility for raising children. All of these beliefs lead to mothers being blamed when bad things befall children. For example, starting at least in the early 1900s—and continuing today—mothers have been blamed when their children are victims of incest.[75] Similarly, a recent study looked at families in which a son had been sexually abused. The researchers found that many family members, as well as social service agencies, blamed the mothers. Sadly, many of the mothers blamed themselves as well.[76]

Not surprisingly, poor women receive the most scrutiny as mothers. They are essentially caught in a trap—they are expected to rise to cultural standards of motherhood, but their poverty means that they don't have the resources to do so. For example, poor women are often unable to pay for quality childcare. Rather than seeing this as a societal problem, we blame the mother for not supervising her children. When it comes to abuse, poor women are in a bind as well. They, like all mothers, are expected to protect their children. If they discover their children are being abused and report it, however, they risk being blamed for lax supervision. This can result in the children's removal from the home.[77]

For all of these reasons, some domestic abuse prevention groups have argued that failure-to-protect laws are problematic. They also point out that many abusers target the mother as well as the child, causing the mother to legitimately fear violence if she makes a report. While most of these laws specify an exception to mandatory reporting in these cases, it is very hard to prove that fear of

---

75. Linda Gordon, "The Politics of Child Sexual Abuse: Notes from American History," *Feminist Review* 28 (1988): 56–64, https://www.jstor.org/stable/1394894?seq=1.

76. C. Shawn McGuffey, "Engendering Trauma: Race, Class, and Gender Reaffirmation after Child Sexual Abuse," *Gender & Society* 19, no. 5 (2005): 621–43, https://www.jstor.org/stable/27640832?read-now=1&refreqid=excelsior%3Ac86405337d848a7dda7d67633bd121a5&seq=1#page_scan_tab_contents.

77. Christine Parton and Nigel Parton, "Women, the Family and Child Protection," *Critical Social Policy* 8, no. 24 (1988): 38–49.

harm outweighed the risk to the child from abuse.[78] An additional criticism of failure-to-protect laws is that domestic violence shelters are often full, and there are few other resources available for women who leave abusive situations. Mothers' failure to report can be a rational response to individual and societal oppression and a lack of other options.

CONCLUSION

This chapter examined the criminal justice process from the time a CSA accusation is made through criminal sentencing. Some accusations do not result in criminal charges because CPS, the police, or the prosecutor analyze the evidence and decide that it is too weak to convict the accused person. Alternately, some families decide not to go forward with prosecution. This was the case with Natalie, whom we met at the start of the chapter. When criminal charges are filed, the vast majority end in plea bargains. Plea bargains have the advantage of shortening the justice process and freeing child victims from stressful courtroom testimony but may result in misrepresentative charges on offenders' records. The sentences offenders receive from judges are shaped by mandatory minimums and sentencing guidelines, as well as by risk assessments and victim impact statements. While prison sentences are effective at incapacitating offenders, their length does not appear to have a deterrent effect.

When most people think about criminal sanctions, they just think as far as the sentence that is imposed. The assumption is that people serve their terms, are released back into society, and move on. But the legal impact of a CSA conviction can last well past release—following many people for the rest of their lives. The

---

78. Leah Bartos, "Failure to Protect: Should Victims of Domestic Violence Face Child Abuse Charges?" *California Health Report* (blog), October 28, 2015, https://www.calhealthreport.org/2015/10/27/failure-to-protect-should-victims-of-domestic-violence-face-child-abuse-charges/.

next chapter discusses those post-prison prevention measures, their efficacy, and their unintended consequences.

FURTHER READING

Alexander, Michelle. *The New Jim Crow: Mass Incarceration in the Age of Colorblindness*. New York: New Press, 2012.

Bogira, Steve. *Courtroom 302: A Year Behind the Scenes in an American Criminal Courthouse*. New York: Vintage, 2006.

Bazelon, Emily. *Charged: The New Movement to Transform American Prosecution and End Mass Incarceration*. New York: Random House, 2019.

Ceci, Stephan J., and Maggie Bruck. *Jeopardy in the Courtroom*. Worcester, MA: American Psychological Association, 1995.

CHAPTER FIVE

LEGAL RESTRICTIONS POST-PRISON

In 2018, Richard Gartner was released from prison after serving thirty years for the sexual abuse of a child. He moved into a neighborhood in Providence, Rhode Island, hoping to quietly start over. Instead, dozens of people started protesting outside his house every night, telling him to get out of the neighborhood.[1] This reaction to Gartner's release was extreme, but it is not unusual. As discussed in earlier chapters, the public holds deep fears about sex offenders and believes that most will reoffend. This fear has led to the passage of a number of restrictive measures. In this chapter, I explore the efficacy and unintended consequences of the most common: registries, location restrictions, internet limitations, Halloween bans, chemical castration, and civil confinement.

---

1. Steven Brown, "City Officials Stoke Mob Mentality in Front of Sex Offender's Home," American Civil Liberties Union, October 24, 2018, https://www.aclu.org/blog/free-speech/rights-protesters/city-officials-stoke-mob-mentality-front-sex-offenders-home.

REGISTRIES AND COMMUNITY NOTIFICATION

Upon their release from prison, most people who have been convicted of sexual offenses are required to report to local police. They must log their address as well as other information such as their car's model, color, and license number. In many states, people with sex convictions must also inform the police about where they are employed or attending school. This process is called *registering*, and if a registrant changes addresses, they must reregister. Registrants also have to check in with the police at regular intervals, based on the type of crime they committed, their home state, and whether or not they are homeless.

The first registry was implemented in California in 1947 and, by 1974, four other states had created their own.[2] Today, they exist in every state. Community notification laws mandate that information about people on the registry be provided to the public or to some segment of the public. Before notification laws, the police just used the registry internally as a tool for crime investigation. Washington State passed the first community notification law in 1990. In the original legislation, local law enforcement was allowed to inform the community about people with sexual convictions, but they could decide what information to release and to whom.[3] The state government did, however, suggest that localities use risk-assessment scores to make decisions. Their risk-assessment tool sorted people with convictions for sexual offenses into three tiers, with tier one being the lowest risk. The state guidelines

---

2. Trevor Hoppe, "Punishing Sex: Sex Offenders and the Missing Punitive Turn in Sexuality Studies," *Law & Social Inquiry* 41, no. 3 (2016): 573–94, https://scholar.google.com/scholar?hl=en&as_sdt=0%2C36&q=Punishing+Sex%3A+Sex+Offenders+and+the+Missing+Punitive&btnG=.

3. Washington State Institute for Public Policy, *Washington State's Community Notification Law: 15 Years of Change* (Olympia: Washington State Institute for Public Policy, 2006), https://www.wsipp.wa.gov/ReportFile/936/Wsipp_Washington-States-Community-Notification-Law-15-Years-of-Change_Full-Report.pdf.

recommended that information about those at level one not be publicized at all, and level two information should only be released to nearby childcare centers and schools. Finally, the state recommended full community notification only in the case of a level three. Over the next four years, five other states passed similar bills.

The Jacob Wetterling Crimes Against Children and Sexually Violent Offender Registration Act of 1994 was the first time the federal government became involved in the creation and maintenance of registries. Jacob Wetterling was an eleven-year-old who was abducted and murdered in Minnesota in 1989. The bill in his name required that all states create a sexual offender registry. While the original bill was silent on the issue of community notification, it was later addressed through a 1996 amendment. Named Megan's Law after Megan Kanka, this amendment required all states to implement some form of community notification. Today, somewhat confusingly, people use the term *Megan's Law* to refer both to the federal amendment as well as to the myriad state laws that were drafted to meet its requirements.

In the early years of community notification, police officers would distribute flyers in a neighborhood, visit local day-care centers, or host a community meeting. Even today, some communities hold neighborhood public-notification meetings or post fliers. For example, Minnesota sometimes uses this method when someone with a risk level of three moves to a new address.[4] Here is an example of a community notification posted in Mississippi County, Arkansas, in 2018. I cropped the image so that individual case details are not visible.

In 1997, Minnesota, Mississippi, and Tennessee decided to

4. Mara H. Gottfried, "St. Paul Notification Meeting Wednesday to Detail 12 Predatory Offenders, Alarming Some Residents," *Twin Cities Pioneer Press*, September 24, 2018, https://www.twincities.com/2018/09/24/st-paul-notifi cation-meeting-will-feature-12-predatory-offenders-raising-community-con cerns/.

Community Notification

The Mississippi County Sheriff Department is releasing information pursuant to section 13 of Act 989 of 1997. Known as the "Sex and Child Offender Registration and Community Notification Guidelines," promulgated by the commission on Abuse, this act authorizes law enforcement agencies to inform the public of a sex offender's presence, when the release of such information will enhance public safety and protection.

Individuals appearing on these notifications have been convicted of an offense requiring registration with the Arkansas Crime Information Center. Further, their previous criminal history places them in a classification level that reflects the potential to re-offend.

The named offender is not wanted by the police at this time. This notification is not intended to increase fear. Rather, it is our belief that an informed public will be a safer public. *Please do not take it upon yourself to notify anyone other than the people, specified in this notice.* This offender has advised the agency issuing this fact sheet that he will be living at the location given. It is the intention of this department to pursue every reasonable means to provide for the safety of the public. It is also our intention to do this in a responsible manner and attempt to avoid any unnecessary over reaction or fear. The Mississippi County Sheriff Department has no legal authority to direct where a sex offender lives. Unless court order restrictions exist, this offender is constitutionally free to live wherever he/she chooses.

Sex offenders have always lived in our communities, but not until the passage of the Sex and Child Offender Registration Act were law enforcement agencies informed of where they are living. In many cases, law enforcement agencies can now share this information with the public. **Citizen abuse of this information to threaten, intimidate or harass offenders will not be tolerated.** Such abuse could potentially end law enforcement's ability to share this information with the public. If notification ends, the only person who wins is the offender, since they derive power through secrecy.

Four risk levels apply. **Level One** means an offender is considered to pose a *low risk of re-offense.* **Level Two** means offender is considered to pose a *moderate risk.* **Level Three** means an offender is considered to pose a *high risk.* **Level Four** status is reserved for offenders who are deemed *sexually violent predators.*

Information is now available through a state website maintained by the Arkansas Crime Information Center which can be found at www.acic . Please feel free to contact this department with any comments, suggestions or concerns.

Figure 9. Community Notification from Mississippi County, Arkansas.

employ the internet as a more efficient way to give the public access to the registry. Other states quickly followed their lead and created searchable online databases.[5] In 2006, the Adam Walsh Child Protection and Safety Act was passed. Its first part (known as SORNA, short for the Sex Offender Registration and Notification Act) created a national internet database of sex offenders. Over the years, there have been a lot of changes in state registries, many driven by federal law. SORNA has had a particularly strong impact. For example, it requires states to use three-tier categorization based on crime-related factors (like the seriousness of crime, the age of the victim, and the length of the sentence). This particular classification scheme was new to some states, like Washington, and forced them to reclassify selected registrants. Oftentimes, the new

5. Amanda Y. Agan, "Sex Offender Registries: Fear without Function?" *Journal of Law and Economics* 54, no. 1 (2011): 207–39, https://safervirginia.org/wp-con tent/uploads/2019/08/Registry-Fear-without-Function.pdf.

classification is more stringent than before, putting some people on the registry for the first time and extending the time for others. This has caused considerable controversy, especially when people are suddenly put on the registry, sometimes decades after their crime.

Some Examples from Nevada's Reclassification of Offenders

In 2018, the following people were mandated to register for the first time:

A man who, in his twenties, attempted to proposition a thirteen-year-old over the internet. He was convicted in 1997 and has not committed any other offenses. He married in 2004 and started a successful business in 2015.

A man who was convicted of statutory rape in the 1950s. He then went on to marry the woman and keep his record clean.[6]

Prior to 1996, people who had been convicted of sex crimes as juveniles were not required to register. SORNA changed this, mandating registration for some categories. Today's version of the law requires states to register anyone fourteen or older who was sentenced for a sex crime as an adult or who was "adjudicated delinquent" in juvenile court for serious sexual crimes.[7] Because the offenses that require registration are quite serious, all juvenile registrants are categorized into tier three. This means that they remain on the registry for life, although they can petition to be

---

6. Michelle Rindels, "Nevada to Embark on New Sex Offender Registry System, but Critics Say It's Overly Harsh," *Nevada Independent*, September 2018, https://thenevadaindependent.com/article/nevada-to-embark-on-new-sex-offender-registry-system-but-critics-say-its-overly-harsh.

7. Richard A. Paladino, "The Adam Walsh Act as Applied to Juveniles: One Size Does Not Fit All," *Hofstra Law Review* 40, no. 1 (2014): 269–307, https://scholar.google.com/scholar?hl=en&as_sdt=0%2C36&q=The+Adam+Walsh+Act+as+Applied+to+Juveniles%3A+&btnG=.

removed after twenty-five years.[8] Jurisdictions are allowed to post information about the juveniles on the public registry, but they are not required to do so.

It should be noted that there has been considerable pushback from states to aspects of SORNA. Some object to the financial burden the increased registration entails, and others simply object to putting juveniles, who have a very low average recidivism rate and who generally respond well to treatment, on a registry. Thus, some states are not in compliance.[9] SORNA has also been criticized because it removes discretion from juvenile judges and does not use risk-based metrics to decide whom to place on the registry.[10]

Minimum Registration Requirements Under SORNA

People categorized as tier one (the least serious level) are required to register for fifteen years and report to law enforcement once a year.

Tier two requires twenty-five years of registration, with a check-in every six months.

People categorized as tier three are required to register for the rest of their lives and must report every six months.

There have been a number of court cases that challenge the constitutionality of registries. For example, in 2002, the US Supreme Court agreed to hear a case filed by two men who were going to be

8. Lori McPherson, *Practitioner's Guide to the Adam Walsh Act* (Alexandria, VA: American Prosecutors Research Institute, 2007), https://putnampros.net/docs/APRI Guide Adam Walsh Act.pdf.

9. US House of Representatives, *Adam Walsh Reauthorization Act of 2017* (Washington, DC: US House of Representatives, 2017), https://www.congress.gov/congressional-report/115th-congress/house-report/142/1.

10. National Council of Juvenile and Family Court Justices, *Resolution Regarding Sex Offender Registration Requirements for Youth Younger than Age 18*, (Reno: National Council of Juvenile and Family Court Justices, 2018), https://www.ncjfcj.org/wp-content/uploads/2019/08/regarding-sex-offender-registration-requirements-for-youth-younger-than-age-18.pdf.

placed on Alaska's new online registry. Both were already listed on the old paper registry, but they made the case that an online registry was more punitive. They argued, for example, that the widespread availability of information about their crimes might result in the loss of their or their spouses' jobs. The case's legal basis involved the Constitution's prohibition of ex post facto punishment. This clause prohibits punishment for acts that were legal when they were committed, and it forbids the retroactive implementation of harsher penalties. In other words, a ten-year sentence cannot be increased to twenty to conform to a new sentencing law.

The Alaska case hinged on the question of whether the registry constituted punishment. If it did not, the ex post facto clause would have no relevance. The lower court ruled that registries were punitive, but in 2003, the US Supreme Court overturned that decision, saying that the registry is not intended to punish people, but rather to enhance public safety. This decision cleared the way for states to post names, photos, locations, employment, and car registration on the internet, regardless of when a person's crime had been committed. In an interesting twist, however, the Pennsylvania Supreme Court ruled in 2017 that registration *is* punishment, and that anyone who committed their offense prior to December 2012 (when the state's registry went online) could petition to be removed. At the time of this writing, it is not clear if this case will be heard by the US Supreme Court. Meanwhile, the Pennsylvania Supreme Court is considering another case about whether registries violate due process.

While the courts continue to debate their constitutionality, the registries grow longer and longer. Estimates suggest that by 2019, there were over nine hundred thousand Americans on sex offender registries.[11] This represents substantial growth over time. For example, the registry increased 24 percent between 2005 and

---

11. Steven Yoder, "Registered Sex Offenders in the United States and Its Territories per 100,000 Population," The Appeal, 2019, https://theappeal.org/why-sex-offender-registries-keep-growing-even-as-sexual-violence-rates-fall/.

2013, even though the sex-crime rate was in decline over the period.[12] It looks like this rapid growth is going to continue for the foreseeable future. This is partly because people are placed on the registry for many years or for life, resulting in a situation where more names are added each year than are removed. The retroactive registration provisions of SORNA also continue to add new names as states come into compliance with the law.

One of the most concerning reasons that registries continue to get longer involves net widening. This term refers to the expansion of a policy beyond what was originally intended. This happens across a wide range of public policies, but it has been particularly notable in the case of both registries and community notification. For example, Washington State created a web-based community notification system for people in risk tier three, but by 2003, they began including level two as well. Another example occurred in Pennsylvania when 2011 amendments to Megan's Law required that people who interfered with custody orders be placed on the registry. This means that a noncustodial parent who commits no sexual abuse but who simply returns their child late after a visit can be subject to registration.[13]

California illustrates some of the problems associated with net widening. By 2018, its registry had ballooned to over 106,000 people. This made it the state with the largest number of registered sex offenders in the nation, although only the twenty-fifth in terms of the number per capita.[14] One of the reasons that California has

12. Trevor Hoppe, "Are Sex Offender Registries Reinforcing Inequality?" The Conversation, August 8, 2017, https://theconversation.com/are-sex-offender-registries-reinforcing-inequality-79818.

13. Thomas Huguenor, "Mother Deemed 'Sex Offender' for Violating Custody," Law Office of Huguenor Mattis APC, February 7, 2018, https://www.familylaw-sd.com/blog/when-sex-offender-registry-gets-it-wrong/.

14. Zac Self, "This Is Where California Ranks on List of States with the Most Sex Offenders," KGTV San Diego, September 2, 2018, https://www.10news.com/news/california-ranks-high-on-list-of-states-with-most-sex-offenders.

such a large registry is that it was one of four states to mandate that most people convicted as sex offenders register for life. Many registered offenders had committed very minor crimes decades ago—some had even been convicted of consensual homosexual activities when homosexuality was illegal. In 2017, California Senator Scott Wiener commented:

> Our sex offender registry is broken and useless to law enforcement, with many nonviolent and low-level offenders who committed their offenses decades ago. If we're serious about monitoring high-risk sex offenders—as we should be—we must reform this registry."[15]

Wiener's comment alludes to the fact that, when a child is abducted, police have to comb through information about large numbers of people, most of whom are extremely unlikely to be involved. This wastes precious time and resources. Additionally, California requires that each offender's file be evaluated yearly, consuming law enforcement time that could be put toward other safety priorities. To address these issues, the California governor recently signed new legislation amending the lifetime requirement. Now, only people in the most serious offense category are required to register for life. People who were convicted of more minor crimes in the past are allowed to petition to be removed from the registry after ten or twenty years, depending on the crime.[16] This is a real improvement, but no other states have taken similar steps to

15. Quoted in Patrick McGreevy, "Bill to Reduce Names on California's Sex Offender Registry Shelved," *LA Times*, September 1, 2017, https://www.latimes.com/politics/essential/la-pol-ca-essential-politics-updates-bill-to-reduce-names-on-california-s-1504292042-htmlstory.html.

16. Patrick McGreevy, "California Will Soon End Lifetime Registration of Some Sex Offenders under Bill Signed by Gov. Jerry Brown," *LA Times*, October 6, 2017, https://www.latimes.com/politics/essential/la-pol-ca-essential-politics-updates-bill-ending-lifetime-registry-of-sex-1507332406-htmlstory.html.

reduce the number of names on the registry. This is the reason why there is an expression for "net widening" but not "net contracting."

EFFICACY OF REGISTRIES

The fact that the registry is large and growing makes it particularly important that we examine its impact. Politicians have routinely expressed support for the registry and community notification as a way to deter sex crimes and make communities safer. But do they accomplish this goal? Most research concludes that they do not. For example, one study looked at crime rates in New Jersey before and after the implementation of community notification. They found that sexual offending did go down over the period—but so did the rates of drug and nonsexual crimes that were not subject to the registry. The study concluded that New Jersey's registry had no impact on the rate of child sexual abuse (CSA) offenses, the number of victims, or the recidivism rate.[17]

The conclusions from New Jersey are mirrored in other states.[18] A researcher at the University of Chicago conducted an innovative study using rape data from forty-eight states. She had information

---

17. Kristen Zgoba et al., Megan's Law: Assessing the Practical and Monetary Efficacy (Trenton, NJ: The Research & Evaluation Unit, Office of Policy and Planning, New Jersey Department of Corrections, 2008), https://www.ncjrs.gov/App/Publications/abstract.aspx?ID=247350.

18. See, for example, Elizabeth J. Letourneau et al., "Effects of South Carolina's Sex Offender Registration and Notification Policy on Deterrence of Adult Sex Crimes," Criminal Justice and Behavior 37, no. 5 (2010): 537–52; Jeffrey C. Sandler, Naomi J. Freeman, and Kelly M. Socia, "Does a Watched Pot Boil? A Time-Series Analysis of New York State's Sex Offender Registration and Notification Law," Psychology, Public Policy, and Law 14, no. 4 (2008): 284–302, https://scholar.google.com/scholar?hl=en&as_sdt=0%2C36&q=Does+a+Watched+Pot+Boil%3F+A+Time-Series+&btnG=; Jeff A. Bouffard and LaQuana N. Askew, "Time-Series Analyses of the Impact of Sex Offender Registration and Notification Law Implementation and Subsequent Modifications on Rates of Sexual Offenses," Crime & Delinquency 65, no. 11 (2017): 483–1512.

about three points in time: before the registry, after the registry was created but not yet publicly available, and after the registry went on the internet. She found no evidence of a relationship between the registry, its public availability, and the rape rate. Additionally, there was no effect on the recidivism rate of people convicted of rape. This suggests that registries deter neither current registrants nor new offenders from crime. The researcher also compared the locations of sex offenders' homes and where sex crimes took place. It turns out there is little correlation. This suggests that knowing where sex offenders live does not help parents protect their children—because offenders often commit their crimes outside their own neighborhoods.[19]

Although most research shows that the registry and community notification do not deter crime, some studies have slightly more nuanced findings. An analysis of the separate effects of registration and community notification, for example, showed that registries are associated with a slight decrease in sexual reoffending. This is because police know where registrants live and are better able to monitor them. Notification is also associated with a slightly reduced rate of sexual offending, but only among people who are not on the registry. Presumably the registry exerts a deterrent effect on this group. Surprisingly, however, the researchers found that people who are on the registry actually increase their rate of offending. This is likely because, as I discuss in the next section, being on the registry often leads to unemployment, homelessness, and shame—all of which are linked to higher recidivism.[20]

---

19. Agan, "Sex Offender Registries," https://safervirginia.org/wp-content/uploads/2019/08/Registry-Fear-without-Function.pdf.

20. J. J. Prescott and Jonah E. Rockoff, "Do Sex Offender Registration and Notification Laws Affect Criminal Behavior?," *Journal of Law and Economics* 54, no. 1 (2011): 161–206, https://scholar.google.com/scholar?hl=en&as_sdt=0%2C36&q=Do+Sex+Offender+Registration+and+Notification+Laws+Affect+Criminal+Behavior%3F+2011&btnG=.

UNINTENDED CONSEQUENCES OF REGISTRIES

Plea Bargains

> Jacob Anderson, a student at Baylor University, was charged
> with four counts of sexual assault after a woman reported that
> he gave her a drugged drink, repeatedly raped her, and left her
> lying in vomit. In December of 2018, the judge allowed the
> case to be pled down to lesser charges, resulting in no prison
> time and no registration requirement.[21] Might the judge have
> made this decision because of registry requirements? Possibly.
> The research is summarized below.

One concern about registries is that they may lead to an increase
in plea bargains, acquittals, or the dismissal of charges. Why
would this happen? Prosecutors and judges, recognizing that the
registry is extremely punitive, may try to avoid sentences that
mandate it. A study of juvenile offenders in South Carolina provided support for this hypothesis. Researchers found that the
implementation of strict registration requirements correlated
with an increase in charges being dismissed or bargained down
to a nonsexual charge. The authors speculate that judges felt
that registration was too harsh a penalty for the crimes that had
been committed. If true, the registry may have the ironic effect
of requiring fewer sex offenders to get treatment that might
help them.[22] A similar phenomenon was found when adults were

---

21. Denise Couture, "Texas Judge Allows Former Baylor Frat President to Sidestep Rape Charge," National Public Radio, December 11, 2018,
https://www.npr.org/2018/12/11/675691750/texas-judge-sentences-
former-baylor-frat-president-to-sidestep-rape-charge.

22. Elizabeth J. Letourneau et al., "Sex Offender Registration and Notification Policy Increases Juvenile Plea Bargains," *Sexual Abuse: A Journal of Research
and Treatment* 25, no. 2 (2013): 189–207, http://citeseerx.ist.psu.edu/viewdoc/
download?doi=10.1.1.994.152&rep=rep1&type=pdf.

charged with sex crimes in South Carolina; after the implementation of registries, the number of plea bargains from sex crime to nonsex crime increased significantly.[23]

It should be noted that not all studies have found an increase in plea bargains after mandatory registration is put into place. A large-scale study conducted in New York State, for example, found that plea bargains did not increase after the implementation of Megan's Law.[24] But New York's laws were less strict than those in South Carolina.[25] If judges are trying to avoid imposing highly punitive sentences, it makes sense that there would be a more dramatic increase in plea bargains in the states with the strictest laws.

A final issue about plea bargains and registration involves bias. It is likely that white people—like Jacob Anderson—are more likely than people of color to be offered plea bargains. There is not yet research available on this question, but in many states, Megan's Law disproportionately affects Black people.[26] In 2017, for example, Black men were registered at twice the rate of white men, resulting in 1 percent of all Black men being on the registry.[27] This means that people of color are more likely to pay the heavy price that registration entails. That price is discussed next.

---

23. Elizabeth J. Letourneau et al., "The Effects of Sex Offender Registration and Notification on Judicial Decisions," *Criminal Justice Review* 35, no. 3 (2010): 295–317.

24. Naomi J. Freeman, Jeffrey C. Sandler, and Kelly M. Socia, "A Time-Series Analysis on the Impact of Sex Offender Registration and Community Notification Laws on Plea Bargaining Rates," *Criminal Justice Studies* 22, no. 2 (2009): 153–65.

25. Letourneau et al., "The Effects of Sex Offender Registration."

26. Daniel M. Filler, "Silence and the Racial Dimension of Megan's Law," *Iowa Law Review* 89 (2004): 1535–94, https://papers.ssrn.com/sol3/papers.cfm?abstract_id=648261.

27. Hoppe, "Are Sex Offender Registries Reinforcing Inequality?" https://theconversation.com/are-sex-offender-registries-reinforcing-inequality-79818.

Stigma and Discrimination

Most public debate about the impact of the registry involves crime deterrence; other possible effects are rarely discussed. Research says, however, that the registry has a significant adverse impact on people convicted of sexual offenses. For example, in a large survey taken of people on the registry, about a third reported at least one "very negative" effect, including losing a house or job, being harassed, or having property damaged. More than half reported a negative but less serious impact like stress, the loss of a relationship, or embarrassment.[28] Another study found that 42 percent had lost a job when an employer found them on the registry, 45 percent were denied housing, 40 percent were treated "rudely" in a public place, and 47 percent reported in-person harassment.[29] All of these data are worrying because housing, employment, and social support serve as deterrents to further crime.[30] In other words, the registry might serve to increase rather than decrease sexual offending.

Sexual offenders are not the only people to feel the effect of the registries. Their families also suffer negative effects. In a survey of 584 family members of registrants, 44 percent reported being harassed by neighbors and 53 percent reported financial effects

---

28. Jill S. Levenson and Leo P. Cotter, "The Effect of Megan's Law on Sex Offender Reintegration," *Journal of Contemporary Criminal Justice* 21, no. 1 (2005): 49–66, https://scholar.google.com/scholar?hl=en&as_sdt=0%2C36&q=The+Effect+of+Megan's+Law+on+Sex+Offender+Reintegration&btnG=.

29. Richard Tewksbury, "Collateral Consequences of Sex Offender Registration," *Journal of Contemporary Criminal Justice* 21, no. 1 (2005): 67–81, http://citeseerx.ist.psu.edu/viewdoc/download?doi=10.1.1.864.6141&rep=rep1&type=pdf.

30. Sarah Lageson and Christopher Uggen, "How Work Affects Crime—and Crime Affects Work—Over the Life Course," in *Handbook of Life-Course Criminology*, ed. Chris L. Gibson and Marvin D. Krohn (New York: Springer New York, 2013), 201–12, https://scholar.google.com/scholar?hl=en&as_sdt=0%2C36&q=How+Work+Affects+Crime—And+Crime+Affects+Work&btnG=; Christopher Uggen, "Ex-Offenders and the Conformist Alternative: A Job Quality Model of Work and Crime," *Social Problems* 46, no. 1 (February 1999): 127–51, https://scholar.google.com/scholar?hl=en&as_sdt=0%2C36&q=Ex-Offenders+and+the+Conformist+Alternative%3A+&btnG=.

when their family member lost a job due to the registry. Even more disturbing, 47 percent of the children of registrants reported being harassed because their parent was on the list.[31]

Documentary Film about Being on the Registry

Here is a link to a short film by director David Feige about some of the unintended outcomes of being on the registry. It features individual people's stories: https://www.themarshallproject.org/2017/09/17/shawna-a-life-on-the-sex-offender-registry.

As discussed above, the Supreme Court ruled that registries are legal because they are preventative, not punitive. This logic assumes that people will simply use registries to take precautions and will not harass registrants or their families.[32] The studies described in this section, however, demonstrate that this is not the reality. Instead, people disregard warnings from law enforcement (like that in the community notification flier shown above), and use the registries as a way to exact further punishment on people with sexual offense convictions and their families.

Juvenile Registrants

Jacob was eleven when he touched his sister's genitals. The juvenile court in Michigan convicted him of criminal sexual conduct, required him to register for life, and decreed that he could no longer live near other children. This meant that

---

31. Jill S. Levenson and Richard Tewksbury, "Collateral Damage: Family Members of Registered Sex Offenders," *American Journal of Criminal Justice* 34 (2009): 54–68, https://link.springer.com/article/10.1007/s12103-008-9055-x.

32. Ron Levi, "The Mutuality of Risk and Community: The Adjudication of Community Notification Statutes" *Economy and Society* 29, no. 4 (2000): 578–601.

he was forced to live in foster care because he could not live with his sister. When he turned eighteen, his registration became public and parents at his high school tried to have him expelled. He went on to college but was harassed so badly about being on the registry that he dropped out.[33]

Current data are hard to come by, but estimates suggest that there are at least two hundred thousand people on registries because of sex crimes committed as children or teenagers.[34] In some states, children as young as eight can be listed on the registry. Jacob's case illustrates the severe and often lifelong effects the registry can have on these juveniles, and research confirms that his experiences are not unique. For example, 44 percent of juvenile registrants reported becoming homeless due to residential restrictions on housing, and 52 percent experienced violence when others discovered that they were on the registry.[35]

While people on the registry are allowed to attend college, they must inform the institution of their status. In 2010, Lake Michigan College enacted a blanket ban preventing all registrants from taking classes on campus. Under pressure from the American Civil Liberties Union (ACLU), however, they—like many other colleges—began conducting an individual review of each case.[36] School policies vary in terms of housing. Many schools preclude

33. Nicole Pittman, Alison Parker, and Human Rights Watch (HRW), *Raised on the Registry: The Irreparable Harm of Placing Children in Sex Offenders Registries in the US* (New York: Human Rights Watch, 2013), https://www.hrw.org/sites/default/files/reports/us0513_ForUpload_1.pdf.

34. Juvenile Law Center, "Juvenile Sex Offender Registry (SORNA)," Juvenile Law Center, 2018, https://jlc.org/issues/juvenile-sex-offender-registry-sorna.

35. Pittman, Parker, and HRW, *Raised on the Registry*, https://www.hrw.org/sites/default/files/reports/us0513_ForUpload_1.pdf.

36. American Civil Liberties Union, "Lake Michigan College Agrees to Individualized Review of Students with Criminal Records, ACLU Announces," American Civil Liberties Union, June 22, 2011, https://www.aclu.org/press-releases/lake-michigan-college-agrees-individualized-review-students-criminal-records-aclu.

Figure 10. Self Offense. 2011 by Nina Paley. Mimi and Eunice. CC-BY-SA. https://mimiandeunice.com/category/violence/

registrants from living on campus altogether; others only allow those who have been convicted of low-level offenses and who have been approved by a committee vote. Recently, the Texas legislature passed a bill that prevents almost all registrants from living on either public or private campuses.[37] The federal government requires all colleges to inform students about how to access the registry in case they want to see if there are offenders attending classes or living on campus.

False Sense of Security

One of the most ironic effects of the registries is that they may increase abuse because they cause parents to reduce protective behaviors.[38] In other words, some parents might believe, consciously or not, that the registry contains a complete list of anyone who might abuse their children. Keeping children safe then becomes a simple matter of keeping them away from those particular individuals. While this idea may make parents feel better,

---

37. Emma Platoff, "New Texas Law Keeps Sex Offenders Out of College Dorms," *Texas Tribune*, September 25, 2017, https://www.texastribune.org/2017/09/25/books-sex-offenders-kept-out-campus-dorms/.

38. Alvin Malesky and Jeanmarie Keim, "Mental Health Professionals' Perspectives on Sex Offender Registry Web Sites," *Sexual Abuse: A Journal of Research and Treatment* 13, no. 1 (2001): 53–63.

Figure 11. False Sense of Security. Source: Kieran Meehan.

their sense of security is false because the registry contains only the subset of offenders who have been caught. It does not include people who are currently offending without detection, nor does it include people who will begin offending in the future. In fact, research suggests that registries only contain the names of a small proportion of the people who go on to commit sex crimes. In one study in New York State, 95 percent of all sex crimes were committed by people who were not on the registry.[39] When parents rely on the registry to identify danger, they may fail to see the actual dangerous people who are standing right in front of them—often relatives, family friends, or other people close to their child.

Economic Costs

It seems like registration and notification should be cheap. How much could it possibly cost to keep a list of names? The reality is, however, that registries are expensive to create and maintain. One study found that the implementation of Megan's Law in New Jersey cost $555,565 (in 2007 dollars). And by 2013, after six years of operation, the state had paid about $3.9 million.[40] This figure, however, does not include what economists call "opportunity costs." Any time people decide to take part in one activity, it precludes them from engaging in others. Opportunity cost refers to what one would have gained had they taken another path. In other words, it is possible the $3.9 million that New Jersey spent on the registry could have been used to implement much more effective measures.

Opportunity costs are hidden—as are other costs of the registry. For example, it appears that property values decrease in neighborhoods where registrants live. Houses that are directly adjacent to

39. Sandler, Freeman, and Socia, "Does a Watched Pot Boil?" https://scholar.goo gle.com/scholar?hl=en&as_sdt=0%2C36&q=Does+a+Watched+Pot+Boil%3F+A+ Time-Series+&btnG=.

40. Zgoba et al., *Megan's Law*, https://www.ncjrs.gov/App/Publications/ abstract.aspx?ID=247350.

the registrant's home decrease in value by 12 percent, and homes as far as one-tenth of a mile away decrease in value by 4 percent. The researchers who discovered this speculate that there are several reasons: people fear living near a registrant, they overestimate the risk associated with it, and they assume that there will be social costs such as friends being hesitant to visit the neighborhood.[41] A decrease in property values affects all the people in the neighborhood, but it also impacts the state and local governments (and therefore schools) by lowering property tax revenue.

INTERNET RESTRICTIONS

> In 2010, North Carolinian Lester Packingham was arrested for logging onto Facebook and posting about being thankful to God for his parking ticket being dismissed. How could such an innocuous Facebook post result in an arrest? Under state law, registrants were not allowed to access any social media platform that minors might use. Because Packingham was on the registry for a 2002 conviction for a sexual crime against a minor, his brief venture onto Facebook resulted in another felony conviction.[42]

The Adam Walsh Act allows a wide range of restrictions on offenders' use of technology. For example, law enforcement officials are allowed to search or put monitoring software on registrants'

---

41. Leigh Linden and Jonah E. Rockoff, "Estimates of the Impact of Crime Risk on Property Values from Megan's Laws," *American Economic Review* 98, no. 3 (2008): 1103–27, https://scholar.google.com/scholar?hl=en&as_sdt=0%2C36&q=Estimates+of+the+Impact+of+Crime+Risk+on+Property+Values+from+Megan%E2%80%99s+&btnG=.

42. Derek Gilna, "Supreme Court Voids North Carolina Law barring Sex Offenders from Facebook," *Prison Legal News*, June 30, 2017, https://www.prisonlegalnews.org/news/2017/jun/30/supreme-court-voids-north-carolina-law-barring-sex-offenders-facebook/.

computers, and they can even prohibit registrants from using electronic communication entirely.[43] These types of internet laws have come under recent legal scrutiny. In fact, Lester Packingham sued North Carolina, and the case went all the way to the US Supreme Court. He ultimately prevailed, and the North Carolina statute was struck down as violating the right to free speech. Justice Samuel Alito commented that the statute was overly broad, prohibiting people from doing things like online shopping. Similarly, in 2017, a federal judge overturned two Kentucky laws that required offenders to stay off social network sites and to report all of their online and e-mail identities to their parole officer.[44] As in North Carolina, these laws were overturned on free speech grounds and because they were too broad. There remain, however, other states and localities with internet restrictions.

There is not a lot of research on the efficacy of internet restrictions, so it is hard to assess their impact. As discussed in chapter 3, a small percentage of offenders do use the internet to meet children or to communicate with them. It is certainly possible that restrictions prevent some of these activities, but it is hard to know if they reduce the rate of offending overall. In other words, offenders who want to contact children but can't use technology might just turn to other methods. What we do know, however, is that the restrictions appear to have a negative impact on the lives of people convicted of sexual crimes. For example, one study surveyed people who were completely prohibited from using the internet. They reported that the restriction made it difficult to locate and

43. United States Courts, "Overview of Probation and Supervised Release Conditions" (Washington, DC: Administrative Office of the United States Courts Probation and Pretrial Services Office, 2016), http://www.uscourts.gov/services-forms/computer-internet-restrictions-probation-supervised-release-conditions.

44. Bruce Schreiner, "Judge Strikes down Kentucky's Internet Restrictions for Sex Offenders," *Courier Journal*, October 20, 2017, https://www.courier-journal.com/story/news/local/2017/10/20/judge-strikes-down-kentuckys-internet-restrictions-sex-offenders/786270001/.

apply for jobs and to communicate with family and friends.[45] It is concerning that internet restrictions mean that people are cut off from two potential paths to maintaining crime-free lives.

RESIDENTIAL RESTRICTIONS

Residency restrictions limit where people on the registry can live. One common law prohibits former offenders from living within five hundred feet of a school, park, playground, or day-care center. In some places, that distance is set as high as a half mile or mile. Many communities have also adopted rules that disallow more than one person on the registry from living in a household. This rule is intended to prevent people with convictions for sexual offenses from colluding with each other to commit new crimes.

There is not a lot of research on residency restrictions, but, in general, studies indicate that they are not very effective at preventing CSA. The Colorado Department of Public Safety, for example, conducted a study for the state legislature as it was considering implementing residency requirements. They compared the rates of recidivism of people who had convictions for sexual crimes living in different kinds of arrangements (alone, with family, with a non-offending roommate, etc.). Contrary to expectations, they found that people living together in supportive communities had notably lower levels of recidivism than people in other types of households. It appears that when people live together and pledge to support each other in recovery, they hold each other accountable for their behavior. For example, the study found that housemates in the

---

45. Richard Tewksbury and Kristen M. Zgoba, "Perceptions and Coping with Punishment: How Registered Sex Offenders Respond to Stress, Internet Restrictions, and the Collateral Consequences of Registration," *International Journal of Offender Therapy and Comparative Criminology* 54, no. 4 (2010): 537–51, https://safervirginia.org/wp-content/uploads/2019/08/Collateral-Damage-Perceptions-and-Coping-With-Punishment.pdf.

supportive communities called the police quickly when they suspected criminal behavior or parole violations. While this study did not assess the effect of rules prohibiting residency near schools, it did find that when there are no rules, people with sexual convictions do not tend to cluster around schools or parks. Instead, they are spread out in a seemingly random pattern across cities.[46]

> PBS produced a movie called *Pervert Park*, about a supportive community-living situation in Florida. You can't access the whole movie for free, but you can see the trailer here: https://www.youtube.com/watch?v=9qOhXyfodpY.

A study by the Minnesota Department of Corrections more directly tested the impact of residency requirements. Researchers examined 224 cases of sexual offenders who were released from prison and went on to commit another sexual offense. There was not a single case that involved an offender making contact with a child at a school or a park. In the vast majority of cases, the abuse happened through adult connections, such as a mother introducing her children to a new boyfriend.[47]

Residency requirements have significant effects on people with CSA convictions. Due to stigma, it is already difficult for them to find housing, and the residency restrictions further limit their choices. Often, registrants are forced to live in the most impoverished and socially disorganized areas of town because these areas have less infrastructure (including parks and schools).[48] This

---

46. Colorado Department of Public Safety, *Report on Safety Issues Raised by Living Arrangements for and Location of Sex Offenders in the Community* (Denver: Division of Criminal Justice, Colorado Department of Public Safety, 2004).

47. Minnesota Department of Corrections, *Residential Proximity & Sex Offense Recidivism in Minnesota* (St. Paul: Minnesota Department of Corrections, 2007), https://ccoso.org/sites/default/files/import/SexOffenderReport-Proximity.pdf.

48. Elizabeth Ehrhardt Mustaine, Richard Tewksbury, and Kenneth M. Stengel, "Social Disorganization and Residential Locations of Registered Sex Offenders:

is particularly true for people of color. They are discriminated against both because of their race and their offender status, making it extremely difficult to find housing in anywhere but the most socially disorganized neighborhoods.[49]

> In Miami-Dade County in 2009, more than one hundred people who had been convicted of sexual crimes were living together under a freeway overpass. Why? The county had enacted so many residential restrictions that no affordable units were left in the few unrestricted areas. While the law was changed to make restrictions less onerous, localities then responded by categorizing more institutions as "schools" and increasing the radius inside which people with convictions for sexual crimes could not live. As a result, people have continued to live in camps outside the city limits.[50]

Miami is not alone in having a tent city caused at least partly by residency rules. My own small Ohio town also had an encampment, leading to numerous health and hygiene issues. The city ultimately forced the residents to leave. While they helped some of the residents find housing, it was extremely difficult to assist those with convictions for sexual abuse. Residency requirements, landlords refusing to rent to them, and our local shelter's rule barring registrants all proved to be impediments.[51] A study conducted in four states found that 72 percent of homeless shelters had similar policies.[52]

Is This a Collateral Consequence?" *Deviant Behavior* 27, no. 3 (2006): 329–50.

49. Elizabeth Ehrhardt Mustaine and Richard Tewksbury, "Registered Sex Offenders, Residence, and the Influence of Race," *Journal of Ethnicity in Criminal Justice* 6, no. 1 (2008): 65–82.

50. Nicole Flatow, "Inside Miami's Hidden Tent City for 'Sex Offenders,'" ThinkProgress, October 23, 2014, https://thinkprogress.org/inside-miamis-hidden-tent-city-for-sex-offenders-5c9356a45d1f/.

51. Linda Hall, "Wooster Tent City: Sheltering Options Limited and Restricted for People with Series of Records," *Daily Record*, September 2, 2014, https://www.the-daily-record.com/article/20140902/NEWS/309029363.

52. Shawn M. Rolfe, Richard Tewksbury, and Ryan D. Schroeder,

HALLOWEEN LAWS

Halloween laws restrict the movement and behavior of people with CSA convictions—but only on one day a year—October 31. For example, California's Operation Boo gives police permission to check up on registrants on Halloween. In New York State, several counties require people on the registry to attend hours-long educational presentations during that evening.[53] People convicted of sexual offenses who live in New Jersey are not allowed to open their doors or give out candy. If they do so, it is counted as a parole violation that can result in up to three years of incarceration.[54] In Tennessee, registrants must be in their houses by 6 p.m., cannot display decorations or turn on their porch light, and cannot attend Halloween events or pass out candy.[55]

Cities pass Halloween laws out of a fear that former offenders might lure trick or treaters into their homes. This fear, however, is not based in reality. Halloween is not associated with an increase in sex crimes against children, nor is there an elevated risk during the three-day window around the holiday. A study by Chaffin et al. even looked separately at family and nonfamily abuse and found no rise in nonfamily incidents. The researchers point out that the real danger to children on Halloween is being hit by a car, but

"Homeless Shelters' Policies on Sex Offenders: Is This Another Collateral Consequence?" *International Journal of Offender Therapy and Comparative Criminology* 61, no. 16 (2017): 1833–49, https://scholar.google.com/scholar?hl=en&as_sdt=0,5&q=Rolfe+Tewksbury+Homeless+Shelters.

53. Mark Chaffin et al., "How Safe Are Trick-or-Treaters?: An Analysis of Child Sex Crime Rates on Halloween," *Sexual Abuse: A Journal of Research and Treatment* 21, no. 3 (2009): 363–74, https://journals.sagepub.com/doi/pdf/10.1177/1079063209340143.

54. Chaffin et al., "How Safe Are Trick-or-Treaters?" https://journals.sagepub.com/doi/pdf/10.1177/1079063209340143.

55. Ron Maxey, "Sex Offenders Have a List Of 'Don't's' on Halloween Night, TDOC Officers Will Be Checking for Compliance," *Commercial Appeal*, October 12, 2018, https://www.commercialappeal.com/story/news/2018/10/12/tennessee-department-correction-officers-keep-eye-sex-offenders-halloween-night/1613989002/.

Halloween laws force some police officers to monitor offenders rather than direct traffic.[56]

CASTRATION

While castration sounds like something out of the Middle Ages, it is very much a topic of discussion and policy-making today. In fact, the governor of Alabama signed a bill in 2019 that requires chemical castration as a condition of parole for anyone with a sexual conviction involving a child under the age of thirteen. Alabama joins a number of other states, such as California, Florida, and Oregon, with similar statutes. States vary somewhat in the categories of people who are required to undergo this treatment and who pays for it.[57]

There are two types of castration: physical and chemical. Physical castration is the removal of a man's testes or a woman's ovaries. Chemical castration, in contrast, involves taking drugs that block testosterone and other hormones associated with the libido. One often-cited study found that men who are chemically castrated have lower sex drives and fewer sexual fantasies than do those who do not receive the treatment.[58] The fact that this study relied on self-report, however, raises the concern that it might not be accurate.[59] In a review of the literature, Karen Harrison found that there is evidence to suggest that chemical castration decreases recidivism,

---

56. Chaffin et al., "How Safe Are Trick-or-Treaters?" https://journals.sagepub.com/doi/pdf/10.1177/1079063209340143.

57. Alan Blinder, "What to Know about the Alabama Chemical Castration Law," *New York Times*, June 11, 2019, https://www.nytimes.com/2019/06/11/us/politics/chemical-castration.html.

58. Kyo Chul Koo et al., "Treatment Outcomes of Chemical Castration on Korean Sex Offenders," *Journal of Forensic and Legal Medicine* 20, no. 6 (2013): 563–66.

59. Blinder, "What to Know about the Alabama Chemical Castration Law." https://www.nytimes.com/2019/06/11/us/politics/chemical-castration.html.

but that many of the studies have methodological flaws.[60] Because testosterone increases libido in both men and women, women can also take certain castration drugs but not much is known about its effect because its use is rare. Fewer women than men commit sex crimes, and many of the laws that result in castration are written in such a way that men are more likely to violate them. There is also evidence that, in some cases, women are sentenced less harshly than men and might be less likely to trigger mandatory castration requirements.[61]

A number of criticisms have been levied against mandatory chemical castration. First, the ACLU argues that it violates the Constitution's Eighth Amendment against cruel and unusual punishment. Second, chemical castration has side effects, including osteoporosis, cardiovascular disease, metabolic changes, and infertility. A law like Alabama's exposes all people with CSA convictions to these risks, even though most would not have gone on to recidivate. Third, research shows that while castration reduces sexual impulses, it does not necessarily take them away altogether. For example, in a study with voluntarily castrated men, 37 percent reported having sex several times a week.[62] It appears that physical castration may be more effective at reducing sex drive and recidivism, but its permanence increases the ethical issues, and it is not currently required in any state.[63] A final problem with castration

---

60. Karen Harrison, "The High-Risk Sex Offender Strategy in England and Wales: Is Chemical Castration an Option?" *Howard Journal of Criminal Justice* 46, no. 1 (2007): 16–31.

61. Zachary Edmonds Oswald, "'Off with His __': Analyzing the Sex Disparity in Chemical Castration Sentences," *Michigan Journal of Gender and Law* 19, no. 2 (2013): 472–503, https://scholar.google.com/scholar?hl=en&as_sdt=0%2C36&scio q=Registered+Sex+Offenders%2C+Residence%2C+and+the+Influence+of+Race& q=Off+with+His+__'%3A+Analyzing+the+Sex+Disparity+in+Chemical+&btnG=.

62. Ariel B. Handy et al., "Gender Preference in the Sexual Attractions, Fantasies, and Relationships of Voluntarily Castrated Men," *Sexual Medicine* 4 (2016): 51–59, https://www.sciencedirect.com/science/article/pii/S2050116116000106.

63. Walter J. Meyer and Collier M. Cole, "Physical and Chemical Castration of Sex Offenders: A Review," *Journal of Offender Rehabilitation* 25, no. 3–4 (1997):

is that it assumes that the reason people commit CSA is sexual. As we learned in previous chapters, CSA is associated with other issues such as drug use, power, and intimacy deficits. Castration only addresses sex drive, perhaps explaining why it is not entirely effective.

ELECTRONIC MONITORING

GPS technology has a huge range of applications. It enables phones to give directions, it navigates planes, and it even warns lifeguards about potential shark attacks.[64] GPS has also led to a revolution in criminal justice. Today, electronic monitoring (EM) uses GPS to track the movements of people who are awaiting trial, are serving house arrest, or—increasingly—who are on parole for sex offenses. People on EM wear an ankle bracelet that transmits location information. There are three different types of monitoring. Active monitoring means that data are sent continuously to law enforcement. In passive monitoring, data are only transferred at intervals (such as once a day). A hybrid system sends information at intervals but goes active if a violation is detected. While active systems would seem ideal because they operate in real time, they are also very expensive.[65]

The first mandatory ankle monitoring bill for people convicted of sexual crimes was passed in Florida in 2005. It was called Jessica's Law in memory of nine-year-old Jessica Lunsford who, earlier

---

1–18; Linda E. Weinberger et al., "The Impact of Surgical Castration on Sexual Recidivism Risk Among Sexually Violent Predatory Offenders," *Journal of the American Academy of Psychiatry and the Law* 33, no. 1 (2005): 21, http://citeseerx. ist.psu.edu/viewdoc/download?doi=10.1.1.517.6776&rep=rep1&type=pdf.

64. Patrick Kiger, "10 Unconventional Uses for GPS," HowStuffWorks, July 28, 2014, https://electronics.howstuffworks.com/10-unconventional-uses-gps.htm.

65. International Association of Chiefs of Police, *Tracking Sex Offenders with Electronic Monitoring Technology: Implications and Practical Uses for Law Enforcement* (Alexandria, VA: International Association of Chiefs of Police, 2008), https://www.theiacp.org/sites/default/files/2018-08/TrackingOffenders.pdf.

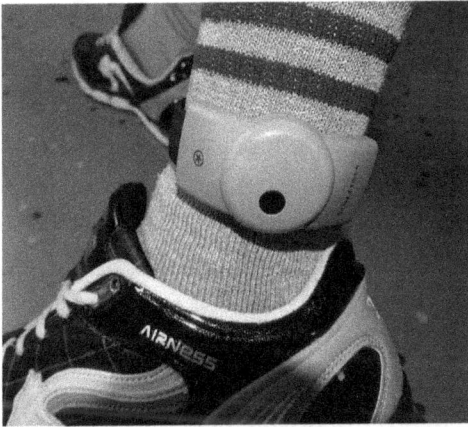

Figure 12. Bracelet électronique. Author: Jérémy-Günther-Heinz Jähnick, from Wikimedia Commons, License: Creative Commons Attribution-ShareAlike 3.0.

that year, had been sexually abused and murdered by a neighbor who had a prior sex conviction. People also sometimes use Jessica's name to refer to legislation in other states that was modeled after Florida's law. Jessica's Law expanded registration requirements for people convicted of sexual abuse against a child, increased their sentence lengths, and mandated that, post-prison, they wear electronic monitoring devices. While some states mandate electronic monitoring for a restricted period of parole, Florida puts people with CSA convictions on indefinite parole, meaning that they have to wear the monitoring device for the rest of their lives.[66] In 2006, California quickly followed Florida's lead. They legislated that all people convicted of a sex offense must wear a monitor while on parole, and those who are convicted of a felony sex offense have to wear one for life.[67]

66. Associated Press, "Fla. Gets Tough New Child-Sex Law—CBS News," CBS News, May 2, 2005, https://www.cbsnews.com/news/fla-gets-tough-new-child-sex-law/.

67. California Department of Corrections, "Laws Related to Sex Offender Parolees," Division of Adult Parole Operations (DAPO), 2020, https://www.cdcr.ca.gov/parole/sex-offender-laws/.

EFFICACY OF ELECTRONIC MONITORING

Proponents of EM make a number of arguments. They point out that both jails and prisons are severely overcrowded. EM can potentially reduce these populations and, because it is cheaper than incarceration, it can also save money. Another argument is that EM decreases recidivism since users are not able to leave their homes or jobs without alerting law enforcement. Because users know this, they refrain from crime.

The argument that EM is less expensive than prison is absolutely true, but it is not a simple apples-to-apples comparison. This is because EM is rarely used in place of prison for people convicted for sexual offenses. Instead, it is used once they are released on parole, so the more appropriate question is whether EM saves money over traditional parole. Surprisingly, a study published in 2012 estimated that EM costs about eight dollars and fifty cents per day, per person, more than traditional parole.[68] In addition to taking a long time to train wearers, it takes time for law enforcement to deal with the massive amount of data produced by the tracking. Furthermore, monitors sometimes report that someone has left their home when they have not, causing police to be sent.[69] Finally, when a state monitors huge numbers of people (as do California and Florida), they end up including a lot of offenders who have a very low risk of reoffense and would likely not have been put on traditional parole.

Does EM have a positive effect on behavior? The research results

---

68. Stephen V. Gies et al., *Monitoring High-Risk Sex Offenders with GPS Technology: An Evaluation of the California Supervision Program, Final Report* (Washington, DC: National Institute of Justice, 2012), https://pdfs.semanticscholar.org/6333/49d0abd658f9113f9299b09bc7bb64c1f309.pdf.

69. Brian K. Payne and Matthew DeMichele, "Sex Offender Policies: Considering Unanticipated Consequences of GPS Sex Offender Monitoring," *Aggression and Violent Behavior* 16, no. 3 (2011): 177–87; Deeanna M. Button, Matthew DeMichele, and Brian K. Payne, "Using Electronic Monitoring to Supervise Sex Offenders: Legislative Patterns and Implications for Community Corrections Officers," *Criminal Justice Policy Review* 20, no. 4 (2009): 414–36.

are somewhat mixed, so it is hard to draw firm conclusions. A large study in Florida of over seventy-five thousand participants, about 3.9 percent of whom were convicted of sexual offenses, found that EM reduced parole violations, new criminal convictions, and people absconding from parole. The study was impressive because of its large sample size. It was also conducted early enough in the state's transition to using EM that they were able to compare the monitor-wearers to similar parolees who had not been assigned to wear one.[70] Unfortunately, the study did not separate out sexual and nonsexual reoffenses. As discussed in chapter 3, when people who have been convicted of sex crimes recidivate, the new crime is often nonsexual.

Two studies were conducted with former sex offenders determined to be at high risk for recidivism. The studies, although both conducted in California, took place in different counties and led to somewhat different conclusions. One found that EM reduced the chances of recidivism for sex crimes as well as for parole violations.[71] The other found that EM was not associated with fewer sex crimes. Those offenders who were on EM, however, were more likely to register as sexual offenders (as required by law) and were slightly less likely to go AWOL from parole.[72] Both studies compared two groups of people convicted of a sexual crime: one group was mandated to wear a GPS tracking device, and the other was not. Unfortunately, the two studies differed in terms of time period, location, and composition of the control group. It is likely that these differences explain the divergent conclusions.

So, what is the answer? Two researchers decided to review all

70. Kathy G. Padgett, William D. Bales, and Thomas G. Blomberg, "Under Surveillance: An Empirical Test of the Effectiveness and Consequences of Electronic Monitoring," *Criminology & Public Policy* 5, no. 1 (2006): 61–91, http://www.antoniocasella.eu/nume/Padgett_electronic_2006.pdf.

71. Gies et al., Monitoring High-Risk Sex Offenders with GPS Technology.

72. Susan Turner et al., "Does GPS Improve Recidivism among High Risk Sex Offenders? Outcomes for California's GPS Pilot for High Risk Sex Offender Parolees," *Victims & Offenders* 10, no. 1 (2015): 1–28.

the studies that had been published through 2002. They found that the vast majority were methodologically unsound and should not be used for the development of policy. Only two studies out of the twelve assessed were strong enough for inclusion; they indicated that EM might be linked with a decrease in reoffending among people determined to be at medium and high risk.[73] At the same time, the authors commented that "after 20 years, it is clear that EM has been almost desperately applied without adequate vision, planning, program integration, staff training, and concurrent research."[74] This quote referred to the situation eighteen years ago, but there is little evidence that things have improved in the intervening years. At the same time, I think the jury is still out on the efficacy of EM. It is quite possible that it reduces recidivism and parole violations but probably only among certain populations and under certain conditions.

UNANTICIPATED CONSEQUENCES OF ELECTRONIC MONITORING

Electronic monitoring may share a downside with registries: they both lull the community into a false sense of security.[75] In a recent national survey, researchers found that most people think that monitoring is effective (32 percent said it was "very effective" and 47 percent said it was "somewhat effective").[76] Research suggests,

---

73. Marc Renzema and Evan Mayo-Wilson, "Can Electronic Monitoring Reduce Crime for Moderate to High-Risk Offenders?" *Journal of Experimental Criminology* 1, no. 2 (2005): 215–37, http://www.correcttechllc.com/articles/14. pdf.

74. Renzema and Mayo-Wilson, "Can Electronic Monitoring Reduce Crime?" http://www.correcttechllc.com/articles/14.pdf.

75. Payne and DeMichele, "Sex Offender Policies."

76. Kristen M. Budd and Christina Mancini, "Public Perceptions of GPS Monitoring for Convicted Sex Offenders: Opinions on Effectiveness of Electronic Monitoring to Reduce Sexual Recidivism," *International Journal of Offender Therapy and Comparative Criminology* 61, no. 12 (2017): 1335–53.

however, that people do not have a good sense of how the trackers work and may overestimate their abilities. For example, they may think that all trackers are active when many are not.[77]

A second possible downside to EM involves the use of extrinsic motivators. Ideally, we want people to engage in good behavior because they know it is the right thing to do and they have a desire to feel good about themselves. This is intrinsic motivation. Monitoring, however, encourages people to focus on external motivators. They may desist from CSA, but only because somebody is watching them. This does not help them learn to control their own behavior, leading to the question of what happens when the monitor is removed.[78] Similarly, EM in and of itself does nothing to rehabilitate anyone; it simply incapacitates them for a period of time.[79] Using EM as the whole solution for post-prison control fails to address the multiple causes of CSA.[80]

What are the effects of EM on those required to wear it and their families? First, it should be said that most people vastly prefer EM to prison. At the same time, EM is associated with some negative effects on families.[81] For example, it shifts the balance of power in households because the partner of the person being monitored has to do the bulk of the chores outside the house. Depending on the EM restrictions, users can no longer take their partners out to dinner, nor can they attend a child's sporting event. This causes strain on the very relationships that have the potential to deter people from further crime.[82] Finally, states are increasingly turning

---

77. Payne and DeMichele, "Sex Offender Policies."

78. Payne and DeMichele.

79. Mike Nellis, "Surveillance, Rehabilitation, and Electronic Monitoring: Getting the Issues Clear," *Criminology & Public Policy* 5, no. 1 (2006): 103–8.

80. Button, DeMichele, and Payne, "Using Electronic Monitoring to Supervise Sex Offenders."

81. Brian K. Payne and Randy R. Gainey, "A Qualitative Assessment of the Pains Experienced on Electronic Monitoring," *International Journal of Offender Therapy and Comparative Criminology* 42, no. 2 (1998): 149–63.

82. Nellis, "Surveillance, Rehabilitation, and Electronic Monitoring."

to private companies to provide EM and allowing them to charge users. If a person is required to wear a monitor and is unable to pay, they end up back in prison.[83] This effectively punishes poor people more than those who are financially stable.

CIVIL CONFINEMENT

The most restrictive post-prison sexual abuse prevention strategy is called civil confinement. It involves a court order that declares a person a continuing threat to public safety. After their prison sentence is complete, they are confined in mental hospitals. The first laws of this type were dubbed "sexual psychopath laws." Michigan, Illinois, Ohio, California, and Minnesota passed the first of these laws between 1935 and 1939, but, by 1967, twenty-six states and the District of Columbia had them on the books. Some of the laws were rescinded in the 1960s over concerns that the "sexual psychopath" label was ambiguous and that due process was not being followed in making decisions about civil confinement.[84] There were also criticisms that states failed to provide treatment, making it virtually impossible for people to get help or to prove that they had ceased to be a threat to society. By the 1990s, only thirteen states still retained these laws.[85]

---

83. Ava Kofman, "Digital Jail: How Electronic Monitoring Drives Defendants into Debt," ProPublica, July 3, 2019, https://www.propublica.org/article/digital-jail-how-electronic-monitoring-drives-defendants-into-debt.

84. Estelle B. Freedman, "'Uncontrolled Desires': The Response to the Sexual Psychopath, 1920–1960," *Journal of American History* 74, no. 1 (1987): 83–106, https://pdfs.semanticscholar.org/4ef2/88e27c4a90b7f069735e193bee17c52809e4.pdf; Tamara Rice Lave, "Only Yesterday: The Rise and Fall of Twentieth Century Sexual Psychopath Laws," *Louisiana Law Review* 69 (2009): 549–91, https://scholar.google.com/scholar?hl=en&as_sdt=0%2C36&scioq=Registered+Sex+Offenders%2C+Residence%2C+and+the+Influence+of+Race&q=Only+Yesterday%3A+The+Rise+and+Fall+of+Twentieth&btnG=.

85. Lave, "Only Yesterday," https://scholar.google.com/scholar?hl=en&as_sdt=0%2C36&scioq=Registered+Sex+Offenders%2C+Residence%2C+and+the+Influence+of+Race&q=Only+Yesterday%3A+The+Rise+and+Fall+of+Twentieth&btnG=.

A second wave of civil confinement began in the 1990s under a new name. These laws identify and confine "sexually violent predators" (some states use different terms) past the end of their sentences. The first of these laws was passed in Washington State. That law allows for indefinite confinement, but, interestingly, it precludes it when the victim is a family member or acquaintance of the person convicted of the crime. When asked, legislators said that they made this decision because if people were aware that their relative or friend might be confined indefinitely, they might not report the abuse at all.[86]

Today, twenty states plus the District of Columbia allow for the civil confinement of people convicted of very serious sexual crimes.[87] The Adam Walsh Act also makes federal prisoners eligible. In general, to trigger civil confinement, a court must find that a person has a mental disorder that makes it likely that they will offend again. As in the earlier period of these kinds of laws, the definition of *mental disorder* is often not well specified. The Kansas civil confinement law applies the predator label for *mental abnormality* rather than *mental disorder*, but their term is not clearly defined either. Critics of the Kansas law argue that prosecutors are given a lot of power to define mental abnormality.[88] It is important to note that the label *sexually violent predator* and its equivalents are legal terms, not clinical terms, and court personnel rather than therapists decide whether or

---

86. Neil Websdale, "Predators: The Social Construction of 'Stranger Danger' in Washington State as a Form of Patriarchal Ideology," in *Making Trouble: Cultural Constructions of Crime, Deviance, and Control*, ed. Jeff Ferrell and Neil Websdale (New York: Aldine de Gruyter, 1996).

87. Arielle W. Tolman, "Sex Offender Civil Commitment to Prison Post-Kingsley," *Northwestern University Law Review* 113, no. 1 (2018): 115–91, https://scholar.google.com/scholar?hl=en&as_sdt=0%2C36&scioq=Registered+Sex+Offenders%2C+Residence%2C+and+the+Influence+of+Race&q=Tolman+sex+offender+civil&btnG=

88. Jonathan Simon, "Managing the Monstrous: Sex Offenders and the New Penology," *Psychology, Public Policy, and Law* 4, no. 1/2 (1998): 452–67.

not it applies to a particular person. Psychologists, however, do testify at hearings.[89]

A group of researchers surveyed experts who are charged with assessing people for civil confinement. They found that 95 percent used actuarial risk-assessment tools all or most of the time (only 2 percent rarely used them), and 79 percent used more than one tool. When the tools gave different results, some experts reported the higher-risk result, some the lower-risk result, and some averaged the scores. The experts also relied heavily on offenders' treatment records, records from prison, and victim reports.[90]

Although there have been many legal challenges to civil confinement, the US Supreme Court has upheld it three times.[91] Their decisions, much like those about registries, were based on the argument that civil confinement is not punitive but is instead intended to enhance public safety.[92] The courts have declared that, to be civilly confined, one must not just be in need of treatment, but must be deemed a danger to oneself and to others. If psychiatrists have an effective treatment for a person's mental illness, it must be provided, but if no treatment is known, none must be provided.

There are no reliable national records of the number of people

89. Corey Rayburn Yung, "Civil Commitment for Sex Offenders," *AMA Journal of Ethics* 15, no. 10 (2013): 873–77, https://journalofethics.ama-assn.org/article/civil-commitment-sex-offenders/2013-10.

90. Rebecca L. Jackson and Derek T. Hess, "Evaluation for Civil Commitment of Sex Offenders: A Survey of Experts," *Sexual Abuse: A Journal of Research and Treatment* 19, no. 4 (2007): 425–48, http://citeseerx.ist.psu.edu/viewdoc/download?doi=10.1.1.913.201&rep=rep1&type=pdf.

91. Association for the Treatment of Sexual Abusers, "Civil Commitment," Association for the Treatment of Sexual Abusers, 2017, http://www.atsa.com/civil-commitment-2.

92. Ryan W. Porte, "Sex Offender Regulations and the Rule of Law: When Civil Regulatory Schemes Circumvent the Constitution," *Hastings Constitutional Law Quarterly* 45 (2018): 715–38, https://scholar.google.com/schol ar?hl=en&as_sdt=0%2C36&scioq=Registered+Sex+Offenders%2C+Resi dence%2C+and+the+Influence+of+Race&q=Sex+Offender+Regulations+and+th e+Rule+of+Law%3A+When&btnG=.

living under civil confinement orders in the United States. Counting is complicated by the fact that there are a number of reasons that people end up in civil confinement—sexual offending is just one of those reasons. In 2016, the Marshall Project calculated that there were five thousand four hundred people being held in civil confinement for sexual crimes. They point out that this number includes people in thirteen states who were convicted as juveniles.[93] A study in 2017 in New York State found that there were 322 people convicted of sexual offenses living under its civil commitment law. Two thirds of them had no prior convictions (aside from the one that landed them in prison in the first place), and Black people were disproportionately represented. The study estimated that the costs of confining these 322 individuals was $65 million a year.[94] In Minnesota, there are over seven hundred people who are civilly committed. The US Supreme Court declined to hear a case in 2017 that claimed that Minnesota's civil confinement was unconstitutional because only a handful of people had been released since the program began in the 1990s. A lower court ruled that the practice is constitutional because it is treatment, not punishment, and there is a way to petition for release.[95]

Civil commitment raises huge ethical and practical issues—far too many for me to effectively address here. The state sees it as the control measure of last resort, but it is clear that net widening has occurred, and today we confine far more than just a few very serious offenders. In the last fifteen years, for example, California,

93. George Steptoe and Antoine Goldet, "Why Some Young Sex Offenders Are Held Indefinitely," The Marshall Project, January 27, 2016, https://www.themarshall project.org/2016/01/27/why-some-young-sex-offenders-are-held-indefinitely.

94. David Robinson, Jonathan Bandler, and Avram A. Billig, "Civil Commitment: The Cost of Locking up Sex Offenders," Journal News, June 8, 2017, https://www.lohud.com/story/news/investigations/2017/05/31/civil-commitment-sex-offenders/325390001/.

95. Amy Forliti, "Supreme Court Won't Hear Minnesota Sex Offender Case," Twin Cities Pioneer Press, October 2, 2017, https://www.twincities.com/2017/10/02/supreme-court-wont-hear-minnesota-sex-offender-case/.

Minnesota, and Wisconsin expanded their programs. SORNA actually provides incentives to states to expand civil confinement, further increasing the chances for net widening.[96]

CONCLUSION

This chapter has highlighted the most common restrictions applied to people who have left prison with CSA convictions. All of the measures have the stated goal of reducing sexual offending. Unfortunately, research shows that a number of them—including registries, community notification, and residential restrictions—are not only ineffective but might actually increase offending. Electronic monitoring shows more promise to deter offending, although it mostly functions as a way to incapacitate people temporarily. It does not provide any sort of rehabilitation. Chemical castration appears to inhibit offending in a subgroup of men, but it raises significant ethical concerns. Similarly, civil confinement has been criticized by some as ex post facto punishment and as a violation of due process. States do not have clear standards for imposing civil confinement, and few people are ever released.

Readers might be feeling rather dispirited by this chapter. If most of the common methods used to reduce recidivism are ineffective or problematic, what can be done? In chapter 8, I discuss some actions that may reduce CSA and its harms. I also talk about programs that have had success in helping people convicted of sexual offenses maintain crime-free lives. First, however, I will turn to policies child-serving organizations have adopted to reduce offending.

---

96. Richard G. Wright, "Sex Offender Post-Incarceration Sanctions: Are There Any Limits," *New England Journal on Crime and Civil Confinement* 34 (2008): 17–50, https://scholar.google.com/scholar?hl=en&as_sdt=0%2C36&scioq=Regis tered+Sex+Offenders%2C+Residence%2C+and+the+Influence+of+Race&q=Sex +Offender+Post-Incarceration+Sanctions%3A+Are+&btnG=.

FURTHER READING

Horowitz, Emily. *Protecting Our Kids? How Sex Offender Laws are Failing Us*. New York: Praeger, 2015.

Wright, Richard G. *Sex Offender Laws: Failed Policies, New Directions*. New York: Springer, 2009.

CHAPTER SIX

PREVENTING ABUSE IN
ORGANIZATIONS AND WORKPLACES

In 2018, the public's attention was riveted by the televised courtroom testimony of over one hundred gymnasts. The women spoke about the abuse they had suffered at the hands of Dr. Larry Nassar, the team doctor of USA Gymnastics and a faculty member at Michigan State University. The stories were heartrending and showed how abuse can have far-reaching consequences. As has occurred in other organizations, high-level administrators at USA Gymnastics and Michigan State University had covered up the abuse. Because they ignored credible allegations against Nassar, it continued over decades.

By the time the gymnastics story broke, organizations were already well aware of the potential for child sexual abuse (CSA) by their employees and volunteers. Many, including USA Gymnastics, had implemented protective measures. In this chapter, I examine how organizations have adopted background checks, interviews, and reference checks as ways to protect children. States have also adopted mandatory reporter laws that require many categories of

workers, such as teachers and social workers, to report CSA suspicions. As I have done in the last two chapters, I will ask whether
these actions are effective and what their unintended consequences are.

BACKGROUND CHECKS

Of all the measures organizations take to prevent CSA, criminal
background checks are the most common. Laws regarding background checks are complicated and vary by state. Many states,
however, have laws that require all child-serving organizations to
perform the checks before hiring people to work with children.
In 2015, the US Government Accountability Office (GAO) surveyed state governments about their background check policies.
They received responses from forty-five states and the District of
Columbia and found that:

- Forty-five of forty-six require FBI checks for teachers.
- Forty-five of Forty-six require the checks for day-care workers, including those who provide care to senior citizens.
- Only thirty-eight require checks for "youth development
  positions" at organizations such as the Boys & Girls Clubs of
  America.
- The states who lack background check requirements say it
  is because they do not have the administrative capacity to
  review them.[1]

There is no federal law that mandates background checks, but
the federal Fair Credit Reporting Act (FCRA) sets out guidelines
for how they are to be conducted. For example, employers must

---

1. General Accounting Office, Criminal History Records: Additional Actions
Could Enhance the Completeness of Records Used for Employment-Related
Background Checks, (Washington, DC, February 2015), https://digitalcommons.
ilr.cornell.edu/key_workplace/1393/.

inform applicants that they are conducting the check. They must also tell them if they are denying them a job based on information that is revealed. The employer does not, however, have to hold a job open if an applicant challenges the accuracy of their background check.[2]

Even when their states do not require it, most child-serving organizations mandate background checks for their employees. Some large national organizations, such as the Boy Scouts of America (BSA) and the Catholic Church, require background checks for both employees and volunteers. Organizations that require checks for employees, but not for volunteers, say that the primary reason is due to cost.[3] Some also fear that the request will insult or annoy potential volunteers.

Fun Facts about Fingerprinting

1. Thousands of years ago, Babylonians used fingerprints to sign contracts.
2. The first fingerprint bureau was established in Argentina in 1892 and the second in India in 1897.
3. The US military started using fingerprinting early in the 1900s, partly to help identify soldiers who died in combat.
4. Since 1953, all positions in the federal government have required that applicants submit fingerprints to be run through a national criminal database.

Oddly, background checks became available to child-serving organizations as a result of the *Oprah Winfrey Show*. Andrew Vachss, a lawyer and children's advocate, was invited on the show

---

2. Privacy Rights Clearinghouse, "Employment Background Checks: A Jobseeker's Guide," Privacy Rights Clearinghouse, 2019, https://privacyrights.org/consumer-guides/employment-background-checks-jobseekers-guide.

3. Michelle Waul Webster and Julie Whitman, *Who's Lending a Hand? A National Survey of Nonprofit Volunteer Screening Practices* (Washington, DC: The National Center for Victims of Crime, 2008).

to talk about a terrible rape of a four-year-old girl in Chicago. As a CSA survivor herself, Oprah vowed to do something to make a difference. She hired a law firm to draft what became the National Child Protection Act.[4] The act created the first national database of criminal CSA convictions that organizations could access.

Today, most of us simply accept background checks as part of the application process for work in child-serving organizations, but this was not the case initially. Teachers in some states actively protested fingerprinting.[5] In Maine, for example, the debate was so intense it became a central issue in the gubernatorial election. Teachers worked with the Maine Civil Liberties Union to argue that the proposed background check requirement was burdensome and vague. They also felt that it implied a fundamental distrust in them. Some went so far as to resign in protest.[6] The governor vetoed the law because he said it was "overregulation" and would be too costly for small businesses.[7] The legislation later overturned his veto. Although the law was enacted in 1999, it was not until 2018 that the legislation was extended to include childcare workers as well as teachers.

Many of the early objections to background checks involved cost and oversight. Who should pay? Who should review them? One solution was to require job applicants to pay. Maine's original proposal was framed this way, resulting in significant pushback

4. David Mills, "Oprah, Children's Crusader," *Washington Post*, November 13, 1991, https://www.washingtonpost.com/archive/lifestyle/1991/11/13/oprah-childrens-crusader/b388a5a3-85f4-41f1-89fe-93e31a940521/.

5. Christina Buschmann, "Mandatory Fingerprinting of Public School Teachers: Facilitating Background Checks or Infringing on Individuals' Constitutional Rights?" *William & Mary Bill of Rights Journal* 11, no. 3 (2003): 1273–1307, https://scholar.google.com/scholar?hl=en&as_sdt=0%2C36&q=Mandatory+Fingerprinting+of+Public+School+Teachers%3A+&btnG=.

6. Brad Morin, "Teachers, Staff Resent Fingerprint Law," *Ellsworth American*, November 25, 1999.

7. Group One, "Maine Child Care Workers Support New Background Checks," Group One, July 18, 2018, https://gp1.com/maine-child-care-workers-support-new-background-checks/.

from teachers. The problem was temporarily solved in 2003, when Congress allocated money to provide background checks for teachers and other childcare workers. The National Center for Missing and Exploited Children agreed to review the results of the checks, obviating the need for organizations to do it themselves. Although President Barack Obama extended parts of this program in 2010, the funding for background checks was not reauthorized. Today, organizations either pay or they can pass the cost on to individual employees and volunteers.

Ideally, a background check provides organizations with complete information about applicants' criminal histories. FBI fingerprinting comes the closest to this ideal. Their program is called Next Generation Identification (NGI). NGI collects fingerprints from people seeking a background check (called "civil prints") as well as from those who are arrested ("criminal prints").

Today there are over 145 million fingerprints in the NGI.[8] In the past, the FBI destroyed most civil prints after they sent out the requested background check.[9] They now keep them indefinitely, unless a court or the agency who initially requested them asks that they be removed. This means that the FBI can offer employers a continuing criminal check on their employees without the employees needing to submit new fingerprints. Called the Retained Applicant Fingerprint Database, or Rapback, this program saves organizations money and administrative hassle.

---

8. Federal Bureau of Investigations, *June 2019 next Generation Identification System Fact Sheet*, (Washington, DC: Federal Bureau of Investigations, June 2019).

9. Ernest J. Babcock, "Next Generation Identification (NGI)—Retention and Searching of Noncriminal Justice Fingerprint Submissions," FBI, February 20, 2015, https://www.fbi.gov/services/records-management/foipa/privacy-impact-assessments/next-generation-identification-ngi-retention-and-searching-of-noncriminal-justice-fingerprint-submissions.

Figure 13. Fingerprinting. Source: Ivan Semenovych at Shutterstock.

Problems with FBI Fingerprint Checks[10]

The FBI relies on local agencies to report arrests and dispositions (outcomes) of cases. Sometimes agencies fail to report information, especially about dispositions. This means that an arrest might be listed but not the fact that the charges were dropped. Overall, in 2016, disposition information was missing for just about half of the cases. States vary widely in the rate at which they report dispositions. For example, only 14 percent of cases from Mississippi have both the arrest and disposition listed, but the equivalent number in Maryland is 98 percent.

In some cases, local law enforcement agencies fail to report an arrest or conviction to the FBI at all.

---

10. Marina Duane et al., *Criminal Background Checks* (Washington, DC: The Urban Institute, 2017), https://www.urban.org/sites/default/files/publication/88621/2001174_criminal_background_checks_impact_on_employment_and_recidivism_1.pdf.

> It sometimes takes time for local agencies to report information to the FBI. This means that if the background check is requested immediately after an arrest, the arrest will not appear.
>
> People who submit their prints to the FBI will become part of the database searched for a match for criminal suspects.

While the FBI provides the most comprehensive and reliable background checks, organizations have other options. For example, they can purchase a fingerprint check from their state government. While this is cheaper than going through the FBI, these records only include in-state crimes, greatly limiting their utility. Another less expensive option is to contract with a commercial vendor. These vendors operate entirely over the internet, with the applicant entering their name, birthdate, address, and social security number into a secure server. The vendors then match the information with their own repositories of criminal records. To compete with the Rapback program, most vendors now keep applicant information on file so that they can provide periodic updates to the requesting organization.

> **Problems with Commercial Background Checks**[11]
>
> Companies sometimes associate a name with the wrong person. In other words, they get records for the wrong "John R. Smith." Lawsuits have been filed by people who have been denied jobs based on someone else's criminal record.
>
> Some companies do not update their records very often (even though there are regulations in place that require them do so).
>
> The criminal records vendors obtain are not necessarily

11. Duane et al., *Criminal Background Checks*, https://www.urban.org/sites/default/files/publication/88621/2001174_criminal_background_checks_impact_on_employment_and_recidivism_1.pdf.

reliable. They might, for example, contain arrest but not disposition information.

People sometimes accidentally or intentionally submit false information to the vendor, causing them to run a check on the wrong person.

Once an organization receives a background check for a prospective employee or volunteer, they must decide what to do with the information. What crimes should preclude someone from service? There is little debate about CSA, but organizations often choose to prohibit other categories of crime as well. A 2008 survey found that one-fifth of nonprofits disqualified applicants just for having been arrested (regardless of the type of crime and the outcome of the case). About half reported that they disqualified people based on specific crime types, usually those involving CSA or violent felonies.[12]

It appears that very few organizations consider the timing of crimes when they make eligibility decisions. This means that a person who committed a crime yesterday and one who committed the same crime forty years ago will both be precluded from service. There are some exceptions, however. For example, the school district in Washington County, Kentucky, only bans people from volunteering for four years after a drug conviction. After that, they can be "approved with caution," and after seven years, the offense no longer has any effect.[13] A few states—like California—place limits on the number of years of criminal history an employer can access. California has also made it illegal for employers to consider

---

12. Michelle Waul Webster and Julie Whitman, *Who's Lending a Hand? A National Survey of Nonprofit Volunteer Screening Practices* (Washington, DC: The National Center for Victims of Crime, 2008).

13. Devin Katayama, "JCPS Background Checks Block Parents from Volunteering, Even for Years-Old Offenses," 89.3 WFPL News Louisville, August 25, 2013, http://wfpl.org/jcps-background-checks-block-parents-volunteering-even-years-old-offenses/.

any arrest that did not lead to a conviction. At the federal level, the FCRA makes it illegal for employers to consider arrests (but not convictions) that are more than seven years old—although some states have placed salary caps on that rule. For example, in Colorado, any job offering a salary of more than $75,000 a year is exempt from the time limits.[14]

> **State Laws on Use of Criminal Records**
>
> There is wide variation between states in their regulations about employers' use of criminal records. Some states have enacted "ban the box" provisions that disallow employers from asking about criminal records in the early stages of the hiring process. Others limit how employers can use records once they have them. Here's a website with all the different state laws: https://www.nolo.com/legal-encyclopedia/state-laws-use-arrests-convictions-employment.html.

EFFICACY OF BACKGROUND CHECKS

To cut right to the chase, it is clear that background check requirements are effective in preventing some people with criminal records from working with children. This happens when an organization bans someone based on one or more convictions listed on a background check. It also happens when people who have been convicted of crimes do not to apply for a job at all because they know that a check is required. It is not possible to measure how often the second scenario occurs, but one can count the number of background checks that reveal prior convictions. A study of 3.7 million background checks conducted by a large private background check company of potential employees and volunteers at nonprofit organizations found that about

14. RiskAware, "State Legal Compliance," RiskAware, LLC, 2020, http://riskaware.com/resources/understanding-the-laws/state-legal-compliance/.

5 percent returned a criminal conviction, but only a minority of these (about 1.7 percent of the total) returned a sexual offense. The most common offenses were driving under the influence, theft/larceny, and check fraud.[15]

Organizations can increase the efficacy of background checks by requiring applicants to get a national search rather than a state-level or local one. As described, state records only include crimes committed within their own borders. One study looked at background checks for potential volunteers at youth-serving organizations. Of the crimes that were detected, about 42 percent had been committed outside the state where the person had applied to volunteer.[16] A tragic example of an organization not getting a national-level background check involved Larry Gordon, who became the infamous Berrien County Courthouse shooter. He was able to volunteer in his daughter's classroom even though he had been sentenced twice to prison on violent felony charges. Those charges, however, were not in his current home state of Michigan.[17]

National checks are vastly superior to local or state checks, but they only work if organizations use them properly. A government study compared the social security numbers of teachers working in public and private schools to the sexual offender registry. They found "hundreds of cases of potential sexual offenders working in schools." A deeper dive into fifteen of these cases indicated that sometimes schools did not actually run the required background check. Others simply ignored information about prior convictions.

---

15. LexisNexis, *The Importance of Background Screening of Nonprofits: An Updated Briefing* (New York: LexisNexis, 2009), http://www.idwlcms.org/got odownloadfile.php?file=180.

16. Kristen D. Anderson and Dawn Daly, *What You Need to Know about Background Screening* (Washington, DC: US Department of Justice and the National Center for Missing and Exploited Children, 2013), https://rems.ed.gov/docs/COPS_NCMEC_Background-Screening.pdf.

17. Jennifer Guerra, "Who's Allowed to Volunteer in Schools? It Depends," State of Opportunity, July 27, 2016, http://stateofopportunity.michiganradio.org/post/whos-allowed-volunteer-schools-it-depends.

Disturbingly, schools sometimes discovered that a teacher or other worker was molesting children, fired them, and then proceeded to write a positive letter of recommendation. Because the police were never notified, no record appeared on the person's background check when they applied to work at another school.[18]

A final factor limiting the efficacy of all kinds of background checks is that they do not include most juvenile records. Juvenile records are accorded special protections in order to give children who have committed a crime a chance to have a fresh start in adulthood. Juvenile courts were created early in the 1900s because society believed that children are fundamentally different from adults.[19] To this day, juvenile courts operate differently from those for adults. For example, there are no jury trials, and sentences are more flexible to encourage rehabilitative programming. The problem, of course, is that juveniles often serve as volunteers and employees in child-serving organizations (think about camp counselors, for example), and, as discussed in chapter 3, a significant percentage of CSA is committed by this group.[20] At the same time, relatively low recidivism rates among juveniles make this a somewhat less pressing concern than it might be otherwise.[21]

---

18. Government Accountability Office , *Selected Cases of Public and Private Schools That Hired or Retained Individuals with Histories of Sexual Misconduct* (Washington, DC: Government Accountability Office, 2010), https://www.gao.gov/products/GAO-11-200.

19. Barry C. Feld, "Abolish the Juvenile Court: Youthfulness, Criminal Responsibility, and Sentencing Policy," *Journal of Criminal Law and Criminology* 88, no. 1 (1997): 68–136, https://scholarship.law.umn.edu/cgi/viewcontent.cgi?article=1350&context=faculty_articles.

20. David Finkelhor, Richard Ormrod, and Mark Chaffin, "Juveniles Who Commit Sex Offenses against Minors," *Juvenile Justice Bulletin* (Washington, DC: US Government Printing Office, 2009), http://scholars.unh.edu/ccrc/15/.

21. Michael F. Caldwell, "Quantifying the Decline in Juvenile Sexual Recidivism Rates," *Psychology, Public Policy, and Law* 22, no. 4 (2016): 414–26.

UNANTICIPATED CONSEQUENCES OF BACKGROUND CHECK REQUIREMENTS

There are a number of unanticipated consequences associated with using background checks for CSA prevention. First, like sexual offender registries and electronic monitoring, background checks can give parents and organizations a false sense of security. It is easy to assume that a person who has a clean background check will not abuse children. Of course, this is faulty reasoning because background checks do not identify offenders who have never been caught or who have not begun to abuse children yet. Counting solely on background checks for CSA prevention is a serious mistake.

A second possible unanticipated consequence of requiring background checks is that it might drive law-abiding potential volunteers away. There is little research on this topic, so it is not known for sure, but there are several legitimate reasons a volunteer might object to a background check. For example, private companies often require social security numbers to be submitted over the internet, opening up the possibility of hacking. Another concern involves the ability of nonprofits to keep their records confidential. What if the information is stolen or accidentally revealed to others? In addition to these privacy concerns, some potential volunteers might be unwilling or unable to pay for the background check. Or, like the Maine teachers discussed above, they could be insulted when asked to submit to a check. This is particularly likely with longtime trusted volunteers, but it could be true of new volunteers as well.[22]

---

22. Privacy Rights Clearinghouse, "Volunteer Background Checks: Giving Back Without Giving Up on Privacy," Privacy Rights Clearinghouse, 2017, https://www.privacyrights.org/consumer-guides/volunteer-background-checks-giving-back-without-giving-privacy.

Privacy and Identity Theft

Lori Lipke wanted to volunteer to be the room parent in her son's class. Her husband also wanted to occasionally volunteer in the classroom. Their child's school, however, required that they submit their social security numbers for a background check. The Lipkes refused to do this, in part because Mrs. Lipke had been the victim of identity fraud in the past. The school barred her from the room-parent position and her husband was not allowed past the front desk of the school. Three months later, they were allowed into the classroom but only after obtaining FBI fingerprint checks.[23]

A final unanticipated issue regarding background checks involves net widening. As described, some organizations disqualify people from service for a wide range of criminal offenses. For example, a person who was convicted of one long-ago drug possession charge could be disallowed from a job at a day care. Similarly, a father who got in a bar fight in college could be precluded from volunteering in his child's classroom, affecting both the father and his child.[24] Screening volunteers and employees based on drug convictions is particularly problematic because it disproportionately affects the poor and people of color. The war on drugs has targeted those groups while well-off white people have been better able to avoid detection or hire top-notch lawyers to get charges dropped or reduced. There is a huge amount of evidence indicating, for

23. Tracy Dell'Angela, "Schools Embrace Parents' Help—after Background Check," *Chicago Tribune*, June 2002.

24. See, for example, Cheryl L. Porter Decusati and James E. Johnson, "Parents as Classroom Volunteers and Kindergarten Students' Emergent Reading Skills," *Journal of Educational Research* 97, no. 5 (2004): 235–46, http://www2.connectseward.org/edu/shs/da1/research/kindergarten.pdf; Marco A. Munoz, "Parental Volunteerism in Kindergarten: Assessing Its Impact in Reading and Mathematics Tests," *ERIC Document Reproduction Service*, no. ED464745 (2000): 1–11, https://eric.ed.gov/?id=ED464745.

example, that Black people are overrepresented in drug arrests and prosecutions even though their rates of use are about equivalent to other racial/ethnic groups.[25] On the surface, a background check requirement is color-blind, but a deeper look shows how it can function to reinforce biases introduced by the criminal justice system.

Blanket Prohibitions

Jessica Doyle was a heroin addict during her early twenties but went into recovery and became sober. She worked as a rehabilitation counselor and publicly promoted drug prevention education. Yet, when she asked to volunteer in her daughter's classroom, she was denied because of two felony drug possession charges from the period of her addiction. The American Civil Liberties Union (ACLU) of Rhode Island sued the school district on her behalf and won. Today, Doyle's district no longer has a blanket prohibition against people with drug convictions working in classrooms. The superintendent is empowered to make decisions about individual cases based on characteristics of the crime and when it took place.[26]

---

25. Michelle Alexander, *The New Jim Crow: Mass Incarceration in the Age of Colorblindness*, rev. ed. (New York: New Press, 2012); Kenneth B. Nunn, "Race, Crime and the Pool of Surplus Criminality: Or Why the War on Drugs Was a War on Blacks," *Journal of Gender, Race and Justice* 6 (2002): 381, https://scholar. google.com/scholar?hl=en&as_sdt=0%2C36&q=Race%2C+Crime+and+the+Pool +of+Surplus+Criminality%3A&btnG=.

26. American Civil Liberties Union of Rhode Island, "ACLU Settles Lawsuit over Cranston School District Volunteer Policy," American Civil Liberties Union, December 27, 2012, https://www.aclu.org/news/ aclu-settles-lawsuit-over-cranston-school-district-volunteer-policy.

LOCAL FILES AND OFFENDER SEARCHES

While many states mandate that child-serving organizations run background checks for employees, they rarely require the same for volunteers. Official background checks are costly and subject to FCRA rules, so there are incentives for organizations to avoid them whenever possible. As a result, some choose to forgo the official route and conduct informal background checks instead. A simple Google search usually reveals people's arrest records, and it is also easy to run names through the national sex offender database. These methods of investigation are free and do not require that organizations inform potential employees or volunteers. While this may be beneficial for organizations in the short term, it does not do much to mitigate their legal liability, nor does it allow the potential workers an opportunity to contest or explain findings.

National Registry

The national registry is called the Dru Sjodin National Sex Offender Public Website. It was created as part of the Adam Walsh Act and is named after a twenty-two-year-old woman who was abducted and murdered by a sex offender in Minnesota in 2003. The link to the registry is www.nsopw.gov.

Another low-cost way that organizations try to screen for CSA offenses is to maintain their own lists of people who are prohibited from working with children. For many years, the BSA kept such records, often called the "perversion files," of people who had engaged in abuse in the past. The files were not very effective, however, due to clerical errors, supervisors failing to check them, and offenders changing their names. Some BSA personnel who abused children never even made it into the files, even though the abuse took place at BSA events. Others were listed as being on "probation" but were allowed to continue with the organization. Today, the BSA has dramatically strengthened their policies; they stopped using probation in 1988, they require FBI checks of employees and volunteers, and they also require that the police be informed of all accusations.[27]

OTHER SCREENING TOOLS

The Centers for Disease Control (CDC) publishes a comprehensive set of recommendations for how child-serving organizations should screen potential employees and volunteers. They argue that simply running background checks is not enough. Applications, interviews, and reference checks are other ways to assess whether people are a risk to children.[28] The CDC specifically advises organizations to ask applicants about prior CSA or other criminal violations. While offenders may be unwilling to disclose past offenses, bringing the topic up sends a message that the organization cares about protecting children. The CDC also recommends that organizations ask references about how well the applicant interacts with young people and whether there is any reason that the person should not work with them.

A much more controversial method of screening involves administering questionnaires designed to identify potential volunteers and employees who are at high risk for abusing children. These questionnaires ask applicants about factors that researchers correlate with abuse. For example, as learned in chapter 3, people who were abused as children are at heightened risk for abusing children themselves. Thus, a small number of churches ask applicants about their own abuse histories.[29] The problem, of course, is

27. Jason Felch and Kim Christensen, "Boy Scout Files Reveal Repeat Child Abuse by Sexual Predators," *Los Angeles Times*, August 4, 2012, http://www.latimes.com/local/la-me-boyscouts-20120805-m-story.html.

28. Janet Saul and Natalie C. Audage, *Preventing Child Sexual Abuse within Youth-Serving Organizations: Getting Started on Policies and Procedures* (Atlanta, GA: Centers for Disease Control, 2007), https://www.cdc.gov/ViolencePreven tion/pdf/PreventingChildSexualAbuse-a.pdf.

29. Zack Kopplin, "Abused? You Can't Work at These Churches," The Daily

that most victims do not go on to abuse others. Consequently, this screening tool essentially punishes victims for their own abuse by precluding them from working with children.

> **In the Best Interests of Children?**
>
> This chapter focuses on steps organizations have taken to protect children, but it is also important to note that organizations do not always operate with child welfare as their primary goal. For example, a bill was proposed in 2012 in New York State that would extend the statute of limitations for CSA cases. At the time, New York was one of three states with the most restrictive statute of limitations laws in the country. A number of organizations actively opposed the proposed law, delaying its passage until 2019. The Catholic Church was notable for its public opposition, claiming that the bill singled out Catholics and would put so much financial stress on the Church that it would be unable to fulfill its mission. They paid $1.8 million to lobbyists and only withdrew their public opposition when the state agreed to include both private and public institutions in the bill. The BSA worked more quietly, paying a former state senator $12,500 a month to lobby in opposition to the bill.[30]

BOUNDARY AND CONTACT RULES

Organizations are increasingly implementing rules that limit and structure adult contact with children. The BSA was a pioneer in this area with their "two-deep leadership" policy. Two-deep

Beast, April 15, 2016, https://www.thedailybeast.com/abused-you-cant-work-at-these-churches.

30. Kenneth Lovett, "Opponents of Child Victims Act for Adults Sexually Abused as Kids Mostly Operated in the Shadows to Kill the Bill," Daily News (New York), June 24, 2017, https://www.nydailynews.com/news/politics/child-victims-act-adults-sexually-abused-kids-quietly-dies-article-1.3274973.

leadership, as it sounds, requires that at least two adults be present on any scout outing. BSA supplements this rule with a "no one-on-one contact" policy that states that no adult leader can be alone with any child, either in person or electronically. Electronic communication must go to a group of children or include a parent or another scout leader. The contact rule prohibits either adult from meeting privately with a scout at the outing; an adult talking to a child must remain visible to others.[31]

Catholic dioceses and other organizations have begun to follow the lead of the BSA and add their own rules about in-person and electronic communication. They also talk with workers and volunteers about "boundary violations."[32] The boundary violation concept is a response to research showing that offenders often groom their victims. As discussed in chapter 3, grooming can include gift-giving or sharing of personal information. It can also include touching, often starting with innocuous pats on the back and moving on to sexual touching. In order to decrease the possibility of grooming, organizations try to define clear boundaries for adults. For example, they are not allowed to give a child a gift or hug them. The hope is that these rules encourage adults to monitor their own behavior as well as the behavior of others. However, there is no research looking at how effective these rules are in decreasing CSA in organizations.

Boundary rules are controversial because it can be very difficult to look at a behavior and determine whether it is grooming or whether it is simply something a caring adult is doing for a child. Unfortunately, prohibiting behaviors that can be associated with

---

31. Bryan Wendell, "Youth Protection: 'Two-Deep Leadership' vs. 'No One-on-One Contact,'" *Scouting Magazine*, January 19, 2018, https://blog.scoutingmag azine.org/2018/01/19/whats-the-difference-between-two-deep-leadership-and-no-one-on-one-contact/.

32. See, for example, Diocese of Victoria, "Misconduct Reporting," The Catholic Diocese of Victoria in Texas, 2019, https://victoriadiocese.org/misconduct-reporting.

grooming may inhibit adults from engaging in healthy relationships with children. For instance, many would argue that a coach hugging a child after a championship is absolutely appropriate. Similarly, while a priest could take a child to lunch to groom them, he could also do it to talk through a difficult problem the child is having at school. Offenders groom children exactly because it can be indistinguishable from healthy behavior.[33]

MANDATORY REPORTING LAWS

Mandatory reporting laws require that specific groups of people report suspicions of child abuse to their supervisors, to police, or to a child protection agency. I discuss this here because the laws primarily affect professionals in organizations such as schools and day-care centers. The federal United States Children's Bureau proposed the first reporting law in 1962. This date matches closely with the first reports of battered child syndrome. Four states enacted reporting laws in 1963, and all states had them by 1967.[34] Almost all of the early laws designated physicians and other medical personnel as mandatory reporters, but three states included all citizens.[35]

The federal Child Abuse Prevention and Treatment Act (CAPTA) was passed in 1974. It provided states with funds to support CSA prevention and investigation. States could only receive funding,

33. Natalie Bennett and William O'Donohue, "The Construct of Grooming in Child Sexual Abuse: Conceptual and Measurement Issues," *Journal of Child Sexual Abuse* 23, no. 8 (2014): 957–76.

34. John E. B. Myers, "A Short History of Child Protection in America," *Family Law Quarterly* 42, no. 3 (2008): 449–65, https://www.jstor.org/sta ble/25740668?read-now=1&refreqid=excelsior%3A58cod8880331e786dce 7bad43e2bd130&seq=14#page_scan_tab_contents.

35. Leonard G. Brown III and Kevin Gallagher, "Mandatory Reporting of Abuse: A Historical Perspective on the Evolution of States' Current Mandatory Reporting Laws with a Review of the Laws in the Commonwealth of Pennsylvania," *Villanova Law Review* 59 (2015): 45, https://scholar.google.com/schol ar?hl=en&as_sdt=0%2C36&q=Mandatory+Reporting+of+Abuse%3A+A+Histori cal+Perspective++&btnG=.

however, if they had a mandatory reporting law on the books. This legislation marked the first time the federal government became seriously involved in child abuse issues. It was also the first time that the government specifically included sexual abuse in the definition of child abuse.[36]

Today, state laws vary widely in terms of mandatory reporting. The vast majority require that various categories of professionals such as social workers, counselors, teachers, childcare workers, police, and doctors report suspicions. Fewer than half of states designate all citizens as mandatory reporters. It is important to note that the reporting requirement just involves reasonable suspicions of abuse; it does not require reporters to have proof. Reporters are protected from lawsuits if they make the report in good faith—even if their suspicion turns out to be unfounded. To further protect reporters, many states allow them to remain anonymous, but in states that do not have anonymous reporting, no names are included in the final report. [37] Failure to report can result in a criminal charge in most states.[38]

Penn State and Mandatory Reporting Requirements

In 2011, the media broke the story of serial child sexual abuse perpetrated by Jerry Sandusky, former defensive coordinator for the Penn State football team. He met his victims through a nonprofit he founded to help at-risk kids, and he sometimes brought them to the Penn State locker room to abuse them. Although a number of people at Penn State knew about the abuse, it was not reported to law enforcement. Weren't they

---

36. Myers, "A Short History of Child Protection in America."

37. Child Welfare Information Gateway, *Mandatory Reporters of Child Abuse and Neglect* (Washington, DC: US Department of Health and Human Services, Children's Bureau, 2016), https://www.childwelfare.gov/pubpdfs/manda.pdf.

38. Steven R. Smith and Robert G. Meyer, "Child Abuse Reporting Laws and Psychotherapy: A Time for Reconsideration," *International Journal of Law and Psychiatry* 7, no. 3-4 (1984): 351-66.

mandatory reporters? It turned out that some, like the athletic director Tim Curley, were legally required to report the abuse to police and were prosecuted for their failure to do so. Others, however, were only required to report the abuse to their supervisors. This was the case with Joe Paterno, the head football coach. He complied with the law and was not prosecuted. His supervisors, however, were prosecuted. While it is not clear that stronger mandatory reporting laws would have stopped Jerry Sandusky earlier, Pennsylvania expanded and clarified their laws in the wake of the scandal.[39]

It appears that mandatory reporting laws are an effective way to increase the number of child abuse reports. A study in Australia tracked reports over seven years, both before and after a mandatory reporting law went into effect. The number almost quadrupled after the implementation of the law and then stabilized.[40] Research suggests, however, that not all cases of CSA are equally likely to be reported. For example, a report is more likely when abuse is severe and the victim young. Women and people who have experienced abuse themselves are more likely to report suspicions to officials.[41]

---

39. John Keilman, "Penn State Scandal Spotlights Debate over Who Must Report Abuse," *Chicago Tribune*, November 11, 2011, https://www.chicagotribune.com/news/ct-xpm-2011-11-11-ct-met-mandated-reporters-20111111-story.html.

40. Ben Mathews, Xing Ju Lee, and Rosana E. Norman, "Impact of a New Mandatory Reporting Law on Reporting and Identification of Child Sexual Abuse: A Seven Year Time Trend Analysis," *Child Abuse & Neglect* 56 (2016): 62–79.

41. Wesley B. Crenshaw, "When Educators Confront Child Abuse: An Analysis of the Decision to Report," *Child Abuse & Neglect* 19, no. 9 (1995): 1095–1113; Allison C. Howe, Sharon Herzberger, and Howard Tennen, "The Influence of Personal History of Abuse and Gender on Clinicians' Judgments of Child Abuse," *Journal of Family Violence* 3, no. 2 (1988): 105–19; David J. Hansen et al., "The Influence of Case and Professional Variables on the Identification and Reporting of Child Maltreatment: A Study of Licensed Psychologists and Certified Masters Social Workers," *Journal of Family Violence* 12, no. 3 (1997): 313–332, https://scholar.google.com/scholar?hl=en&as_sdt=0%2C36&q=The+Influence+of+-

Participation in CSA prevention training also may increase the chances that a person files a report.[42]

Mandatory reporting laws can help some children escape abusive situations. At the same time, the laws have unintended effects. One study looked at adults in therapy in Maine before and after psychiatrists became mandated reporters. While some adults had referred themselves to therapy for CSA prior to the law, this kind of self-report dropped to zero after the law was implemented. This suggests that, in some cases, mandatory reporting laws for psychiatrists result in fewer offenders seeking help. Alternately, it is possible that offenders continued to seek out therapy but started lying about why they were there, making it more difficult to treat them.[43] This problem has led some mental health professionals to argue that psychiatrists should not be mandated to report in cases where the abuser is actively trying to change their behavior.[44]

A second unintended consequence of mandatory reporting laws involves unsubstantiated cases. It turns out that laws that designate a wide range of people as mandatory reporters cause an increase in the percentage of cases that investigators cannot prove to be abuse. These unsubstantiated cases result either from a lack of strong evidence or from a report simply being wrong. Every case the state has to investigate costs money, and large numbers of

---

Case+and+Professional+Variables+on+the&btnG=; Seth C. Kalichman and Mary E. Craig, "Professional Psychologists' Decisions to Report Suspected Child Abuse: Clinician and Situation Influences," *Professional Psychology: Research and Practice* 22, no. 1 (1991): 84–89.

42. Linda L. Lawrence, "The Impact of Physician Training of Child Maltreatment Reporting: A Multi-Speciality Study," *Military Medicine* 165, no. 8 (2000): 607-11, https://academic.oup.com/milmed/article/165/8/607/4832483; Russell Hawkins and Christy McCallum, "Effects of Mandatory Notification Training on the Tendency to Report Hypothetical Cases of Child Abuse and Neglect," *Child Abuse Review* 10, no. 5 (2001): 301–22.

43. Fred S. Berlin, Martin Malin, and Sharon Dean, "Effects of Statutes Requiring Psychiatrists to Report Suspected Sexual Abuse of Children," *American Journal of Psychiatry* 148, no. 4 (1991): 449–53, http://citeseerx.ist.psu.edu/viewdoc/download?doi=10.1.1.464.8896&rep=rep1&type=pdf.

44. Smith and Meyer, "Child Abuse Reporting Laws and Psychotherapy."

cases can overwhelm the system. Additionally, when accusations are filed against innocent families, it can cause them considerable trauma.[45] As discussed above, Pennsylvania expanded the scope of their reporting laws after the Sandusky scandal. Its new laws resulted in a dramatic increase in the total number of reports, but no increase in the number of substantiated reports.[46] While this does not necessarily mean that mandatory report laws should be abandoned, it does suggest that lawmakers should take care to craft them narrowly.

JUVENILE PRISONS: A SPECIAL CASE

Juvenile prisons are similar to other organizations in the preventative measures they have adopted. All employees and volunteers, for example, must pass a criminal background check. Staff and volunteers must undergo prevention training. Prisons, however, are unlike other organizations because the clients are unable to leave, and they have very little power to change conditions. There are also notably high levels of violence.[47] Here, I briefly discuss this unique situation and the special policies that the government has adopted to try and stem sexual abuse in these institutions.

In 2003, the federal government passed the Prison Rape Elimination Act (PREA). PREA set up a national committee to research the issue, and finally, in 2012, the US Department of Justice released a set of standards for all correctional facilities. States that do not

---

45. Mical Raz, "Unintended Consequences of Expanded Mandatory Reporting Laws," *Pediatrics* 139, no. 4 (2017): e20163511, https://pediatrics.aappublications. org/content/139/4/e20163511.

46. Jeff Hawkes, "After the Sandusky Case, a New Pennsylvania Law Creates Surge in Child Abuse Reports," LancasterOnline, February 20, 2015, https://lan casteronline.com/news/local/after-the-sandusky-case-a-new-pennsylvania-law-creates-surge/article_03541f66-b7a3-11e4-81cd-2f614d04c9af.html.

47. See, for example, Alan Judd, "Georgia's Juvenile Prisons: Assaults by Guards, Strip Searches, Chaos," *Atlanta Journal-Constitution*, November 17, 2019, https://www.ajc.com/news/crime--law/violence-permeates-youth-prisons/7YRQTDEnIT2ohGVEnjqybP/.

comply are at risk the of losing some of their federal funds. Here are just some of PREA's requirements.

- Correctional facilities must provide an easily reachable contact person outside the facility to allow incarcerated people to report sexual abuse.
- Facilities must inform incarcerated people about how to report sexual abuse.
- There is a zero-tolerance policy for staff who engage in sexual activity with incarcerated people.
- Facilities must provide training for all staff about both the dynamics of sexual abuse as well as the zero-tolerance policy.
- Facilities must assess new arrivals for high risk of abuse while incarcerated. They are instructed to use a standardized risk-assessment inventory that includes items such as the inmate's sexual orientation, age, and own feelings of vulnerability
- Juveniles cannot be housed with adults.[48]

Is PREA effective? The jury is still out because states are still struggling to come into compliance with the law. If the number of reports changes over time, it is important to be aware that PREA itself may cause abuse reports to increase—not because levels of abuse have changed, but because reporting has become easier. Researchers will need to monitor reports for several years before conclusions can be drawn.

CONCLUSION

This chapter reviewed common preventative measures organizations have taken in response to CSA scandals. It appears that criminal background checks are an effective way to preclude people with

---

48. United States Department of Justice, *Prison Rape Elimination Act: Prisons and Jail Standards* (Washington, DC: USDOJ, 2012), https://bja.ojp.gov/sites/g/files/xyckuh186/files/media/document/PREA-Prison-Jail-Standards.pdf.

CSA convictions from working with children, but they do nothing to screen out offenders who have never been caught. Organizations are quick to widen the net and use background checks to exclude people with a wide variety of criminal convictions. Like background checks, mandatory reporting laws are also useful because they increase the number of CSA cases that come to the attention of authorities. Overbroad laws, however, increase the number of unsubstantiated cases. Applications and reference checks can provide organizations with valuable information about prospective workers and volunteers. Screening people based on having been a victim of CSA, however, is problematic because it effectively makes victims suffer for abuse that was not their fault. The jury is still out on the efficacy of organizations' new steps to patrol boundary violations.

In the next chapter, I explore another way that organizations try to prevent CSA: adult and child prevention training. I mentioned this topic briefly in the preface because it was just such a training that piqued my own interest in studying CSA prevention. It's likely that you or your child may also have taken part in one. They occur in a range of organizations, including schools, churches, and scouts. Their increasing popularity means that they reach many Americans each year. I'll take a look at what these programs teach and how effective they are.

FURTHER READING

Bernstein, Nell. *Burning Down the House*. New York: New Press, 2014.

Johnson, Robert T. *Hands Off: The Disappearance of Touch in the Care of Children*. Bern: Peter Lang, 2000.

Pesta, Abigail. *The Girls: An All-American Town, a Predatory Doctor, and the Untold Story of the Gymnasts Who Brought Him Down*. New York: Seal Press, 2019.

CHAPTER SEVEN

CHILD SEXUAL ABUSE PREVENTION TRAINING

Every year, millions of Americans—both adults and children—learn about child sexual abuse (CSA) in prevention training provided by schools, churches, and sports leagues. Thirty years ago, this kind of training was unusual, but today it is common. Prevention training is based on the assumption that when people have accurate knowledge about CSA, they will be better able to identify it and intervene to stop it. But is that the case? In this chapter, I look at a wide range of prevention programs and discuss which are effective. I also look deeply at the unintended consequences of prevention training. Through these programs, child-serving organizations have become an important interpreter and disseminator of CSA knowledge. Programs do not simply provide neutral information about CSA—they frame the problem for participants. In other words, they select which facts to present as well as which not to present. When programs are conducted in group settings rather than online, they also provide an opportunity for discussion to shape messages.

TRAINING FOR CHILDREN

The first CSA prevention training programs for children were developed in the late 1970s by a diverse group of organizations. Their number and scope were greatly expanded in the 1980s, partly due to federal funding provided through the National Center on Child Abuse and Neglect (NCCAN). NCCAN funded five demonstration projects in the area of child education. Some states, like New York and California, made CSA prevention training mandatory in public schools. By 1990, estimates suggested that as many as 85 percent of all districts had implemented abuse prevention in at least some schools.[1]

While prevention programs for children spread quickly, they were not without controversy. Parents expressed concerns that the programs might cause undue fear or prompt children to make false accusations. Some felt that any discussion about sex should happen in the family, not in schools. There were even arguments over what language to use. Should children be told to protect their "private parts" or should body parts be referred to by their proper names? Another area of controversy involved whether abuse programs should be paired with sexual education more generally. Critics worried that if they were combined, schools might focus on information about abuse, not covering the positive aspects of sex.[2] Finally, concerns were raised that prevention training unfairly places the burden on children to stop abuse when it should be an adult responsibility.[3]

Today, it is difficult to estimate the percentage of children who receive school-based CSA prevention training because it is often

---

1. Deborah A. Daro, "Prevention of Child Sexual Abuse," *Future of Children* 4, no. 2 (1994): 198–223, https://www.jstor.org/stable/1602531?seq=1.

2. Carol A. Plummer, "The History of Child Sexual Abuse Prevention: A Practitioner's Perspective," *Journal of Child Sexual Abuse* 7, no. 4 (1999): 77–95.

3. K. J. Topping and I. G. Barron, "School-Based Child Sexual Abuse Prevention Programs: A Review of Effectiveness," *Review of Educational Research* 79, no. 1 (2009): 431–63, https://www.ncbi.nlm.nih.gov/books/NBK77496/.

combined with other parts of the school curriculum (like a health class or a sex education course). It is likely that the numbers are high and increasing, partly due to the passage of Erin's Laws, which vary somewhat by state but either require or recommend that public schools train children to tell someone if they have been touched inappropriately. As of late 2020, thirty-seven states had passed some version of Erin's Law.

Who Is the Erin of Erin's Law?

From the time she was six until she was eight, Erin Merryn's adult neighbor periodically raped her, and she was later sexually abused by an older cousin. As a teenager, she began to speak out about the abuse she had endured. Through appearances in the media and meetings with politicians, she has worked to get public school education laws passed. You can check out her website here: http://www.erinmerryn.net/.

What are children taught in CSA prevention courses? Most teach how to recognize abuse, how to tell which kinds of touch are appropriate or inappropriate, and how to differentiate between secrets children should keep (like information about a birthday present) and those they should not (abuse). These programs also teach children what to do if they find themselves in a potentially abusive situation. They are advised to say "no" loudly and to tell an adult or report it to an official person (like the police, a teacher, or a hotline). Curricula also emphasize that children are not to blame for abuse. Most school-based programs last one to two sessions.[4]

In addition to schools, some child-serving organizations also provide prevention education. One example is the Boy Scouts of America (BSA). The very first section of their handbook teaches parents how to address the issue of physical as well as sexual abuse

---

4. Topping and Barron, "School-Based Child Sexual Abuse Prevention Programs," https://www.ncbi.nlm.nih.gov/books/NBK77496.

with their children. It provides basic information, abuse scenarios, and prevention strategies for parents to discuss with their child. Interestingly, in addition to giving advice about how parents should respond when children disclose abuse, the handbook also provides tips to parents on how they can avoid abusing children during their own times of stress.

In 1989, the BSA produced a short film intended for eleven- to fourteen-year-olds. Called *A Time to Tell*, the original version presented three short vignettes of boys being abused. The video has been updated over the years, and additional vignettes are now available. Each vignette is narrated by a group of children who discuss the situations frankly with each other. They also talk directly to the viewer, urging him to "refuse, resist, and report."

BSA's Prevention Work

You can see the original film *A Time to Tell* at

https://www.youtube.com/watch?v=l7boW5LOrUw.

Here's a link to one of the new vignettes: https://www.you tube.com/watch?v=J5EkLOqBtBo.

If you want to see the other new vignettes, search for "A Time to Tell BSA" on YouTube.

It Happened to Me (for Cub Scouts) is here: https://www.you tube.com/watch?v=B5QRSqBEFeo.

Parent guidebooks are here:

https://www.scouting.org/training/youth-protection/ parents-guides/.

There are several aspects of *A Time to Tell* that make it unusual. First, it employs language that is particularly direct and clear. Second, the movie makes an effort not to *other* the offenders by reminding viewers that offenders can be anyone. The offenders portrayed in the movie are shown as multidimensional people, not just as evil figures. Third, the original version of the movie appears to endorse therapy as a way to deal with offenders. A teenager who molests younger boys is shown going to therapy and coming to understand that the abuse he suffered as a child may have led him to abuse others. The therapy theme does not appear in the later vignettes, nor does it appear in other child and adult programs I have reviewed.

In addition to a *Time to Tell*, the BSA produced a film for Cub Scouts (who are ages six to nine). The prologue to the film clearly states that the film should be shown with children's parents present. It teaches children four safety rules: to check with an adult before changing plans, to go places with a friend, to say no to uncomfortable touches, and to tell an adult if they are hurt, scared, or uncomfortable. The vignettes involve an older teenager trying to convince a young boy to go to a deserted area during a school field trip, a boy and his older brother being approached by an overly friendly man on the bus, and a teenage girl inappropriately touching a boy in after-school care. None of the videos, however, acknowledge that abuse has happened within the organization itself. This is problematic given revelations of widespread abuse in the BSA. It will be interesting to see whether and how their prevention material changes now that the organization accepts girls as members.

EFFECTIVENESS OF TRAINING FOR KIDS

While many researchers have studied child prevention-training programs, there are no clear answers about whether or not they are effective. Part of the problem is that it is difficult to define effectiveness. Is a program effective if children learn new facts about CSA? Or is it only effective if it lowers rates of abuse? This is even more complicated because there do not seem to be consistent effects across programs, making it difficult to generalize. It is safe to say, however, that most child prevention programs (at least the ones that have been evaluated) increase children's knowledge about CSA.[5] Sometimes, however, the knowledge gained is quite minimal—probably as a result of curricula being pitched too low.[6] Programs that employ instructors with specialized knowledge of CSA seem to be more effective than programs whose teachers normally teach another subject.[7] Finally, it appears that children retain their new knowledge but benefit from refresher sessions.[8]

The fact that prevention training increases knowledge seems like a positive outcome. At the same time, the ultimate goal of programs is not just to disseminate information—it's to reduce the incidence of CSA through behavior change. One study measured this outcome by asking two thousand young adults about their childhood prevention-training experiences. The youth who attended comprehensive school-based, antivictimization programs were more likely to have disclosed incidents of abuse and to have used "self-protective strategies" (like demanding to be left alone or telling an adult) than youth who had more limited training. It should be noted, however, that the differences between groups were small. At the same time, researchers found that when

5. Donna M. Brown, "Evaluation of Safer, Smarter Kids: Child Sexual Abuse Prevention Curriculum for Kindergartners," *Child and Adolescent Social Work Journal* 34, no. 3 (2017): 213–22; Jan Rispens, Andre Aleman, and Paul Goudena, "Prevention of Child Sexual Abuse Victimization: A Meta-Analysis of School Programs," *Child Abuse & Neglect* 21, no. 10 (1997): 975–87, https://www.ncbi.nlm. nih.gov/books/NBK67045/; Topping and Barron, "School-Based Child Sexual Abuse Prevention Programs," https://www.ncbi.nlm.nih.gov/books/NBK77496/; David Finkelhor and N. Strapko, "Sexual Abuse Prevention Education: A Review of Evaluation Studies," in *Prevention of Child Maltreatment: Developmental and Ecological Processes*, ed. D. Willis, E. Holder, and M. Rosenberg (New York: Wiley, 1987).

6. Topping and Barron, "School-Based Child Sexual Abuse Prevention Programs," https://www.ncbi.nlm.nih.gov/books/NBK77496/.

7. Topping and Barron, https://www.ncbi.nlm.nih.gov/books/NBK77496/.

8. Topping and Barron, https://www.ncbi.nlm.nih.gov/books/NBK77496/.

parents took an active role in educating their children about CSA, it boosted the impact of prevention programs.[9] Another retrospective study of women undergraduates found that school-based prevention programs do not increase the number of children who disclose abuse, but it encourages them to disclose more quickly.[10]

A somewhat controversial way to test whether child prevention programs result in behavioral change is to simulate an abusive situation and see how children react. One recent study examined a program for five- through seven-year-olds that covered a range of dangerous situations, including CSA and bullying. After the program, individual children (some of whom had participated in the training, others of whom had not) were invited to come to the school office to meet with a familiar administrator. During this meeting, the administrator claimed to have forgotten something and left the office. A male adult stranger entered the room and asked the child to come with him. The stranger waited for a response but then abruptly said he had forgotten something. As he was leaving the room, he asked the child not to mention his presence to anyone. He also dropped a pen on the floor. The administrator returned and prompted the child to disclose the stranger's presence by asking how the pen had gotten on the floor. Contrary to expectations, the children who had participated in the training program were not more likely than nontrained children to disclose the presence of the stranger, nor were they more likely to refuse to go with him.[11]

9. David Finkelhor, Nancy Asdigian, and Jennifer Dziuba-Leatherman, "The Effectiveness of Victimization Prevention Instruction: An Evaluation of Children's Responses to Actual Threats and Assaults," *Child Abuse & Neglect* 19, no. 2 (1995): 141–53, https://calio.org/wp-content/uploads/2014/05/The_effective ness_of_victimization_prevention_instructionFinkelhor-Asdigan.pdf.

10. Laura E. Gibson and Harold Leitenberg, "Child Sexual Abuse Prevention Programs: Do They Decrease the Occurrence of Child Sexual Abuse?" *Child Abuse & Neglect* 24, no. 9 (2000): 1115–25.

11. Codi White et al., "Promoting Young Children's Interpersonal Safety Knowledge, Intentions, Confidence, and Protective Behavior Skills: Outcomes of

Another simulation study with kindergartners and first graders explored a program designed to prevent stranger abduction. Children who received no training were compared with those who received it in different forms—as a videotape presentation, a video-training module-plus-behavioral practice, and a talk by a plainclothes police officer. The experiment took place one to two days after the training. The kids were told to go outside one at a time to learn a new sports skill with the school's physical education instructor. While there, the instructor briefly left the playground and a male stranger appeared and asked the children to come with him. In the untrained group, 75 percent agreed to go. This compared with 10.5 percent in the videotape-plus-behavior practice condition, 21 percent of those who only saw a videotape, and 44 percent in the police-presentation condition. This study indicates that training may lead to behavioral change but that its efficacy varies by method of delivery. It should also be noted that the sample size for this experiment was very small (seventy-four children total).[12]

Not surprisingly, in addition to the method of delivery, course content affects how much impact a program has on behavior. For example, many of the early programs employed a "bad touch, good touch" method to help children distinguish between loving and abusive touch. Unfortunately, children under the age of seven do not seem to be able to make this distinction, likely because they focus on the outcome of the act rather than on the intention. In other words, if a touch is not painful and is accompanied by kind words, most young children are not able to identify it as abuse.

a Randomized Controlled Trial," *Child Abuse & Neglect* 82 (2018): 144–55, https://scholar.google.com/scholar?hl=en&as_sdt=0%2C36&q=Promoting+Young+Children's+Interpersonal+Safety+&btnG=.

12. C. Poche, P. Yoder, and R. Miltenberger, "Teaching Self-Protection to Children Using Television Techniques," *Journal of Applied Behavior Analysis* 21, no. 3 (1988): 253–61, https://www.ncbi.nlm.nih.gov/pmc/articles/PMC1286121/pdf/jabao0097-0031.pdf.

Similarly, kids are not very good at using their feelings to determine appropriateness. Programs are more effective when they teach clear rules; for example, genital touching is always inappropriate unless done for medical or hygiene reasons.[13] Children also respond well to a combination of role play, group discussion, and modeling (seeing a demonstration of someone effectively combatting abuse).[14] Specific programs that the National Sexual Violence Resource Center found particularly effective include Body Safety Training; Talking about Touching; Feeling Yes, Feeling No; and Who Do You Tell?[15]

Like all the other prevention policies discussed, child training is associated with a number of unanticipated consequences. Researchers looked at the results from twenty-two studies of CSA prevention training. One-third concluded that the training was associated with emotional benefits such as an increase in self-esteem.[16] The same researchers, however, also found that about half the studies identified mild short-term negative effects, including anxiety and dependency, fear of strangers, aggression, embarrassment, upset, and wariness of touch. Additionally, programs appear to have the potential to trigger bad memories or upset kids who had been abused in the past but did not resist.[17]

On balance, it appears that child prevention training can be

13. Sandy K. Wurtele et al., "Comparison of Programs for Teaching Personal Safety Skills to Preschoolers," *Journal of Consulting and Clinical Psychology* 57, no. 4 (1989): 505–11, https://scholar.google.com/scholar?hl=en&as_sdt=0%2C36&q=Wurtele+comparison+programs+skills+preschoolers&btnG=.

14. Topping and Barron, "School-Based Child Sexual Abuse Prevention Programs," https://www.ncbi.nlm.nih.gov/books/NBK77496/.

15. Hallie Martyniuk and Emily Dworkin, *Child Sexual Abuse Prevention: Programs for Children* (Harrisburg, PA: National Sexual Violence Resource Center, 2011), https://www.nsvrc.org/publications/child-sexual-abuse-prevention-programs-children.

16. Topping and Barron, "School-Based Child Sexual Abuse Prevention Programs," https://www.ncbi.nlm.nih.gov/books/NBK77496/.

17. Finkelhor and Strapko, "Sexual Abuse Prevention Education: A Review of Evaluation Studies."

effective in increasing children's knowledge. Some studies have identified positive behavioral impacts as well. The National Sexual Violence Resource Center warns, however, that placing the full burden of CSA prevention on children is ethically problematic as well as ineffective. Children's programs must be part of a larger package of initiatives that reach adults and communities and address societal conditions that lead to violence and abuse.[18]

TRAINING FOR ADULTS

Some of the people most likely to receive prevention training are school employees (including teachers, school nurses, counselors, and administrators). These groups are mandated by their states to receive this specialized training, although the specifics vary by location. In Ohio, for example, school professionals must complete four hours of training every five years. Not all of the hours are devoted to CSA, however, because the state curriculum also includes modules on mental and behavioral issues, depression, and bullying/harassment. As mentioned above, a large number of states have also implemented Erin's Law, requiring or recommending that certain categories of employees receive CSA prevention training.

One of the earliest nonprofit organizations to provide training for adults was the BSA. In the mid-1980s, they named child abuse as one of five "compelling societal problems" and piloted a prevention training program for their employees. The goal was to teach the signs of CSA, the techniques that offenders use to gain the trust of children, and the way to report child abuse suspicions. In 1986, the BSA expanded their efforts with an informational pamphlet sent to its more than one million adult volunteers. They later created an educational video that both volunteers and employees must

18. Martyniuk and Dworkin, "Child Sexual Abuse Prevention: Programs for Children," https://www.nsvrc.org/publications/child-sexual-abuse-prevention-programs-children.

watch every two years.[19] In 2018, the requirement was expanded to include all adults who participate in scouting activities for more than seventy-two hours. This would, for example, include a parent who wants to attend a weeklong BSA camping trip with their child.

The Catholic Church is another major organization with broad requirements for adult training. In 1998, the National Catholic Risk Retention Group—an insurance company—sponsored a conference to explore ways the Church could prevent the abuse of children. They created an education program designed for adults who work with children. Expert consultants, including academics, psychologists, and clergy, created the curriculum. The program, now called Protecting God's Children (PGC), is based on the assumption that properly trained adults can recognize dangerous situations and keep children safe. PGC was initially a voluntary program but was made mandatory for employees and volunteers in 2002. Today, all dioceses have training programs. PGC is the most popular, but there are other programs in use as well.

Sports organizations have recently increased their efforts to train adults. There are a number of possible reasons why they have lagged somewhat behind other organizations. First, there are logistical difficulties because there are many different leagues with relative autonomy, and there is often a communication gap between the national and local levels.[20] Another problem involves sports staff. In response to a survey, sports administrators attending a training program in the United Kingdom said prevention is important but that they lacked the training and competence to tackle the problem.[21] Sports administrators in Canada worried that

---

19. Lawrence F. Potts, "The Youth Protection Program of the Boy Scouts of America," *Child Abuse & Neglect* 16, no. 3 (1992): 441–45.

20. Celia H. Brackenridge, "'. . . So What?' Attitudes of the Voluntary Sector towards Child Protection in Sports Clubs," *Managing Leisure* 7, no. 2 (2002): 103–23, https://bura.brunel.ac.uk/bitstream/2438/543/4/804.pdf.

21. K. Malkin, L. Johnston, and Celia H. Brackenridge, "A Critical Evaluation of Training Needs for Child Protection in UK Sports," *Managing Leisure* 5, no. 3

implementing prevention training would suggest to parents that there was an abuse problem.[22] Some coaches fear that bringing up the topic with kids or parents might lead to unfounded accusations.[23] Finally, prevention has been hard to implement in sports because many coaches are unaware of the rules, lack specialized knowledge about sexual abuse, and sometimes have "lax attitudes toward intimacy" with athletes.[24]

Two National Sports CSA Prevention Programs

US Center for Safe Sports at

https://www.safesport.org/.

Safe4Sports at

http://safe4sports.com/.

While I have certainly not participated in every adult prevention program available, I am extremely familiar with several of them. As described in the preface, I attended over twenty sessions of PGC as part of a research project. I have also (unofficially) completed the BSA's training program as well as that provided by the Episcopalian Church (Safeguarding God's Children or SGC). All of these programs are very similar: they present information about CSA,

(2000): 151–60, https://bura.brunel.ac.uk/bitstream/2438/614/3/Malkin+paper.pdf.

22. Sylvie Parent and Guylaine Demers, "Sexual Abuse in Sport: A Model to Prevent and Protect Athletes," *Child Abuse Review* 20, no. 2 (2011): 120–33, https://scholar.google.com/scholar?hl=en&as_sdt=0%2C36&q=Sexual+Abuse+in+Sport%3A+A+Model+to+Prevent+and+Protect&btnG=.

23. Brackenridge, "' . . . So What?" https://bura.brunel.ac.uk/bitstream/2438/543/4/804.pdf.

24. Anne M. Nurse, "Coaches and Child Sexual Abuse Prevention Training: Impact on Knowledge, Confidence, and Behavior," *Children and Youth Services Review* 88 (2018): 395–400; Jan Toftegaard Nielsen, "The Forbidden Zone: Intimacy, Sexual Relations and Misconduct in the Relationship between Coaches and Athletes," *International Review for the Sociology of Sport* 36, no. 2 (2001): 165–82.

with a focus on how offenders groom children for abuse. They also inform participants about the organization's rules regarding child contact and the importance of reporting child abuse suspicions to both the organization and to local law enforcement. The programs use videos to convey key information, with actors illustrating common risky situations. Both PGC and SGC feature interviews with actual offenders. PGC is unique in organizing its program around correcting common myths. For example, they teach that homosexuals are not more likely than heterosexuals to commit CSA, and that people who are known to children are more likely to abuse them than are strangers.

The goal of all the training programs is the same: to prevent abuse by providing adults with accurate information. As described in earlier chapters, many Americans hold significant misperceptions that could misdirect them from recognizing abuse.[25] Training programs increase knowledge and try to boost participants' confidence in that knowledge. Confidence is important because it appears to increase people's willingness to report abuse suspicions.[26]

---

25. Kiranjeet K. Sanghara and J. Clare Wilson, "Stereotypes and Attitudes about Child Sexual Abusers: A Comparison of Experienced and Inexperienced Professionals in Sex Offender Treatment," *Legal and Criminological Psychology* 11, no. 2 (2006): 229–44; Cátula Pelisoli, Steve Herman, and Débora Dalbosco Dell'Aglio, "Child Sexual Abuse Research Knowledge among Child Abuse Professionals and Laypersons," *Child Abuse & Neglect* 40 (2015): 36–47, https://scholar.google.com/scholar?hl=en&as_sdt=0%2C36&q=Child+Sexual+Abuse+Research+Pelisoli&btnG=; James F. Calvert and Michelle Munsie-Benson, "Public Opinion and Knowledge about Childhood Sexual Abuse in a Rural Community," *Child Abuse & Neglect* 23, no. 7 (1999): 671–82; Rita Laura Shackel, "The Beliefs Commonly Held by Adults about Children's Behavioral Responses to Sexual Victimization," *Child Abuse & Neglect* 32, no. 4 (2008): 485–95, https://www.nationalcac.org/wp-content/uploads/2020/01/The-beliefs-commonly-held-by-adults-about-childrens-behavioral-responses-to-sexual-victimization.pdf.

26. Seth C. Kalichman, Mary E Craig, and Diane R. Follingstad, "Professionals' Adherence to Mandatory Child Abuse Reporting Laws: Effects of Responsibility Attribution, Confidence Ratings, and Situational Factors," *Child Abuse & Neglect* 14, no. 1 (1990): 69–77.

EFFECTIVENESS OF ADULT TRAINING

Over the last thirty years, researchers have conducted numerous evaluations of adult training programs. As with child prevention training, the results have been mixed and appear to depend on the program and the measures of effectiveness used. Unfortunately, few studies follow up with respondents after the program is completed to assess whether new knowledge or behaviors are retained over time.

It appears that training programs directed toward teachers improve knowledge about warning signs of abuse, appropriate ways to respond to a child who reports it, and whom to contact to report suspicious behavior.[27] Two particularly strong studies with a randomly selected control group as well as a follow-up assessment (at two and three months, respectively) found that teachers who received training increased their CSA knowledge more than did teachers in the control group. The trained teachers also retained their knowledge over the period of the study.[28] The findings for parent-training programs are similar. While one small study showed that parents do not gain knowledge,[29] other evaluations

27. Ann Hazzard et al., "Child Sexual Abuse Prevention: Evaluation and One-Year Follow-Up," *Child Abuse & Neglect* 15, no. 1 (1991): 123–138; Carol Kleemeier et al., "Child Sexual Abuse Prevention: Evaluation of a Teacher Training Model," *Child Abuse & Neglect* 12, no. 4 (1988): 555–61; Patrick McGrath et al., "Teacher Awareness Program on Child Abuse: A Randomized Controlled Trial," *Child Abuse & Neglect* 11, no. 1 (1987): 125–32; Alyssa A. Rheingold et al., "Child Sexual Abuse Prevention Training for Childcare Professionals: An Independent Multi-Site Randomized Controlled Trial of Stewards of Children," *Prevention Science* 16, no. 3 (2015): 374–85, https://www.d2l.org/wp-content/uploads/2017/06/Prevention-Science-An-independent-multi-site-randomized-controlled-trial-of-Stewards-of-Children.pdf.

28. McGrath et al., "Teacher Awareness Program on Child Abuse"; Rheingold et al., "Child Sexual Abuse Prevention Training for Childcare Professionals," https://www.d2l.org/wp-content/uploads/2017/06/Prevention-Science-An-independent-multi-site-randomized-controlled-trial-of-Stewards-of-Children.pdf.

29. Jill Duerr Berrick, "Parental Involvement in Child Abuse Prevention Training: What Do They Learn?" *Child Abuse & Neglect* 12, no. 4 (1988): 543–53.

indicate improved knowledge of CSA and specific preventative strategies.[30]

In the study I conducted of PGC, I gave over five hundred participants a pretest at the beginning of the session and a posttest at the end. I also sent them a follow-up test six months after the conclusion of the program. The data indicated that parents, teachers, and coaches all increased their knowledge about CSA and retained that knowledge over time. They learned new information about a wide range of topics, but learning was greatest about offender characteristics and behaviors. This was at least partly because participants came into the program with comparatively low levels of knowledge about offenders.[31]

Does adult prevention training lead to decreased rates of CSA? There are at least two ways it might. First, programs could encourage the use of protective behaviors, stopping abuse before it begins. Second, programs could increase the participants' willingness to report CSA suspicions, disrupting ongoing abuse. Unfortunately, researchers have found it methodologically difficult to explore these possibilities directly. Instead, many rely on the indirect method of abuse vignettes. Participants arrive at training and are asked to respond to stories about potentially abusive situations. What would they do if they were confronted with these situations in real life? Upon the conclusion of the training session, they are asked to respond to the stories again. The researchers compare the two sets of answers to see if the posttest responses reflect a

30. Martine Hébert, Francine Lavoie, and Nathalie Parent, "An Assessment of Outcomes Following Parents' Participation in a Child Abuse Prevention Program," *Violence and Victims* 17, no. 3 (2002): 355–72; Robin A. McGee and Susan L. Painter, "What If It Happens in My Family? Parental Reactions to a Hypothetical Disclosure of Sexual Abuse," *Canadian Journal of Behavioural Science/Revue canadienne des sciences du comportement* 23, no. 2 (1991): 228–40.

31. Anne M. Nurse, "Knowledge and Behavioral Impact of Adult Participation in Child Sexual Abuse Prevention: Evaluation of the Protecting God's Children Program," *Journal of Child Sexual Abuse* 26, no. 5 (2017): 608–24, https://open works.wooster.edu/cgi/viewcontent.cgi?article=1230&context=facpub.

higher willingness to intervene. In general, these studies find that training improves the ability to detect abuse and that it increases the number of protective measures participants believe they would take if confronted with particular situations.[32]

Vignette analysis is valuable but only provides a hypothetical measure of behavioral change. A more direct method is to follow up with participants several weeks or months after a training session. For example, six weeks after a group of teachers finished training, researchers administered a survey asking them how much they had read about abuse, discussed it with a colleague or an individual child, implemented prevention activities in the classroom, or reported suspected abuse. They compared the responses with those from a group of teachers who did not participate in the training and found that the only significant difference involved participants being more likely to read about abuse.[33] It is possible, however, that the short time frame of the research did not allow for other types of behavioral change to occur. In a different study with a three-month follow-up, researchers found that trained teachers were more likely than a control group to be able to identify abuse, to talk with children about abuse, and to report suspicious behavior.[34] A second study with a three-month follow-up found that childcare workers who received CSA prevention training reported being more vigilant about supervising children than did the workers in the control group. They were also more likely to talk to other adults about CSA. There were not significant differences in reporting however.[35]

---

32. See Kleemeier et al., "Child Sexual Abuse Prevention: Evaluation of a Teacher Training Model."

33. Kleemeier et al.

34. M. K. Randolph and C. A. Gold, "Child Sexual Abuse Prevention: Evaluation of a Teacher Training Program," *School Psychology Review* 23, no. 3 (1994): 485–95, http://www.aspponline.org/docs/sex_abuse_2spr233randolph.pdf.

35. Rheingold et al., "Child Sexual Abuse Prevention Training for Childcare Professionals," https://www.d2l.org/wp-content/uploads/2017/06/Prevention-Science-An-independent-multi-site-randomized-controlled-trial-of-Stewards-of-Children.pdf.

My evaluation of the PGC program revealed few reported behavioral changes at the six-month mark, except that participants were much more likely to talk to their own children about CSA than were adults who had not attended the training. This is a positive finding because, as described above, school-based education is more effective when it is reinforced by parents at home.[36] Participants were not, however, more likely to have reported abuse to an official agency or talked to a child or parent about abuse suspicions. In sum, my own findings about the behavioral impact of adult prevention programs—as well as the findings of other researchers— are mixed but indicate that adults at least talk and think more about CSA due to training.

UNANTICIPATED CONSEQUENCES OF ADULT TRAINING[37]

As described, most researchers who study CSA prevention programs focus on intended outcomes. Do participants learn the curricular messages? Do they increase their protective behaviors? While important, these questions provide an incomplete picture of the impact of prevention training because they ignore possible unintended effects. I designed my evaluation of PGC with an eye to capturing both kinds of outcomes. In addition to the standard pre- and posttests, I interviewed over twenty-five participants and facilitators about their experiences and feelings. I also attended twenty-two sessions where, with everyone's permission, I took extensive notes. This combination of methods provided me with

---

36. Sandy K. Wurtele and Maureen C. Kenny, "Partnering with Parents to Prevent Childhood Sexual Abuse," *Child Abuse Review* 19, no. 2 (2010): 130–52, https://scholar.google.com/scholar?hl=en&as_sdt=0%2C36&q=Partnering+with+Parents+to+Prevent+Childhood&btnG=.

37. **Acknowledgement:** This section of the book is derived in part from an article published in the *Journal of Criminal Justice Education*, 2017, ©Academy of Criminal Justice Sciences.

a window into some of the unplanned messages participants took home from training.

The PGC program consists of a three-hour instruction session led by a trained facilitator. The facilitators come from a variety of walks of life—most often they are volunteers, but there are some churches that require a staff person (like a director of religious education) to become PGC certified. All facilitators receive two days of training and are given an instructor's manual that includes frequently asked questions (with answers) and teaching tips. Their primary job in PGC sessions is to introduce two thirty-minute movies. The first movie focuses on the experiences of victims and on how offenders groom children and families. It is very emotional and contains footage of two actual offenders being interviewed about how they abused many victims over long periods of time. There are also stories of real victims played by child actors. The second movie is less emotional, providing information about how adults can identify, prevent, and report CSA.

Because the content of PGC is very similar to other programs, it is likely that the findings from my evaluation are more broadly relevant. There is, however, one important difference: PGC is presented in a group setting with a facilitator, while many other programs (like the BSA's) are online. This means that PGC participants are not just exposed to the official curriculum, they also learn from group discussion and dynamics. The facilitators also take an active part in driving this discussion. While they are told that their job is to handle sign-in and other paperwork, introduce and play the videos, lead the discussion, and answer questions, the reality is much more complicated. Facilitators must do a delicate balancing act as they try to manage the emotions in the room, represent the organization, defuse participant resentment, and remain true to the curriculum.

The facilitators understand that one of the primary goals of the program is to encourage people to question their assumptions about typical offenders. This is essential because the common stereotype

Figure 14. Othering. 2010 by Nina Paley. Mimi and Eunice. CC-BY-SA. https://mimiandeunice.com/2010/07/29/othering/

of offenders as monsters hinders people's ability to recognize that family members or friends might be abusing children. Thus, the videos and the PGC facilitator teaching guide both reinforce the idea that anyone can be an offender. Ironically, however, group dynamics in PGC sessions often result in an *othering* of offenders that effectively contradicts this message. The term *othering* refers to the process of pointing to a group of people and declaring them to be different from one's own group. It is often based on stereotypes and assumptions about what the other group believes or how they behave. Othering can be beneficial when it leads to group cohesion, but it can also result in bias when people posit that another group is so different they are essentially not human.[38]

I witnessed numerous instances of PGC facilitators and participants engaging in othering. The most blatant examples took the form of comments about offenders as evil and different from the rest of us. The quotes below are representative:

> They [offenders] are like animals from the jungle—they should all be taken out and shot.

> [Offenders are] perverted, horrendous.

---

38. Lois Weis, "Identity Formation and the Processes of 'Othering': Unraveling Sexual Threads," *Journal of Educational Foundations* 9, no. 1 (1995): 17–33.

[I was] disgusted, really disgusted. Those people were talking like it was nothing. It was unbelievable.

I couldn't look at the abusers. I wanted to punch them in the face.

The number and vehemence of these types of comments were at least partly a reaction to the detailed testimony given by the two men in the video. At the same time, similar expressions of fear and disgust appear to be routine in contexts where no videos are shown. For example, researchers studying community notification meetings found the same phenomenon even though there was no offender testimony.[39]

How did the facilitators respond to negative talk about offenders? I witnessed only one attempt to stop the direction of the conversation. In fact, more often than not, facilitators participated in and encouraged the discussion. In one class, for example, a participant said that offenders are "horrendous." The facilitator immediately responded, "Horrendous captures it. . . . What you saw on the film is very typical of offenders. That's who they are." Below is another interchange in a class.

Participant: Why aren't the offenders in the movie still in jail?

Facilitator: It's up to the judges, unfortunately. If I had my choice, I'd throw away the key.

Participant: Yes, the offenders should be in jail forever.

There are several reasons that facilitators support or even instigate negative talk about offenders. Given the organizational history of priest abuse, and the potential presence of victims in the

---

39. Richard G. Zevitz and Mary Ann Farkas, "Sex Offender Community Notification: Examining the Importance of Neighborhood Meetings," *Behavioral Sciences and the Law* 18 (2000): 393–408.

room, they do not want to appear to be lenient or sympathetic toward offenders. Additionally, facilitators do not like to contradict participants because it can shut down conversation and embarrass people who are often volunteering their time and may already be resentful. The training manual encourages facilitators to gently correct dangerous misperceptions about victims (like the belief that they bring on their own abuse), but this is not extended to negative talk about offenders.

During many PGC sessions, I watched as one negative remark about offenders turned into an avalanche, with no divergent views offered. This is an example of a common phenomenon social psychologists call the "spiral of silence."[40] Most people do not like conflict and, as a result, they are ready and willing to talk about topics when they are confident that other people agree with them. People are much less willing to broach a subject if they think that others will disagree. People who hold a controversial or minority opinion quickly figure out that their position is unpopular, and this discourages them from talking about it, serving to amplify the majority opinion. Then, as the voices holding the majority opinion become louder, the minority opinion becomes correspondingly quiet, creating a spiral.[41] From chatting with many participants and facilitators at PGC sessions, I know there was some diversity of opinions about offenders, yet nobody was ever willing to challenge their portrayal as monsters. In fact, I interviewed a participant who told me that she had a family member with a past conviction for CSA. She talked about being sad that her PGC session focused so little on restorative judgment and mercy. When I asked her why she had not spoken up, she said that she did not think that the other participants would have supported her views.

40. The term was coined by Elisabeth Noelle-Neumann, "The Spiral of Silence: A Theory of Public Opinion," *Journal of Communication* 24, no. 2 (1974): 43–51.

41. A. F. Hayes, "Willingness to Express One's Opinion in a Realistic Situation as a Function of Perceived Support for That Opinion," *International Journal of Public Opinion Research* 13, no. 1 (2001): 45–58.

> **Video about the Spiral of Silence**
>
> https://www.youtube.com/watch?v=ztVuMKhCkKw

Negative comments were one way that participants and facilitators portrayed offenders as "not like us." But the process of othering also happened in other, more subtle, ways. For example, while all facilitators emphasized that anyone could be an offender, some seemed to amend that message to exempt particular categories of people. Primary among the people to receive a pass were those who were attending the session. Facilitators assured us that the Church trusted us to be around children; the session was required only because it would make us even better protectors of children. Other facilitators thanked us for being at the session, saying that the Church runs because of good people like us. This effectively suggested that the "bad guys" are out there somewhere, not in the room.

The message that participants could not be offenders was reinforced by the complete lack of resources provided for offenders or for people who might be struggling with sexual feelings involving children. This stands in interesting contrast to the assumption that victims are present. Facilitators often used statistics to estimate how many people in the session were abused as children or how many knew a victim. Correspondingly, the handouts given out at the end of the sessions were about how to report abuse and how to get help for victims, not how to get help for offenders or potential offenders.

A second category of people seemingly exempted from suspicion in PGC sessions were family members. This message was primarily telegraphed through silence on the topic of incest. In fact, incest is not mentioned at all in the official curriculum. The topic did, however, come up nine times during the twenty-two sessions. Notably, seven participants asked about it, and two facilitators pointed out that incest is an important issue. When participants raised the incest issue, facilitators acknowledged its existence and moved on. In one case, however, the topic came up when a facilitator asked whom should be contacted in cases of suspected abuse. A participant raised her hand and said, "The parent [pause]. Except if the parent is the problem." Instead of acknowledging that incest could happen, the facilitator simply ignored that part of the women's comment and said that talking to parents is an important part of protecting children.

Facilitators unconsciously signaled that family members do not molest children by telling the participants that they would have a "gut feeling" if a true offender were present. Some examples are below.

> Participant: But parents always seem to be as nice as can be. I am now convinced that I wouldn't know if they were an abuser. Facilitator: Yes, you would; you'd have an uncomfortable feeling.

> You have to trust your gut; God gave us that. Nurture your sixth sense.

> If your gut is telling you there is a problem, it's likely there is.

It should be noted that when facilitators told participants to trust their gut, they were not reflecting an official PGC position. In fact, they were directly contradicting the curricular message that people should look out for particular behavioral warning signs (like gift-giving) rather than vague feelings. Why did facilitators rely on the gut-feeling message so heavily then? The fact that it always came up in the same context offers a clue. Below are some representative comments that prompted the use of the gut feeling message.

> While watching it [the video] I wanted to lock my kids in the house. Maybe I'll just homeschool.

Participant One: It's hard to watch the kids hurting.

Participant Two: It was even harder to watch the adults talk about what they did.

Facilitator: How did it make you feel?

Participant Two: I feel paranoid for my own kids. You never know.I'm feeling like, I trust people so much, then I watch this and it's like an internal battle. How much should I trust? I feel internal turmoil. I feel terrified.

Expressions of fear were quite common in sessions, and even one fearful comment often seemed to heighten the anxiety in the whole room. When this happened, the facilitators felt compelled to calm things down. The gut-feeling message was useful because it made participants believe that CSA was knowable, and thus controllable. But it represented its own type of othering. While it does not, on its face, deny the possibility of family or friend abuse, it diverts attention from them because they are unlikely to engender uncomfortable feelings. It also suggests that there is an inherency about sexual abuse—that offenders somehow exude a different feeling from other people.

The othering of offenders was just one of the unexpected effects of the PGC program. If interested in reading more, access my article about it.[42] When it comes down to it, however, it is simply not possible to categorize adult prevention training as either beneficial or harmful. As with so many well-intentioned programs, it is both. Many training programs, like PGC, do a valuable service by increasing the public's knowledge about CSA and prevention strategies. At the same time, the programs have the potential to transmit

42. Anne M. Nurse, "Construction of the Offender in Child Sexual Abuse Prevention Training for Adults," *Journal of Criminal Justice Education* 28, no. 4 (2017): 598–615, https://openworks.wooster.edu/facpub/392/.

unplanned—and even harmful— messages through group dynamics, how information is framed, and even organizational pressures.

COMMUNITY AWARENESS CAMPAIGNS

In chapter 1, I talked about the media's portrayal of CSA as a criminal justice issue. This framing directs minds to solutions like increased sentencing. But the criminal-justice frame is not the only one possible; CSA can also be seen as a public-health problem. The American Public Health Association says that "public health promotes and protects the health of people and the communities where they live, learn, work and play. While a doctor treats people who are sick, those of us working in public health try to prevent people from getting sick or injured in the first place. We also promote wellness by encouraging healthy behaviors."[43] An example of an issue framed as both a criminal justice and a public-health issue is drunk driving. While it is treated as an individual problem that requires punishment and deterring of offenders, drunk driving is also viewed as a public-health issue that demands a community-prevention response. This is why we see public service announcements about the topic, and there are community-based programs like ride shares that help people avoid driving while inebriated.

Public-health approaches to CSA are not common, but they do exist. Here, I focus on primary prevention—large-scale educational outreach efforts to whole communities. The earliest public-health initiatives began in the 1990s and, since that time, have appeared in several countries around the world.[44] Two states in Australia, for example, conducted a media campaign that employed slogans

---

43. American Public Health Association, "What Is Public Health?" APHA: For Science, for Action, for Health, 2019, https://www.apha.org/what-is-public-health.

44. Bernadette J. Saunders and Chris Goddard, "The Role of Mass Media in Facilitating Community Education and Child Abuse Prevention Strategies," *Child Abuse Prevention Issues*, no. 16 (2002): 1–22, https://aifs.gov.au/cfca/sites/default/files/publication-documents/issues16.pdf.

such as "Child Sexual Assault, It's Often Closer to Home than You Think," and "Child Sexual Assault Is a Crime." An evaluation of the project found that it was effective in making the public more aware of CSA and its seriousness. People also became more aware of organizations that provide help to victims.[45]

Social Media and CSA Prevention

Public outreach isn't limited to organizations or governments—especially in the internet age. Here is an example of an individual artist who created an outreach campaign to encourage the disclosure of incest. After learning that her friend had been raped as a child, she created posters that depict Disney princesses being kissed by their fathers. The tagline reads, "46 percent of minors who are raped are victims of family members. It's never too late to report your attack."

If you want to see the art go to:

https://www.huffpost.com/entry/disney-princess-sexual-abuse_n_5534827.

The state of Massachusetts created another interesting public-health approach to CSA. Called Enough Abuse, it began in the early 2000s as a large-scale effort to reduce CSA through education and community engagement. Program staff worked together with community volunteers to design and implement training programs and create TV and radio ads. While Massachusetts offers prevention training to children, this particular initiative targeted adults as the people who should be most responsible for ending abuse. An evaluation of the program found that it correlated with a decrease in reported incidents of CSA in the state, although it

---

45. Saunders and Goddard, "The Role of Mass Media in Facilitating Community Education and Child Abuse Prevention Strategies," https://aifs.gov.au/cfca/sites/default/files/publication-documents/issues16.pdf.

should be noted that many states without a public-health campaign also saw decreases over the period.[46]

CONCLUSION

Training and educational programs are important because they provide accurate information about a difficult and emotional issue. They provide a forum for people to speak about a topic that—not too long ago—was simply taboo in our society. To date, however, there is not very strong evidence that these training programs do much to prevent CSA, although it may be that their effect is simply difficult to detect with standard short-term research methods. It does appear that programs for adults, children, and whole communities increase knowledge and effectively dismantle common misperceptions. While most researchers have not looked at the unintended messages of prevention training, my observations of the PGC program indicate that they are important to consider. Group discussion and subtle messages sent by facilitators shape what the participants learn. This is problematic when the messages are incorrect or when they lead to the othering of offenders.

In the next chapter, I look at the future. Keeping in mind what works and what does not, what measures should society implement going forward?

FURTHER READING

Jeglic, Elizabeth, and Cynthia Calkins. *Protecting Your Child from Sexual Abuse: What You Need to Know to Keep Your Kids Safe*. New York: Skyhorse, 2018.

Luker, Kristin. *When Sex Goes to School*. New York: WW. Norton, 2007.

---

46. Daniel J. Schober, Stephen B. Fawcett, and Jetta Bernier, "The Enough Abuse Campaign: Building the Movement to Prevent Child Sexual Abuse in Massachusetts," *Journal of Child Sexual Abuse* 21, no. 4 (2012): 456–69.

CHAPTER EIGHT

LOOKING TO THE FUTURE

I have finally arrived at the last, and most important, chapter of the book. How can society and individuals reduce childhood sexual abuse (CSA) and the significant harm associated with it? The good news is that there are many strategies available to tackle the problem. The substantial reduction in rates of CSA over the last thirty years is also encouraging.[1] It signals that some current policies may be having a positive effect. At the same time, as previous chapters of this book have demonstrated, our societal response to CSA has been largely reactive, a response to high-profile extreme cases. Now is an excellent moment for us to step back and use our considerable knowledge about CSA to proactively design new policies and revise some old ones.

Before I turn to a discussion of particular policies, it is useful to know that policy makers view prevention efforts as falling into

---

1. David Finkelhor, Kei Saito, and Lisa Jones, *Updated Trends in Child Maltreatment, 2018* (University of New Hampshire: Crimes against Children Research Center, 2020), http://www.unh.edu/ccrc/pdf/CV203%20-%20Updated%20trends%202018_ks_df.pdf.

three categories.[2] The first, primary prevention, aims to stop a harmful event—like CSA— before it starts. Below are some fictional examples.

> Eight-year-old Alice took part in a training program at school and learned about CSA. When a day-care worker gave her a present and told her to keep it a secret, she told her mother. The mother reported the incident to the head of the day-care center, and the worker received training and increased supervision.
>
> James felt attraction to children and went on the internet to find help. He ultimately found a therapist who taught him ways to control his impulses.

The second category of prevention is designed to stop abuse as quickly as possible. The hope is that informed children and adults can recognize warning signs of abuse and intervene, minimizing the damage.

> Twelve-year-old Henry was being abused by his aunt. He was afraid tell anyone, but his parents noticed that he was acting out more than usual and asked him what was wrong. He told them about the abuse, and they contacted Child Protective Services.
>
> Karen noticed that her fellow teacher often spent time alone with a particular child. She had been trained about grooming and talked to the other teacher's supervisor. An investigation was launched, putting an end to what turned out to be the colleague's abusive behavior.

---

2. Institute for Work and Health, "Primary, Secondary and Tertiary Prevention," IWH, 2015, https://www.iwh.on.ca/what-researchers-mean-by/primary-secondary-and-tertiary-prevention.

The final category of prevention, called tertiary, is the provision of support to victims to help them overcome the negative effects of abuse. It is preventative in the sense that it helps victims to live full lives and avoid engaging in abuse themselves.

> Lila was abused for many years as a child and suffered from depression and anxiety. She participates in two different support groups and speaks to groups of children about abuse. While she still struggles sometimes, her depression is greatly reduced, and she is happily married with children of her own.
>
> Mark was abused by a priest. The priest was successfully prosecuted, and the state provided financial help to Mark's family to pay for therapy. Now twenty-eight, he still thinks about the abuse but recognizes that it was not his fault.

It is clear that CSA requires that people pay attention to all three levels of prevention. The goal is a society with no abuse at all, but in the meantime, survivors and current victims need support and help. In this chapter, I look at a range of policies and assess their efficacy in achieving these different levels of prevention. I have organized the chapter by a number of guiding questions: What polices work and should be retained? Which should be jettisoned? And what new and promising directions are there? At the end, I present some actions that individual people can take to reduce CSA and mitigate its harm.

WHAT WORKS?

Media Coverage

In chapter 1, I discussed that the media is the primary way that the public accesses information about CSA. The media have a powerful voice to dispel myths and provide people with the facts they need to detect, report, and prevent abuse. Because of this, they may deserve some credit for the declining rates of CSA. They also deserve credit when their coverage sends a message to abuse victims and survivors that they are not alone.

Of course, media coverage has the potential to be harmful as well as helpful. The stories that are chosen and how they are framed can lead to dangerous misperceptions about CSA. For example, the media disproportionately cover CSA committed by strangers, suggesting that it is more common than family abuse.[3] Remember that in the 1980s, there were many stories in magazines and on television about repressed memory. Although the idea has been largely discredited, many people continue to believe that it is a frequent response to abuse.[4] The media have influenced our ideas about CSA prevention as well. By focusing on ways children can protect themselves rather than educating about adult or society-wide solutions, people come to believe that children, rather than adults, are responsible for stopping abuse.[5] Finally, when the media use episodic rather than thematic framing, minds are drawn to individual punitive solutions rather than larger-scale interventions.

How can the media use its substantial power to make children safer? An obvious answer is to focus on countering common misperceptions and increasing coverage of a wide range of prevention strategies. Researchers Jenny Kitzinger and Paula Skidmore point out, however, that most reporters who write about CSA are general reporters and do not have specialized knowledge of CSA. This impedes their ability to think critically about the issue and

---

3. Jenny Kitzinger and Paula Skidmore, "Playing Safe: Media Coverage of Child Sexual Abuse Prevention Strategies," *Child Abuse Review* 4 (1995): 47–56, https://scholar.google.com/scholar?hl=en&as_sdt=0,36&q=playing+safe:+Media+coverage+of+child+sexual+abuse+prevention+strategies+kitzinger&btnG=.

4. Lawrence Patihis et al., "Are the 'Memory Wars' Over? A Scientist-Practitioner Gap in Beliefs about Repressed Memory," *Psychological Science* 25, no. 2 (2014): 519–30, https://escholarship.org/uc/item/8d0226zh.

5. Kitzinger and Skidmore, "Playing Safe." https://scholar.google.com/scholar?hl=en&as_sdt=0,36&q=playing+safe:+Media+coverage+of+child+sexual+abuse+prevention+strategies+kitzinger&btnG=.

makes it harder for them to write in a thematic, rather than episodic, way.[6] More reliance on reporters who specialize in abuse issues and increased use of experts as sources could lead to better and more accurate reporting. There also needs to be less coverage of extreme cases and more reporting about family abuse so that the public has a more accurate picture of CSA. Finally, changing the fact that victims of color receive less media attention than white victims is crucial.[7]

Support for Victims and Survivors

Historically, our society has failed to provide CSA victims with the support they need to heal from the effects of abuse. In fact, the criminal justice system has actively harmed victims through practices that demean them or fail to take them into account. This continues to be true today, although the situation has improved. The victim's rights movement can be credited with getting laws passed that mandate communication about court cases and gives victims more of a voice in the process. Societal attitudes have shifted as well, resulting in less blame and suspicion directed toward victims. There is still much that needs to be done, however. The suggestions below are based on research about what helps victims disclose abuse and heal from it.

First, the majority of abused children do not disclose it. While study findings vary, most find that about two-thirds of children do not ever tell anyone. Children who do disclose the abuse often wait for years.[8] This delay in disclosure can be psychologically damaging

---

6. Kitzinger and Skidmore, https://scholar.google.com/scholar?hl=en&as_sdt=0,36&q=playing+safe:+Media+coverage+of+child+sexual+abuse+prevention+strategies+kitzinger&btnG=.

7. Clara Simmons and Joshua Woods, "The Overrepresentation of White Missing Children in National Television News," *Communication Research Reports* 32, no. 3 (2015): 239–45.

8. Kamala London et al., "Disclosure of Child Sexual Abuse: What Does the Research Tell Us about the Ways That Children Tell?" *Psychology, Public Policy,*

because it forces children to carry a terrible secret alone. Delays may also prolong abuse and postpone treatment. So how do we encourage children to disclose? One study found that children will often talk about abuse if they are simply asked. It appears that even a general question about well-being can elicit a disclosure.[9] Thus, when children show signs of distress or unusual behavior, an adult should ask them what is going on in their lives; parents and professionals should not simply assume that the child is "just being a kid." Another option is for physicians to ask children about abuse at their regular yearly check-up. This practice would not be without precedent, since many doctors already screen children for other mental health issues like depression.

A second way to improve the response to abused children is to provide services to their nonabusing caretakers. When children disclose abuse, a supportive response by a parent or caretaker substantially reduces the chance of long-term harm.[10] Sometimes, however, caretakers are not well-equipped to be supportive. For example, a parent might have unresolved issues of their own due to childhood abuse. They may also feel so guilty about their child's abuse that it is hard for them to focus on support. It appears that group therapy can be very helpful to these caretakers and—by extension—is helpful for the abused children as well.[11]

---

and Law 11, no. 1 (2005): 194–226, http://www.wondercatdesign.com/mecasa/images/pdfs/disclosure%20of%20child%20osa.pdf.

9. Rosaleen McElvaney, "Disclosure of Child Sexual Abuse: Delays, Non-Disclosure and Partial Disclosure. What the Research Tells Us and Implications for Practice: Disclosure Patterns in Child Sexual Abuse," *Child Abuse Review* 24, no. 3 (2015): 159–69, https://scholar.google.com/scholar?hl=en&as_sdt=0%2C36&q=Disclosure+of+Child+Sexual+Abuse%3A+Delays%2C+Non-Disclosure+and+Partial+&btnG=.

10. Natacha Godbout et al., "Child Sexual Abuse and Subsequent Relational and Personal Functioning: The Role of Parental Support," *Child Abuse & Neglect* 38, no. 2 (2014): 317–25, https://scholar.google.com/scholar?hl=en&as_sdt=0%2C36&q=Child+sexual+abuse+and+subsequent+relational+and+personal+functioning%3A+The+role+of+parental+support&btnG=.

11. Poonam Tavkar and David J. Hansen, "Interventions for Families Victimized

Third, studies show that some kinds of cognitive behavioral therapy (CBT) are effective in helping victims deal with both emotional and behavioral issues. CBT is a form of psychotherapy that starts by helping people confront and change unhealthy emotions and distorted thoughts. The new emotional and thought patterns provide a foundation to change unhealthy behavior.[12] One CBT program that has shown success is called trauma-focused CBT. It is delivered to children in twelve to sixteen sessions and includes information on stress management, abuse, and trauma. The program also helps victims frame abuse in more healthy ways (for example, it teaches them not to blame themselves). There are modules of trauma-focused CBT available for the parents of abused children as well. Project SAFE is another model of CBT that appears to be effective.

Fourth, as discussed in chapter 7, the investigation and prosecution of CSA can be traumatic for children. Children's Advocacy Centers (CAC) provide a safe, centralized space for various types of investigation and support services. In 2017, these centers served over 334,000 children. About two-thirds of them were victims of sexual abuse. As an example of these centers' efficacy, one study found that 72 percent of children whose cases were handled through a CAC received mental health referrals, compared to only 31 percent of cases handled in communities without a CAC.[13] Extending the reach of these centers could help many children. While most urban areas are well served, many rural areas lack a CAC entirely.

by Child Sexual Abuse: Clinical Issues and Approaches for Child Advocacy Center-Based Services," *Aggression and Violent Behavior* 16, no. 3 (2011): 188–99, https://scholar.google.com/scholar?hl=en&as_sdt=0%2C36&q=Interventions+for+Families+Victimized+by+Child+&btnG=.

12. *Psychology Today*, "Cognitive Behavioral Therapy," *Psychology Today*, 2019, https://www.psychologytoday.com/basics/cognitive-behavioral-therapy.

13. Theodore P. Cross et al., "Evaluating Children's Advocacy Centers' Response to Child Sexual Abuse," *Juvenile Justice Bulletin* 106 (2008), https://scholar.google.com/scholar?hl=en&as_sdt=0%2C36&q=Evaluating+Children's+Advocacy+Centers'+Response&btnG=.

Check out an interactive map of Children's Advocacy Centers in the United States: https://www.nationalchildrensalliance .org/cac-coverage-maps/.

Fifth, there is evidence to suggest that health-care coverage is linked to reduced rates of victimization. The Affordable Care Act (ACA) allowed states to expand their Medicaid programs. Studies show that this led to reductions in some types of crime. Why might this be? ACA coverage, by law, includes mental health services, giving victims access to therapy. Therapy can help these victims recover and—in so doing—enables them to avoid criminal behavior themselves. Medical coverage is also linked to a reduction in parental depression, substance abuse, and stress—all factors that can play a role in abuse.[14]

There are currently opportunities for improving services to victims of CSA. The 1984 federal Victims of Crime Act is the primary funding source for victim support services. It provides block grants to states. In 2015, this funding was increased from $745 million to $2.3 billion dollars—a huge increase that has the potential to reach many more crime victims with expanded services. This is particularly good news because a recent large-scale study with crime victims showed that two-thirds did not receive any help from the government after their victimization.[15]

Background Checks

Background checks provide a valuable means for employers or supervisors of volunteers to identify people with CSA convictions

---

14. Elizabeth Letourneau, "Can Improved Health Care Access Reduce Sexual Violence," *Psychology Today*, 2019, https://www.psychologytoday. com/blog/prevention-now/201901/can-improved-health-care-access-reduce-sexual-violence.

15. Alliance for Safety and Justice, *Crime Survivors Speak: The First-Ever National Survey of Victims' Views on Safety and Justice* (Oakland, CA: Alliance for Safety and Justice, 2016), https://allianceforsafetyandjustice.org/wp-content/uploads/documents/Crime%20Survivors%20Speak%20Report.pdf.

before they are hired to work in positions that involve children. As discussed in chapter 6, when organizations use these checks, they can substantially decrease the chance of hiring someone with a conviction. Today, most schools, day-care centers, and youth organizations require background checks. This has been accomplished through a combination of legal action and voluntary compliance.

There are many ways to improve the background check system. First, the accuracy of records is a continuing problem that needs to be resolved. For example, FBI records often show an arrest but not the case disposition. Background checks from commercial vendors also miss information because they contain only a subset of criminal records. Additionally, commercial vendors use names or social security numbers rather than fingerprints, which can lead to misidentifications.

Reforming Background Check Procedures

Background check reform is a complicated issue. If readers are interested in learning more about it, the National Consumer Law Center has a terrific report with recommendations. Check it out at https://www.nclc.org/images/pdf/pr-reports/broken-records-report.pdf.

Background checks are most effective when used thoughtfully. Instead, many organizations simply prohibit people with any kind of criminal conviction from service, resulting in a wide range of harms. Good workers are rejected for long-ago crimes unrelated to the job they seek. Parents who committed minor crimes are precluded from volunteering in their child's classroom. Perhaps these outcomes would not be so bad if they only affected a small group, but a huge number of people are arrested. In fact, about 23 percent of Americans born between 1979 and 1988 have an arrest record for incidents occurring prior to their twenty-sixth birthdays.[16] These

---

16. James P. Smith, "The Long-Term Economic Impact of Criminalization in

are today's parents and workers. Minorities and poor people are arrested at even higher rates, largely because they are more likely to be caught, arrested, and convicted of certain crimes, particularly those involving drugs. Background check policies that include drug crimes as disqualifiers run the risk of perpetuating this discrimination. For all of these reasons, organizations should use background checks judiciously, and if nonabuse crimes are included on the list of prohibitions, there should be time limits.

Prevention Training for Children and Adults

In the last chapter, I talked about prevention training programs. Some of these programs are delivered to children in schools and in organizations like the Boy Scouts of America. There are also a growing number of programs that target adults. It appears that training both groups can result in higher levels of knowledge and confidence.[17] While the findings are more mixed about behavioral

---

American Childhoods," *Crime & Delinquency* 65, no. 3 (2019): 422–44, https://www.ncbi.nlm.nih.gov/pmc/articles/PMC6874402/.

17. Donna M. Brown, "Evaluation of Safer, Smarter Kids: Child Sexual Abuse Prevention Curriculum for Kindergartners," *Child and Adolescent Social Work Journal* 34, no. 3 (2017): 213–22; Jan Rispens, Andre Aleman, and Paul Goudena, "Prevention of Child Sexual Abuse Victimization: A Meta-Analysis of School Programs," *Child Abuse & Neglect* 21, no. 10 (1997): 975–87, https://www.ncbi.nlm.nih.gov/books/NBK67045/; K. J. Topping and I. G. Barron, "School-Based Child Sexual Abuse Prevention Programs: A Review of Effectiveness," *Review of Educational Research* 79, no. 1 (2009): 431–63, https://www.ncbi.nlm.nih.gov/books/NBK77496/; David Finkelhor and N. Strapko, "Sexual Abuse Prevention Education: A Review of Evaluation Studies," in *Prevention of Child Maltreatment: Developmental and Ecological Processes*, ed. D. Willis, E. Holder, and M. Rosenberg (New York: Wiley, 1987); Martine Hébert, Francine Lavoie, and Nathalie Parent, "An Assessment of Outcomes Following Parents' Participation in a Child Abuse Prevention Program," *Violence and Victims* 17, no. 3 (2002): 355–72; Anne M. Nurse, "Knowledge and Behavioral Impact of Adult Participation in Child Sexual Abuse Prevention: Evaluation of the Protecting God's Children Program," *Journal of Child Sexual Abuse* 26, no. 5 (2017): 608–24, https://openworks.wooster.edu/cgi/viewcontent.cgi?article=1230&context=facpub.

effects, some studies find that children are more likely to resist going away with a stranger after training.[18] It may also be the case that child participants disclose abuse faster.[19] Adults who receive training are more likely to talk to their children about CSA, reinforcing what the children learn in school.[20] For all of these reasons, it is worthwhile to continue prevention training. Given that a significant percentage of abuse is committed by juveniles (such as camp counselors), it is also important to change current policies to require their participation.

Of course, organizations need to be thoughtful about the particular prevention programs they adopt. There are a huge number on the market. However, the most effective ones follow best-practice guidelines developed by researchers. There's a list of these in chapter 7. Organizations should also remember that curricula can convey unplanned messages through what is presented and what is not. As my description of Protecting God's Children illustrated, in-person training can also introduce dynamics that result in a spiral of silence and cause extreme (and sometimes wrong) positions to be embraced by the group.

Various organizations are experimenting with new and different kinds of prevention programs. For example, the Vermont Network Against Domestic and Sexual Violence has created a *Consent Campaign Guidebook* to help middle and high school teachers introduce the concept of consent to students. This provides an opportunity

---

18. C. Poche, P. Yoder, and R. Miltenberger, "Teaching Self-Protection to Children Using Television Techniques," *Journal of Applied Behavior Analysis* 21, no. 3 (1988): 253–61, https://www.ncbi.nlm.nih.gov/pmc/articles/PMC1286121/pdf/jabaoo097-0031.pdf.

19. Laura E. Gibson and Harold Leitenberg, "Child Sexual Abuse Prevention Programs: Do They Decrease the Occurrence of Child Sexual Abuse?" *Child Abuse & Neglect* 24, no. 9 (2000): 1115–25.

20. Sandy K. Wurtele and Maureen C. Kenny, "Partnering with Parents to Prevent Childhood Sexual Abuse," *Child Abuse Review* 19, no. 2 (2010): 130–52, https://scholar.google.com/scholar?hl=en&as_sdt=0%2C36&q=Partnering+with+Parents+to+Prevent+Childhood&btnG=.

for boys and girls to think together about consent and about people's right to control their own body. Prevent Child Abuse Vermont has also created a set of interesting training programs for children and adults. The child program is notable because it teaches about CSA in the context of creating healthy relationships. It also acknowledges that children can be both victims and perpetrators.

Links to Education Resources

Vermont's *Consent Campaign Guidebook*: https://vtnetwork. org/wp-content/uploads/2017/08/ConsentCampaignGuide book_2ndEd.pdf.

The *New York Times* created a compendium of suggestions for teachers interested in teaching the construction of masculinity: https://www.nytimes.com/2018/04/12/learning/les son-plans/boys-to-men-teaching-and-learning-about-mas culinity-in-an-age-of-change.html.

Prevent Child Abuse Vermont's website: https://www.pcavt. org/.

While these new types of prevention programs are exciting, it is important to note that the kind of comprehensive sex education programs that many school districts have been offering for years also appear to provide protection.[21]

Treatment for Offenders and Potential Offenders

One of the keys to reducing CSA is to ensure access to treatment for people who have already abused children as well as for those who fear that they might in the future. A recent meta-analysis of

---

21. David Finkelhor et al., "Sexual Abuse in a National Survey of Adult Men and Women: Prevalence, Characteristics, and Risk Factors," *Child Abuse & Neglect* 14, no. 1 (1990): 19–28.

studies evaluating the impact of treatment demonstrated that therapy can reduce recidivism. While treatment appears to be effective in adults convicted of sexual crimes (reducing recidivism by about 5 percent), the effect is stronger for juveniles (with a 24 percent reduction). When treatment is offered in the community, it tends to be more successful than when it is offered in prison.[22]

Because identities of convicted sex offenders are made public, it is not difficult to locate them for treatment. It is far more challenging, however, to treat those who have not been caught or who have not acted on an attraction toward children. This is because, in the United States, therapists are mandatory reporters. People cannot reveal past abusive behavior without risking law enforcement involvement. While simply having sexual fantasies about children is not a reportable offense, many people do not understand this and are afraid to admit to attraction for fear of being identified and possibly arrested.[23]

Compounding the fear of arrest, people have difficulty figuring out where to go for help. Elizabeth Letourneau, a well-respected researcher, asked people arrested for sex crimes why they did not seek help. She reports,

> The first thing they say is that they really had no idea where to go. They see all these public health announcements: "If you have a drug problem, or a gambling problem, or you think you have HIV, call this number." But you never see a bus go by with an ad that says: "If you're concerned about your attractions to children, call this number." Another reason is the very shame and fear of

---

22. Bitna Kim, Peter J. Benekos, and Alida V. Merlo, "Sex Offender Recidivism Revisited: Review of Recent Meta-Analyses on the Effects of Sex Offender Treatment," *Trauma, Violence & Abuse* 17, no. 1 (2016): 105–17, https://www.research gate.net/profile/Bitna_Kim2/publication/270765529_Sex_Offender_Recidi vism_Revisited/links/567a864608ae7fea2e9a1444.pdf.

23. Jennifer Bleyer, "Sympathy for the Deviant," *Psychology Today*, November 3, 2015, https://www.psychologytoday.com/articles/201511/sympathy-the-deviant.

judgment—"If I open up and tell somebody, what are they going to think of me?"[24]

Germany has experimented with new approaches to voluntary treatment. In 2005, researchers launched a media campaign offering free and anonymous treatment to anyone over eighteen who was troubled by an interest in children or teenagers. Almost six hundred men contacted the program over the following six years, and the waiting list became long, making it possible to form a control group from those people who were waiting for help. Men in the treatment group received weekly cognitive behavioral therapy (CBT), and men in the control group received no treatment (until they were no longer on the wait list). The results of the study indicated that the program was successful in reducing many of the risk factors associated with sexual offending. The official recidivism rate of the project was zero, although it is possible that some treatment-group participants continued to abuse children or looked at child pornography undetected by the criminal justice system.

Story about a Juvenile Seeking Help for Attraction to Children

Here's a link to the National Public Radio show *This American Life*. It's a story about a juvenile who is a self-identified pedophile and his seeking help for his attraction. It's very much worth listening to. It's in act 2 of the radio broadcast: https://www.thisamericanlife.org/522/tarred-and-feathered.

A second public outreach project in Germany targeted juveniles who felt an attraction to children. Using posters with a picture of a dinosaur or a teddy bear, they offered free treatment. The dinosaur poster was directed at those who were attracted to boys. It said,

---

24. Bleyer, "Sympathy for the Deviant," https://www.psychologytoday.com/articles/201511/sympathy-the-deviant.

"He is still dreaming of dinosaurs. You are dreaming of him." The tagline on the teddy bear poster, directed toward attraction to girls, said, "She is sharing her bed with teddy bears. You would like to share it with her." Of course, these taglines were in German on the actual posters. While evaluation results are not yet available, about fifty juveniles contacted the project and received treatment.[25]

Germany has been at the forefront of voluntary treatment, but there are examples in the United States as well. As I mentioned in the preface, there is a hotline that takes calls about CSA—including those from people who are afraid they may act on their attraction to children. Called Stop It Now!, the model originated in the United States and has been exported to other countries, including the United Kingdom and the Netherlands. An evaluation of the programs in the latter two countries found that the hotline was effective in encouraging callers to enter therapy and that it helped them develop plans to avoid offending. Callers, however, reported that it was difficult to find out about the hotline and that shame had kept many of them from calling earlier.[26]

The success of the programs described above provides an argument for their expansion. It is clear that some people who are attracted to children would like help to resist their feelings. When anonymity is guaranteed, they are willing to seek treatment. It should be noted, however, that the two German projects were made possible by a law that exempts therapists from mandatory reporting. This is a difficult idea for most Americans because it appears to give offenders a free pass on punishment.[27] At the

---

25. Klaus M. Beier et al., "'Just Dreaming of Them': The Berlin Project for Primary Prevention of Child Sexual Abuse by Juveniles (PPJ)," *Child Abuse & Neglect* 52 (2016): 1–10.

26. Joan Van Horn et al., "Stop It Now! A Pilot Study Into the Limits and Benefits of a Free Helpline Preventing Child Sexual Abuse," *Journal of Child Sexual Abuse* 24, no. 8 (2015): 853–72, https://scholar.google.com/scholar?hl=en&as_sdt=0%2C36&q=Stop+It+Now%21+A+Pilot+Study+Into+the+Limits+&btnG=.

27. Deborah A. Daro, "Prevention of Child Sexual Abuse," *Future of Children* 4, no. 2 (1994): 198–223, https://www.jstor.org/stable/1602531?seq=1.

same time, it is important to remember that some of the people who sought out therapy in Germany were likely never going to be caught. Voluntary treatment gave them a chance at rehabilitation and therefore enhanced public safety. While it is unlikely that the United States will completely exempt therapists from mandatory reporting, perhaps there could be a middle ground, allowing an exemption for people in therapy who only abused in the past (meaning that the abuse is not actively ongoing). Alternately, public outreach campaigns could be created that are very clear about which actions are reportable and which are not, so that people understand that desires are not illegal.

Electronic Monitoring and Risk Assessment

While much more research needs to be conducted, there are some indications that electronic monitoring (EM) decreases recidivism. In other words, restricting offenders to their homes and workplaces appears to reduce the chance that they will abuse another child. Some caveats are necessary, however. Many states have widened the net, forcing monitors on hundreds of people convicted of low-level crimes and who are extremely unlikely to recidivate. This is expensive, time consuming for law enforcement, and negatively impacts those who wear monitors. Similarly, a number of states require some categories of sex offenders to wear monitors for life— well past the point where they are at significant risk of reoffense.

EM is most appropriately used for limited periods of time with people who have committed very serious crimes and are at high risk of reoffense. How is risk determined? This may be an area where risk assessment is helpful. As discussed in chapter 7, risk-assessment tools are becoming increasingly good at predicting recidivism. While the use of these tools in sentencing is ethically problematic, the issues that arise in decisions about limited-time monitoring are less so. Of course, assessments should include both risk and promotive factors and should be conducted at intervals.

Because factors change over time, risk levels do as well. Remember that EM does not rehabilitate people—it simply limits their opportunities to commit new crimes. EM must be combined with the kinds of therapy discussed in the previous section, and with significant reintegration supports, which are discussed below.

WHAT DOES NOT WORK

The Registry

As discussed in chapter 5, public sex offender registries do not achieve their intended effect; they do not appear to reduce rates of offending, nor do they help protect children. In fact, there is evidence that people on the registries are so stigmatized that it is difficult for them to find places to live or work.[28] This increases their chances of committing further crimes.[29] Further, the children of people on the registry often suffer harassment—a particularly sad and ironic outcome given that the point of the registry is to protect children.[30] Registries may also encourage plea bargains or

---

28. Jill S. Levenson and Leo P. Cotter, "The Effect of Megan's Law on Sex Offender Reintegration," *Journal of Contemporary Criminal Justice* 21, no. 1 (2005): 49–66, https://scholar.google.com/scholar?hl=en&as_sdt=0%2C36&q=The+Effect+of+Megan's+Law+on+Sex+Offender+Reintegration&btnG=.

29. Sarah Lageson and Christopher Uggen, "How Work Affects Crime—and Crime Affects Work—Over the Life Course," in *Handbook of Life-Course Criminology*, ed. Chris L. Gibson and Marvin D. Krohn (New York: Springer New York, 2013), 201-12, https://scholar.google.com/scholar?hl=en&as_sdt=0%2C36&q=How+Work+Affects+Crime—And+Crime+Affects+Work&btnG=; Christopher Uggen, "Ex-Offenders and the Conformist Alternative: A Job Quality Model of Work and Crime," *Social Problems* 46, no. 1 (1999): 127–51, https://scholar.google.com/scholar?hl=en&as_sdt=0%2C36&q=Ex-Offenders+and+the+Conformist+Alternative%3A+&btnG=.

30. Jill S. Levenson and Richard Tewksbury, "Collateral Damage: Family Members of Registered Sex Offenders," *American Journal of Criminal Justice* 34 (2009): 54–68, https://scholar.google.com/scholar?hl=en&as_sdt=0%2C36&q=Collateral+Damage%3A+Family+Members+of+Registered+Sex+Offenders&btnG=.

reduced charges, which can change the categorization of a crime from sexual to nonsexual. Finally, as described earlier, registries only contain a small percentage of the people who actually go on to commit sex crimes.[31]

Politicians created registries based on faulty recidivism statistics. As discussed in chapter 3, Supreme Court Justice Anthony Kennedy used the now infamous, and incorrect, 80 percent recidivism statistic in an opinion. Many states went on to use that same number to justify passing registry laws. Registries are also a result of politics. Sociologist Joseph Gusfield points out that politicians are very interested in voting for policies that can bolster their image while also saving the state money.[32] Registries are expensive, but they are cheaper than other measures the state could take to protect children. The registry effectively allows the state to offload some of the responsibility for children's safety onto parents. In other words, the state creates a list of names, but it is the parents who must engage in the actual prevention.[33]

Unfortunately, there is widespread public support for the registry, so it may be necessary to take some intermediate steps to reduce its harms.[34] First, remove people who have not actually

31. Jeffrey C. Sandler, Naomi J. Freeman, and Kelly M. Socia, "Does a Watched Pot Boil? A Time-Series Analysis of New York State's Sex Offender Registration and Notification Law," Psychology, Public Policy, and Law 14, no. 4 (2008): 284–302, https://scholar.google.com/scholar?hl=en&as_sdt=0%2C36&q=Watched+Pot+Boil%3F+Sandler+time+series&btnG=.

32. Joseph R. Gusfield, "Constructing the Ownership of Social Problems: Fun and Profit in the Welfare State," Social Problems 36, no. 5 (1989): 431–41, https://www.jstor.org/stable/3096810?read-now=1&refreqid=excelsior:4ccf530163bffa18d2820dea7c839161&seq=11#page_scan_tab_contents.

33. Jonathan Simon, "Managing the Monstrous: Sex Offenders and the New Penology," Psychology, Public Policy, and Law 4, no. 1/2 (1998): 452–67.

34. Jill S. Levenson et al., "Public Perceptions about Sex Offenders and Community Protection Policies," Analyses of Social Issues and Public Policy 7, no. 1 (2007): 137–61, https://scholar.google.com/scholar?hl=en&as_sdt=0%2C36&q=+Public+Perceptions+about+Sex+Offenders+and+Community+&btnG=.

committed sexual crimes. As described in chapter 5, some states have expanded their registries to include people who have committed minor, nonsexual crimes. This kind of net widening makes the registry completely meaningless. There are also compelling reasons to restrict the registry to people who committed CSA as adults. Juveniles simply do not have the same capacity as adults to make decisions about their behavior. Neuroscience is increasingly suggesting that children's brains process information in different ways from adult brains.[35] Further supporting the difference between the two groups, therapy is particularly effective with juveniles, and their recidivism rates are lower than those for adults.[36] As described in chapter 3, only a small minority of juvenile sex offenders go on to adult sex crimes.[37] Finally, the effects of the registry on children's lives are enormous and include harassment and a loss of access to education, jobs, and housing.[38] While juveniles who commit serious sexual abuse should certainly receive sanctions and help, the registry is an ineffective and disproportionately punitive way to achieve that.

35. Richard J. Bonnie and Elizabeth S. Scott, "The Teenage Brain: Adolescent Brain Research and the Law," *Current Directions in Psychological Science* 22, no. 2 (2013): 158–61, https://journals.sagepub.com/doi/pdf/10.1177/0963721412471678.

36. Kim, Benekos, and Merlo, "Sex Offender Recidivism Revisited," https://www.researchgate.net/profile/Bitna_Kim2/publication/270765529_Sex_Offender_Recidivism_Revisited/links/567a864608ae7fea2e9a1444.pdf.

37. Franklin E. Zimring, Alex R. Piquero, and Wesley G. Jennings, "Sexual Delinquency in Racine: Does Early Sex Offending Predict Later Sex Offending in Youth and Young Adulthood?," *Criminology & Public Policy* 6, no. 3 (2007): 507–34, https://scholar.google.com/scholar?hl=en&as_sdt=0%2C36&q=Sexual+Delinquency+in+Racine%3A+Does+Early+Sex+&btnG=.

38. Nicole Pittman, Alison Parker, and Human Rights Watch (HRW), *Raised on the Registry: The Irreparable Harm of Placing Children in Sex Offenders Registries in the US* (New York: Human Rights Watch, 2013), https://www.hrw.org/report/2013/05/01/raised-registry/irreparable-harm-placing-children-sex-offender-registries-us.

> In the wake of Polly Klaas's brutal murder, Californians passed a three strikes law mandating life imprisonment for criminals who commit a third felony of any type after having received two "serious" or "violent" felony convictions. While not named after Polly Klaas, her memory was frequently invoked in the campaign to pass the law, and her father, Mark Klaas, was an ardent supporter. Once the bill was passed, however, it became clear that it had serious flaws. For example, there were no limits on what felonies could constitute a third strike. As a result, people ended up with life sentences after stealing a battery or baby food (those are real examples). Both Mark Klaas and his father, Joe, ended up actively working for the rollback of the law that they had helped pass. Read the *Los Angeles Times*'s coverage here: https://www.latimes.com/archives/la-xpm-2004-sep-19-tm-threestrikes38-story.html.

Sometimes, when a particularly horrific CSA case comes to light, politicians create new laws to prevent similar crimes. These laws are often named after the victim and are known as memorial laws or bills. The intention of memorial bills is certainly good; they honor the victim by trying to make the world a safer place. The problem, however, is that memorial laws are often passed hastily and contain flaws that limit their efficacy.

Policy makers worry that if they do not act immediately in the wake of a crime, they will face public criticism. Consequently, they rush to pass poorly written and inadequately researched bills.[39] The fact that the bills memorialize a child victim adds to the pressure to pass them. Politicians worry that any opposition might be read as a

---

39. Brian K. Payne and Matthew DeMichele, "Sex Offender Policies: Considering Unanticipated Consequences of GPS Sex Offender Monitoring," *Aggression and Violent Behavior* 16, no. 3 (2011): 177–87.

lack of empathy toward victims.[40] It is also the case that memorial bills are usually proposed in the wake of extreme CSA cases. Thus, the measures they enact do little to stop the vast majority of cases. If politicians are really interested in protecting children, they need to craft careful legislation that is targeted at the largest number of cases, not the extreme ones.

In addition to resulting in faulty legislation, memorial bills raise ethical questions. The use of a victim's name implies that the bill represents that person's interests and wishes. Yet, when a victim is dead or when they are a young child, it is impossible to know what they really would have wanted. Although not referring to memorial bills specifically, one theorist called this kind of talking for others "usurpatory ventriloquism." Like a ventriloquist, lawmakers talk through a silent other—in this case, the child victim.[41] By claiming that a bill is what a victim "would have wanted," lawmakers can hide the fact that they gain political capital from its passage.

I should note that it is overly simplistic to say that all memorial bills are bad. In theory, it is possible to craft a solid memorial bill that really does protect children and does not exploit the victim's name. The political reality surrounding the bills, however, makes this difficult to achieve. Society would be better off finding other ways to honor victims.

Residency Requirements and Halloween Laws

In chapter 5, I talked about residency rules that limit where people with CSA convictions can live. These rules are based on the assumption that offenders stalk schools and parks looking for victims. This assumption has been shown to be incorrect; abusers usually meet their victims through family connections or through

40. Simon, "Managing the Monstrous."

41. Pierre Bourdieu, *Language and Symbolic Power*, ed. John B. Thompson, trans. Gino Raymond and Matthew Adamson (Cambridge: Harvard University Press, 2003).

work at a school or other child-serving organization.[42] Halloween laws are similarly based on misperceptions. There is no evidence that offenders lure children into their homes during trick or treating.[43] This myth is similar to recurrent, and also incorrect, rumors about tainted Halloween candy. Both residency rules and Halloween laws are the result of irrational fears stoked by media reports of stranger danger.

It is clear that neither residency rules nor Halloween laws reduce CSA in any substantial way. Additionally, they have unanticipated negative effects. Residency rules severely limit where people on the registry can live, resulting in high numbers living in close proximity in particularly poor neighborhoods.[44] In extreme cases, the rules force them to become homeless. The impact of Halloween laws is much less serious, but enforcing the laws is expensive and takes police away from tasks that are much more pressing (like directing traffic so that trick or treaters are safe). Communities would save money and become safer if both kinds of laws were overturned.

Othering People Who Have Committed CSA

In the first chapter of this book, I talked about perceptions of CSA offenders as monsters and evil. This imagery suggests that offenders are a completely different category of people who are nothing like the rest of society. One of the reasons that this is unfortunate

---

42. Minnesota Department of Corrections, *Residential Proximity & Sex Offense Recidivism in Minnesota* (St. Paul: Minnesota Department of Corrections, 2007), https://ccoso.org/sites/default/files/import/SexOffenderReport-Proximity.pdf.

43. Mark Chaffin et al., "How Safe Are Trick-or-Treaters? An Analysis of Child Sex Crime Rates on Halloween," *Sexual Abuse: A Journal of Research and Treatment* 21, no. 3 (2009): 363–74, https://journals.sagepub.com/doi/pdf/10.1177/1079063209340143.

44. Elizabeth Ehrhardt Mustaine, Richard Tewksbury, and Kenneth M. Stengel, "Social Disorganization and Residential Locations of Registered Sex Offenders: Is This a Collateral Consequence?" *Deviant Behavior* 27, no. 3 (2006): 329–50.

is that it may slow down the detection of CSA. When an image of a monster is placed in the minds of the public, it is hard for them to recognize that the person abusing children could be a family member or friend. Demonizing offenders also has the potential to discourage people who might abuse a child from seeking help. When they hear the message that they are evil and unable to change, they may internalize it, and in a self-fulfilling prophecy, do not bother to seek help.[45]

Interestingly, the #MeToo movement might help rethink the othering of people with sexual convictions. Othering causes people to see "sex offenders" as part of one homogeneous group of bad guys. #MeToo has brought to light the fact that many beloved figures, such as Bill Cosby, sexually abuse others. In other words, seemingly nice people can commit abuse. #MeToo is also making people question the homogeneity of offenders. It has encompassed a wide range of accusations, from rape to unwanted advances, sparking heated discussion about how different levels of abuse should be treated. For example, former Senator Al Franken was accused of forcibly kissing a woman. This is quite different from accusations against Senate candidate Roy Moore who faced assault allegations from three women, one of whom was fourteen at the time of the alleged encounter. There are similar distinctions with CSA—a serial child rapist is different from a person who exposes himself once to a child. Both require intervention, but solutions and sanctions should be different.

Portraying Children as Innocent and Nonsexual

In chapter 1, I discussed the image of children as innocent. Research suggests that, at least in part, people understand innocence to mean a lack of knowledge about sex and an absence of sexual

---

45. Bleyer, "Sympathy for the Deviant," https://www.psychologytoday.com/articles/201511/sympathy-the-deviant.

impulses.[46] Parents feel strongly about protecting this aspect of children's innocence. In interviews, they say that they purposefully withhold information about sexuality from their children for this reason.[47] When infants and toddlers touch their genitals, parents usually describe it as "natural and nonsexual." Among preschoolers, the activity is considered to be exploratory. After that, most parents begin to discourage it because of concerns that it might be a sign of problems or lost innocence.[48]

The cultural assumption that children are nonsexual led to the pathologizing of children who engaged in any sort of sexual behavior. Starting in the 1980s, some experts came to believe that these children must have been victims of CSA. How else would they know to do sexual things? It was only a small leap to labeling children who tried to involve other children in sexual behaviors as sexual abusers.[49] It was hard to refute these conclusions because few researchers had conducted studies of the sexual behaviors of "normal" children.[50] Today, it is common knowledge that children engage in a wide range of sexually related behaviors that include masturbation as well as exploring other children's bodies ("playing doctor"), fondling other children, touching women's breasts, and trying to look at naked people. A very small percentage engage in penetration or other highly intrusive acts.

---

46. Laura McGinn et al., "Parental Interpretations of 'Childhood Innocence': Implications for Early Sexuality Education," *Health Education* 116, no. 6 (2016): 580–94, http://researchspace.bathspa.ac.uk/8782/1/8782.pdf.

47. McGinn et al., "Parental Interpretations of 'Childhood Innocence,'" http://researchspace.bathspa.ac.uk/8782/1/8782.pdf.

48. Gail Ryan, "Childhood Sexuality: A Decade of Study. Part 1—Research and Curriculum Development," *Child Abuse & Neglect* 24, no. 1 (2000): 33–48, https://scholar.google.com/scholar?hl=en&as_sdt=0%2C36&q=Childhood+Sexuality%3A+A+Decade+of+Study.+Part+1—Research&btnG=.

49. Richard Beck, *We Believe the Children: A Moral Panic in the 1980s*, 1st ed. (New York: PublicAffairs, 2015).

50. Ryan, "Childhood Sexuality," https://scholar.google.com/scholar?hl=en&as_sdt=0%2C36&q=Childhood+Sexuality%3A+A+Decade+Ryan&btnG=.

The portrayal of children as innocent can lead us to patholo-gize healthy children. Jenny Kitzinger points out that there can be other unintended effects as well.[51] First, projecting innocence onto children may actually make them more appealing sexual targets for adults. Child pornography, for example, often plays off the idea that children's innocence makes them sexy. We also see this link in mainstream advertising when teenage girls are made to look like innocent children.

When we assume that "normal" children are innocent, it can make people less sympathetic to children who do not conform to that expectation. If a child displays sexual knowledge or interest, for example, their allegations of abuse may not be taken as seri-ously. Similarly, if a child acquiesces to sexual activity or appears to have enjoyed it, they may not be protected as vigorously.[52] Finally, as described above, when parents prioritize children's innocence, they might fail to give them information about their bodies or about sex that could help them protect themselves. They could, for example, deprive them of information that would help a child interpret a potential offender's actions as inappropriate.[53]

Extremely Lengthy Sentences

One important policy area for reconsideration involves the length of criminal sentences. The last thirty years have seen dramatic

51. Jenny Kitzinger, "Who Are You Kidding? Children, Power, and the Struggle against Sexual Abuse," in *Constructing and Reconstructing Childhood*, ed. Allison James and Alan Prout (New York: Routledge, 1997), 165–89.

52. Shafiqul Islam, "Ideal Victims of Sexualized Violence: Why Is It Always Female?" *European Journal of Research in Social Sciences* 4, no. 8 (2016): 82–92, https://scholar.google.com/scholar?hl=en&as_sdt=0%2C36&q=Ideal+Vic tims+of+Sexualized+Violence%3A&btnG=.

53. Dona Matthews, "Call Children's Private Body Parts What They Are," *Psychology Today* (blog), 2017, https://www.psychologytoday.com/blog/going-beyond-intelligence/201703/call-children-s-private-body-parts-what-they-are.

increases in mandatory minimums for CSA, resulting in many life sentences.[54] Sentences for sexual offenders tend to be fairly long compared to other types of criminals, although there is no evidence to suggest that sentence length is associated with a convicted sex offender being rearrested for a sexual crime.[55] Additionally, as discussed in chapter 3, recidivism is relatively low for sexual offenses, and most people age out of all types of crime, including CSA.[56] In other words, each year older a former offender is, the lower the risk they pose to society. At a certain point, incarcerating someone makes no sense from a public-safety perspective—it's just expensive.[57] Additionally, research suggests that sentence length is not related to its value as a deterrent. This is because when a person is thinking about committing a crime, they rarely consider the punishment. They might, however, consider how likely they are to be apprehended.[58] Sentence length is of less consequence because most people optimistically assume that they will not be caught.[59]

---

54. Ashley Nellis, "Still Life: America's Increasing Use of Life and Long-Term Sentences," The Sentencing Project, 2017, https://www.sentencingproject.org/publications/still-life-americas-increasing-use-life-long-term-sentences/.

55. Kristen Budd and Scott A. Desmond, "Sex Offenders and Sex Crime Recidivism: Investigating the Role of Sentence Length and Time Served," *International Journal of Offender Therapy and Comparative Criminology* 58, no. 12 (2014): 1481–99.

56. Andrew John Rawson Harris and Robert Karl Hanson, *Sex Offender Recidivism: A Simple Question* (Ottawa: Minister of Public Safety and Emergency Preparedness, 2004), https://www.publicsafety.gc.ca/cnt/rsrcs/pblctns/sx-ffndr-rc dvsm/index-en.aspx?wbdisable=true; Michael F. Caldwell, "Quantifying the Decline in Juvenile Sexual Recidivism Rates," *Psychology, Public Policy, and Law* 22, no. 4 (2016): 414–26.

57. Marc Mauer, "Long-Term Sentences: Time to Reconsider the Scale of Punishment," *UMKC Law Review* 87 (2018): 113–30, https://www.cmcainternational.org/wp-content/uploads/2019/05/UMKC-Law-Review-Scale-of-Punishment.pdf.

58. Daniel S. Nagin, "Deterrence in the Twenty-First Century," *Crime and Justice* 42, no. 1 (2013): 199–263, https://scholar.google.com/scholar?hl=en&as_sdt=0%2C36&q=Deterrence+in+the+Twenty-First+Century+DS+Nagin&btnG=.

59. Mauer, "Long-Term Sentences": Time to Reconsider the Scale of Punishment," https://www.cmcainternational.org/wp-content/uploads/2019/05/UMKC-Law-Review-Scale-of-Punishment.pdf.

Mass Incarceration

Lengthy sentences contribute to mass incarceration, which has had a devastating impact on poor and minority communities. Here is a terrific TED Talk that made me think about punishment and mass incarceration in a new way: https://www.ted.com/talks/bryan_stevenson_we_need_to_talk_about_an_injustice?language=en.

Another excellent resource about mass incarceration is a documentary called *13th*. If you have a Netflix account, it is well worth watching.

Long sentences are appealing to Americans because, as discussed in chapter 5, society tends to support a retribution theory of punishment.[60] In other words, punishment is seen as a way to make people pay for their crimes. Punishment also serves an expressive purpose. For example, one way to symbolize sorrow and guilt over harm done to child victims is by imposing harsh sentences on the offenders.[61] This can easily turn into a dangerous cycle, however. Sorrow and desire for retribution lead to harsh sentences, but then society needs to justify those sentences, so the level of danger offenders present is exaggerated.[62] This tendency, while understandable, creates a system where people are paying a lot of money to incarcerate people who are not actually very threatening.

---

60. Jody L. Sundt et al., "The Tenacity of the Rehabilitative Ideal: Have Attitudes Toward Offender Treatment Changed?" *Criminal Justice and Behavior* 25, no. 4 (1998): 426–42.

61. Judith Kay, "Murder Victims' Families for Reconciliation: Story-Telling for Healing, as Witness, and in Public Policy," in *Handbook of Restorative Justice: A Global Perspective*, ed. Dennis Sullivan and Larry Tifft (New York: Routledge, 2006), 230–45.

62. Mark Chaffin, "Our Minds Are Made Up—Don't Confuse Us with the Facts: Commentary on Policies Concerning Children with Sexual Behavior Problems and Juvenile Sex Offenders," *Child Maltreatment* 13, no. 2 (2008): 110–21, https://ok-rsol.org/resources/Documents/Chaffin%20-%20Policies%20Concerning%20JSOs%20%28May%202008%29%20-%20Child%20Maltreatment.pdf.

One of the justifications that society uses to explain support for harsh penalties is that victims deserve justice. This argument is based on the assumption that victims want offenders punished with maximum penalties. But is that the case? A recent survey of crime victims finds compelling evidence that many of them support rehabilitative, not retributive, sanctions. In fact, two out of three say that they would prefer that the criminal justice system focus on rehabilitation rather than punishment. Six in ten argue that sentences should be decreased so that more money can be spent on prevention and rehabilitation. Two in three want to see more funding for parole and probation and less to prisons.[63]

One Victim's View of Punishment

Lindsay contributed to the national survey of victims described above. She talked about her experiences following the murder of her sister by her sister's husband. Lindsay said:

Victims and families need help recovering from crime. I've also come to realize that focusing too much on punishment can cause us to lose sight of the big picture. Initially, I was very angry at my brother-in-law and wanted retribution. But with time, I began to think about how the system had failed us all. My brother-in-law had substance abuse addiction issues and had been incarcerated. Did his drug addiction and experience in prison play a role in his loss of control? He's not a bad person. Public safety must be the top priority. But I believe we can best achieve that by helping those with substance abuse and mental health problems. Our criminal justice system should do more to help rehabilitate people like my brother-in-law instead of making them worse off and more likely to commit crimes.[64]

---

63. Alliance for Safety and Justice, *Crime Survivors Speak*, https://alliancefor safetyandjustice.org/wp-content/uploads/documents/Crime%20Survivors%20 Speak%20Report.pdf.

64. Alliance for Safety and Justice, https://allianceforsafetyandjustice.

A final reason to reconsider very long sentences is that they encourage innocent people to take plea bargains. A recent survey with attorneys found that the vast majority (89.1 percent) had been involved in cases where a person who maintained their innocence agreed to a plea bargain. Similarly, nearly 45 percent of the attorneys had advised a client they believed to be innocent to take a plea bargain. When asked to explain why, they listed long mandatory sentences as one of their key considerations. Here are quotes from two of the attorneys in the study:

> Many innocent people take deals when facing draconian mandatory penalties. Faced with decades of prison and offered a year or two, rational people don't even gamble.

> Even if the risks of losing are extremely small, the consequences of losing can change a client's life where the consequences of a plea will not.[65]

Given that lengthy sentences fail to deter crime and encourage innocent people to plead guilty, it is time to rethink them. Of course, this leads to the question of what sentence length should be. Comparing the United States to other Western countries can provide some guidance. The United States incarcerates people much longer than the countries we usually compare ourselves to; for example, European countries rarely incarcerate anyone for more than twenty years.[66] There is a continuum of punitive sentencing, with the United States on one end, Germany and other

---

org/wp-content/uploads/documents/Crime%20Survivors%20Speak%20 Report.pdf.

65. Rebecca K. Helm et al., "Limitations on the Ability to Negotiate Justice: Attorney Perspectives on Guilt, Innocence, and Legal Advice in the Current Plea System," *Psychology, Crime & Law* 24, no. 9 (2018): 915–34, https://www.ncbi.nlm. nih.gov/pmc/articles/PMC6368263/.

66. Mauer, "Long-Term Sentences: Time to Reconsider the Scale of Punishment," https://www.cmcainternational.org/wp-content/uploads/2019/05/ UMKC-Law-Review-Scale-of-Punishment.pdf.

countries in continental Europe on the other, and Canada, the United Kingdom, and Australia in the middle. We could use laws drafted in these other countries as a guidepost for scaling back our own sentences so that we are no longer an outlier.[67]

NEW AND PROMISING DIRECTIONS

Circles of Support and Accountability (COSA)

Circles of Support and Accountability (COSA) is an innovative program that shows promise in lowering recidivism rates among former offenders. People who are soon to be released from prison are provided with what is essentially a support team.[68] The team consists of an "inner circle" of four to six volunteers from the community and an "outer circle" of professionals such as therapists, job counselors, and social workers who are specifically trained to work with sex offenders.[69] The inner circle undergoes background checks, interviews, and training to ensure that they are well equipped to help returning citizens.

The team begins working with an offender (called the "core member") before he or she is released from prison. This enables everyone an opportunity to get to know each other and for the group to help the core member formulate a reentry plan. This is important because studies have found that people with convictions

---

67. Michael Petrunik and Linda Deutschmann, "The Exclusion–Inclusion Spectrum in State and Community Response to Sex Offenders in Anglo-American and European Jurisdictions," *International Journal of Offender Therapy and Comparative Criminology* 52, no. 5 (2008): 499–519.

68. R. J. Wilson, F. Cortoni, and A. J. McWhinnie, "Circles of Support & Accountability: A Canadian National Replication of Outcome Findings," *Sexual Abuse: A Journal of Research and Treatment* 21, no. 4 (2009): 412–30.

69. Kathryn J. Fox, "Contextualizing the Policy and Pragmatics of Reintegrating Sex Offenders," *Sexual Abuse: A Journal of Research and Treatment* 29, no. 1 (2017): 28–50, https://scholar.google.com/scholar?hl=en&as_sdt=0%2C36&q=Fox+Contextualizing+the+Policy+and+Pragmatics+of&btnG=.

for sexual crimes who have more extensive reentry plans prior to being released are less likely to recidivate.[70] Upon release, the COSA meets weekly with the core member. Team members provide support, from advice to social outings. The core member can call either inner or outer circle members if they encounter problems in any area of their lives. While there are some other reintegration models in use, they tend to focus on the physical needs of the formerly incarcerated. The COSA model is unique in its recognition that returning citizens also need social support.

COSA in Canada

Reconciliation and Re-entry Ministries in Canada made a short film for the Canadian Correctional Service about COSAs and the people who participate in them. It can be found here: https://www.youtube.com/watch?v=bUv3BNiqrrk.

The first COSA programs began in Canada and have since spread to the United Kingdom and New Zealand. The United States has been slow to adopt them—but both Vermont and Minnesota now have programs. The relative rarity of this model is unfortunate, however, given research showing that participation in a circle significantly decreases recidivism risk. One study compared COSA participants with people who had committed similar crimes but were not in a circle. The researchers found that the COSA participants were considerably less likely than nonparticipants to return to prison.[71] Another, less well-designed, study followed twenty people assessed to be at high risk of sexual reoffense. All participated in a British COSA and none were charged with a new sexual offense over three years.

---

70. Gwenda M. Willis and Randolph C. Grace, "Assessment of Community Reintegration Planning for Sex Offenders: Poor Planning Predicts Recidivism," *Criminal Justice and Behavior* 36, no. 5 (2009): 494–512.

71. Wilson, Cortoni, and McWhinnie, "Circles of Support & Accountability."

Restorative Justice

The term *restorative justice* covers a huge number of programs and approaches. In general, restorative justice programs are an alternative or supplement to the regular criminal justice system. They bring together victims, offenders, and other stakeholders to arrive at a resolution about how to move forward after a crime. These meetings only occur after an offender has admitted guilt—the point is not to find out what happened, but rather to help resolve the issue.[72] For example, a family whose house had been burgled might come together with the offender to talk about why the burglary happened, what the impact of it was, and what would need to be done to "restore justice." Restorative justice models are generally not applied in cases of child abuse (even when the victim has aged into adulthood) because there is a significant power differential between the victim and the offender and because an encounter with the offender could retraumatize the victim. These are the same reasons why restorative justice is only rarely used in cases of domestic violence.

Restorative Justice Podcast

The podcast called *Justice in America* did a worthwhile episode about restorative justice. It starts with some important information about crime rates and moves on to restorative justice: https://podcasts.apple.com/us/podcast/justice-in-america/id14 10847713?i=1000431679906&mt=2.

Despite the risks associated with using restorative justice for CSA, there are reasons to consider it—at least in some cases. First, a study conducted with adult survivors of child sexual abuse revealed that many of them had not reported their abuse to the

---

72. Clare McGlynn, Nicole Westmarland, and Nikki Godden, "'I Just Wanted Him to Hear Me': Sexual Violence and the Possibilities of Restorative Justice," *Journal of Law and Society* 39, no. 2 (2012): 213–40, http://dro.dur.ac.uk/8809/1/8809. pdf.

police because they felt an emotional tie to their abuser (usually a relative) and did not want that person to go to prison. Having a restorative justice option could make family members more willing to report abuse because it opens punishment options that do not involve prison sentences. Restorative justice also has the potential to overcome limitations built into the criminal justice system. Some of the adult survivors in the study reported that they had become deeply upset when the criminal justice system did not allow them to fully tell their story, their offender would not admit guilt, or the sanctions did not appear to address the root causes of the offending.[73] In restorative justice hearings, victims can gain a better sense of closure because they are given a safe space to confront their abuser directly, ask questions, and talk about the harm the abuse caused.

Why Not Report Abuse?

Luz experienced sexual abuse as both a child and as an adult. Here, she explains why she did not contact law enforcement:

As a youth, I never called Child Protective Services or law enforcement to deal with the perpetrators. I don't think knowing the perpetrators are in prison would have helped me heal and it might have added more trauma in my life because I would have had to testify against them, leaving me with the burden of breaking up my family unit. What I do want is for them to receive the help they need to see the impact of their actions and to value women and children, and to learn to love and be loved in healthy and appropriate ways.[74]

---

73. Shirley Jülich, "Views of Justice among Survivors of Historical Child Sexual Abuse: Implications for Restorative Justice in New Zealand," *Theoretical Criminology* 10, no. 1 (2006): 125–38.

74. Alliance for Safety and Justice, *Crime Survivors Speak*, https://alliancefor safetyandjustice.org/wp-content/uploads/documents/Crime%20Survivors%20 Speak%20Report.pdf.

There is at least one program in Australia that uses a restorative justice model with juvenile sexual offenders. A study of its efficacy, while not methodologically strong, indicated that it decreases recidivism among offenders.[75] Additionally, a case study of a restorative justice meeting between an adult survivor of child rape and the man who abused her shows that—when conducted carefully—such meetings can provide an important opportunity for victims to tell their abusers how the abuse affected them and to hear an apology. In that particular case, the victim prepared herself to meet with the abuser by seeing a counselor for three months. Additionally, a very experienced moderator was brought in to run the session to ensure her emotional safety.[76]

In chapter 4, I talked about how victim impact statements are one way to allow victims an opportunity to tell their abusers about the harms they have suffered. I also, however, talked about the many problems with the use of these statements, particularly in the sentencing phase of a trial. Restorative justice programs have the potential to let victims voice their experiences without some of the problems associated with victim impact statements. Restorative justice programs also have fewer restrictions on how long the victim can talk and what they can talk about. For example, victims can ask questions and offenders have a chance to explain their actions and apologize.[77]

75. Kathleen Daly et al., "Youth Sex Offending, Recidivism and Restorative Justice: Comparing Court and Conference Cases," *Australian & New Zealand Journal of Criminology* 46, no. 2 (2013): 241–67, http://citeseerx.ist.psu.edu/viewdoc/download?doi=10.1.1.1034.1565&rep=rep1&type=pdf.

76. McGlynn, Westmarland, and Godden, "'I Just Wanted Him to Hear Me,'" http://dro.dur.ac.uk/8809/1/8809.pdf.

77. McGlynn, Westmarland, and Godden, http://dro.dur.ac.uk/8809/1/8809.pdf.

Talk about Gender and CSA

Although research clearly shows that the majority of CSA offenders are men,[78] people often try to avoid talking about this fact or its implications. Gender becomes the elephant in the room. When gender does come up, a common response is that the problem is not men per se, but rather a few "bad apples." The bad apple theory is comforting because it allows society to avoid the uncomfortable conclusion that something might be wrong with men or with definitions of masculinity. It does little, however, to explain the gender disparity in CSA offending. If CSA is really caused by bad apples, why are so many of them men? Of course, women also abuse children, but at much lower rates and often alongside men.[79]

Comprehensive solutions to CSA, and to the related crimes of rape and to sexual harassment, are going to have to involve an honest engagement with the issues of gender and power. How do we socialize our boys? What does masculinity mean? One place to start this conversation is in schools. Linda Gordon, a prominent feminist historian, suggests that it's essential to talk frankly with children about power so that both boys and girls have tools to contextualize abuse. In other words, they need to understand that power is not equally distributed in society—some groups such as women, children, people with disabilities, and LGBTQ+ people do not get an equal share. Consequently, members of these groups are more likely to be victims of sexual crimes.[80]

---

78. David Finkelhor et al., "Child Maltreatment Rates Assessed in a National Household Survey of Caregivers and Youth," *Child Abuse & Neglect* 38, no. 9 (2014): 1421–35, http://unh.edu/ccrc/pdf/CV316.pdf; Alissa R. Ackerman et al., "Who Are the People in Your Neighborhood? A Descriptive Analysis of Individuals on Public Sex Offender Registries," *International Journal of Law and Psychiatry* 34, no. 3 (2011): 149–59, https://scholar.google.com/schol ar?hl=en&as_sdt=0%2C36&q=Who+Are+the+People+in+Your+Neighbor hood%3F+A+Descriptive+&btnG=.

79. Katria S. Williams and David M. Bierie, "An Incident-Based Comparison of Female and Male Sexual Offenders," *Sexual Abuse: A Journal of Research and Treatment* 27, no. 3 (2015): 235–57, http://citeseerx.ist.psu.edu/viewdoc/ download?doi=10.1.1.918.1750&rep=rep1&type=pdf.

80. Linda Gordon, "The Politics of Child Sexual Abuse: Notes from

Programs to Reduce Male Violence

Here are some programs working to reduce male violence through deconstructing common ideas of masculinity:

Promundo operates in forty countries, including the United States. It is dedicated to eradicating gender-based violence through both research and community-based outreach. The organization educates both men and women about masculinity and promotes "healthy ways to be a man": https://promun doglobal.org/about/#.

Men Can Stop Rape, based in Washington, DC, has a mission to "mobilize men to use their strength for creating cultures free from violence, especially men's violence against women." The organization has a school-based curriculum for youth as well as a college campus education program: https://mcsr.org/our-vision.

Maine Boys to Men provides training to youth to stop the incidence of male violence. Their programs are used in many middle and high schools in the state: https://maineboystomen.org/.

In chapter 3, I talked about how masculinity may be related to the commission of abuse. The power imbalance among men, women, and children can result in a situation where men feel they have a right to women's and children's bodies.[81] Dominant ideas about masculinity also demand that boys not show weakness or ask for help. When they are victimized, it is especially hard for them to reveal abuse or agree to get to therapy.[82] A reconsideration

American History," *Feminist Review* 28 (1988): 56–64, https://www.jstor.org/stable/1394894?seq=1.

81. Anne Cossins, *Masculinities, Sexualities, and Child Sexual Abuse* (The Hague and Boston: Kluwer Law International, 2000).

82. Ramona Alaggia, Delphine Collin-Vézina, and Rusan Lateef, "Facilitators

of masculinity might have the double advantage of reducing rates of CSA and enabling boys to ask for help when they are victims.

Video about the Construction of Masculinity

Here's an interesting trailer for a film called *The Mask You Live In*, about how the current construction of masculinity hurts boys: https://www.youtube.com/watch?v=hc45-ptHMxo.

CONCLUSION

As you may recall, this book was born when I dragged myself to a CSA prevention program. That training made me question myself and my own opinions. What did I think about CSA? Did my beliefs match the research? Was I blindly supporting problematic public policies? Standing here at the end of this project, I know the answers to these questions. I did hold significant misperceptions about CSA, and many of my beliefs and feelings were shaped less by reality than by what I had read in the media and heard from my friends. My opinions led me to support a number of ineffective, and even harmful, public policies.

I hope that this book has been a useful resource in your own thinking about CSA. What now? It is possible to take steps to work toward CSA prevention. Below, I present a list of some possible actions. Perhaps some will interest you as you move forward in your efforts to protect children.

- Intervene when someone mischaracterizes CSA. This suggestion is tough because it requires overcoming the spiral of silence. At the same time, it is important to educate people so that society can make better policy decisions.

---

and Barriers to Child Sexual Abuse (CSA) Disclosures: A Research Update (2000–2016)," *Trauma, Violence, & Abuse* 20, no. 2 (2017): 260–83, https://journals.sage pub.com/doi/pdf/10.1177/1524838017697312.

- Critically analyze media coverage about CSA. When reading an article, think about the frame that is being employed and how it may affect your reaction. Is the coverage episodic? Does the story cover an extreme case? Link the answers to these questions to the feelings of fear and blame discussed in chapters 1 and 5.

- Challenge your own and others' assumptions about children. How, for example, does the view of the ideal victim cause belief in the claims of some children over others? How does the view of children as innocent affect the ability to recognize that children sometimes harm other children? How does it prevent teaching children information about sexuality that could help them protect themselves from CSA?

- Call your congressperson about a policy you find problematic. For example, address the registry, background checks, or residency requirements. You can find contact information for your federal, state, and local representatives at https://www.usa.gov/elected-officials.

- Donate to your local Children's Advocacy Center or other organization that provides support to child victims (like the courthouse dogs program talked about in chapter 4).

- Call the victim assistance department of the local court and find out how to help victims navigate the criminal justice system. Some offer opportunities to become a guardian ad litem. In this capacity, one would accompany a child through a court case and then would have a role in advocating for their interests to the judge.

- Find out about local reentry initiatives. Volunteer to work with people leaving prison. There might even be a COSA in the area. If not, enlist support from the community and start one.

- Sign up to be a facilitator for CSA prevention workshops. The Catholic Church offers this option, but you may be able to find opportunities through your place of worship or through a local scouting or other nonprofit organization.

- Challenge the local school to think about the participation restrictions they put on employees and volunteers. Are these restrictions really necessary for the protection of children? Or are they a result of net widening?

- Before you vote on criminal justice issues, think through your own ideas about sentencing. Are you reacting out of fear or out of mischaracterizations of who offenders really are? What would really help to protect children?

- Consider the restrictions you put on your own children. If they are primarily based on fear and not on an honest assessment of risk, consider loosening those restrictions.

- If you are interested in learning more about initiatives to scale back the registry or to change other public policies toward sex offenders, check out the National Association for Rational Sex Offense Laws (NARSOL). Their website has links to all sorts of up-to-the-minute information at https://narsol.org/.

- Think about whether and how you are talking to your kids about sex and CSA prevention. Make sure that you talk to them about bodily integrity and give them the words they need to describe their own bodies. The Chicago Children's Advocacy Center has a great reading list for children about CSA prevention, sexual development, and healing from abuse. Here is the link: https://www.chicagocac.org/books-children-sexual-abuse/.

- Bring a program that trains boys on how to develop a healthy masculinity to your community or schools (see some examples of these programs in the box above).

Acknowledgments

First, l am grateful to Lever Press. l believe that information about CSA prevention should be free and accessible to everyone. Lever Press is the only academic press that does not charge authors for open access. l appreciate their mission and commitment to social justice.

This book would not have been possible without Heather Fitz Gibbon, Susie Sargent, and Deborah Turner. They read and edited endless drafts and provided invaluable support. Patrick Carr also provided important feedback early on. He died in April of 2020 as l was working on the final revisions. l truly miss his laughter, friendship, and keen sociological mind.

Sharon Minson supported and helped design my evaluation of adult prevention programs. l have come to greatly value her wisdom as well as her friendship.

Much credit goes to the research assistance of Lydia Reedstrom and Melina Mera. They worked diligently and patiently, often catching details that escaped my notice. l look forward to the research they will produce one day.

Two anonymous reviewers took the time to read the manuscript carefully and give me detailed feedback. Lever Press editor Beth Bouloukos also provided helpful advice.

The sections of this book about the Protecting God's Children prevention program were made possible by the hundreds of participants who filled out pre- and posttests and allowed me to take notes during the sessions. The administrators and facilitators of the program were always helpful and welcoming, granting me access to prevention sessions and to facilitator training. I admire their commitment to protecting children.

I have spent my career at the College of Wooster and am deeply indebted to the support it has provided for my work. Without a research leave, I would not have had the time and space to write this book. I am also grateful for the help of the librarians and IT staff.

Thanks and love, as always, to my parents as well as to John, Alexander, and Gabriel Thompson and Jacob Nurse.

Bibliography

Abel, Gene G., Judith V. Becker, Mary Mittelman, Jerry Cunningham-Rathner, Joanne Rouleau, and William D. Murphy. "Self-Reported Sex Crimes of Non-incarcerated Paraphiliacs." *Journal of Interpersonal Violence* 2, no. 1 (1987): 3–25.

Ackerman, Alissa R., Andrew J. Harris, Jill S. Levenson, and Kristen Zgoba. "Who Are the People in Your Neighborhood? A Descriptive Analysis of Individuals on Public Sex Offender Registries." *International Journal of Law and Psychiatry* 34, no. 3 (2011): 149–59.

Agan, Amanda Y. "Sex Offender Registries: Fear without Function?" *Journal of Law and Economics* 54, no. 1 (2011): 207–39.

Alaggia, Ramona, Delphine Collin-Vézina, and Rusan Lateef. "Facilitators and Barriers to Child Sexual Abuse (CSA) Disclosures: A Research Update (2000–2016)." *Trauma, Violence & Abuse* 20, no. 2 (2017): 260–83.

Alexander, Kate, Anne Stafford, and Ruth Lewis. "The Experiences of Children Participating in Organised Sport in the UK." London: National Society for the Prevention of Cruelty to Children, 2011.

Alexander, Michelle. *The New Jim Crow: Mass Incarceration in the Age of Colorblindness*. Rev. ed. New York: New Press, 2012.

Alliance for Safety and Justice. *Crime Survivors Speak: The First-Ever National Survey of Victims' Views on Safety and Justice*. Oakland, CA: Alliance for Safety and Justice, 2016. https://allianceforsafetyandjustice.org/wp-content/uploads/documents/Crime%20Survivors%20Speak%20Report.pdf.

Altheide, David L., and R. Sam Michalowski. "Fear in the News: A Discourse of Control." *The Sociological Quarterly* 40, no. 3 (1999): 475–503.

American Civil Liberties Union. "Lake Michigan College Agrees to Individual-ized Review of Students with Criminal Records, ACLU Announces." American Civil Liberties Union, June 22, 2011. https://www.aclu.org/press-releases/lake-michigan-college-agrees-individualized-review-students-criminal-records-aclu.

American Civil Liberties Union of Rhode Island. "ACLU Settles Law-suit over Cranston School District Volunteer Policy." American Civil Liberties Union, December 27, 2012. https://www.aclu.org/news/aclu-settles-lawsuit-over-cranston-school-district-volunteer-policy.

American Public Health Association. "What Is Public Health?" APHA: For Science, for Action, for Health, 2019. https://www.apha.org/what-is-public-health.

Anderson, Kristen D., and Dawn Daly. *What You Need to Know about Background Screening*. Washington, DC: U.S. Department of Justice and the National Center for Missing and Exploited Children, June 2013. https://rems.ed.gov/docs/COPS_NCMEC_Background-Screening.pdf.

Andrews, D. A., James Bonta, and J. Stephen Wormith. "The Recent Past and near Future of Risk and/or Need Assessment." *Crime & Delinquency* 52, no. 1 (2006): 7–27.

Applegate, Brandon K., Francis T. Cullen, Michael G. Turner, and Jody L. Sundt. "Assessing Public Support for Three-Strikes-and-You're out Laws: Global versus Specific Attitudes." *Crime & Delinquency* 42, no. 4 (1996): 517–34.

Assink, Mark, Claudia E. van der Put, Mandy W. C. M. Meeuwsen, Nynke M. de Jong, Frans J. Oort, Geert Jan J. M. Stams, and Machteld Hoeve. "Risk Factors for Child Sexual Abuse Victimization: A Meta-Analytic Review." *Psychological Bulletin* 145, no. 5 (2019): 459–89.

Associated Press. "Fla. Gets Tough New Child-Sex Law—CBS News." CBS News, May 2, 2005. https://www.cbsnews.com/news/fla-gets-tough-new-child-sex-law/.

———. "Memory Issue Prompts Retrial in Murder Case." *New York Times*, November 21, 1995. https://www.nytimes.com/1995/11/21/us/memory-issue-prompts-retrial-in-murder-case.html.

Association for the Treatment of Sexual Abusers. "Civil Commitment." Association for the Treatment of Sexual Abusers, 2017. http://www.atsa.com/civil-commitment-2.

Babcock, Ernest J. "Next Generation Identification (NGI)—Retention and Searching of Noncriminal Justice Fingerprint Submissions." Federal Bureau of Investigation, February 20, 2015. https://www.fbi.gov/services/records-management/foipa/privacy-impact-assessments/next-generation-identification-ngi-retention-and-searching-of-noncriminal-justice-fingerprint-submissions.

Back, Sudie, and Hilary M. Lips. "Child Sexual Abuse: Victim Age, Victim Gender, and Observer Gender as Factors Contributing to Attributions of Responsibility." *Child Abuse & Neglect* 22, no. 12 (1998): 1239–52.

Bales, William D., and Alex R. Piquero. "Racial/Ethnic Differentials in Sentencing to Incarceration." *Justice Quarterly* 29, no. 5 (2012): 742–73.

Bandes, Susan A. "What Are Victim-Impact Statements For?" *Atlantic*, July 23, 2016. https://www.theatlantic.com/politics/archive/2016/07/what-are-victim-impact-statements-for/492443/.

Barbaree, Howard E., Calvin M. Langton, and Edward J. Peacock. "Different Actuarial Risk Measures Produce Different Risk Rankings for Sexual Offenders." *Sexual Abuse: A Journal of Research and Treatment* 18, no. 4 (2006): 423–40.

Barth, F. Diane. "How Confirmation Bias Affects You Every Single Day." *Psychology Today* (blog), December 31, 2017. https://www.psychologytoday.com/us/blog/the-couch/201712/how-confirmation-bias-affects-you-every-single-day.

Bartos, Leah. "Failure to Protect: Should Victims of Domestic Violence Face Child Abuse Charges?" *California Health Report* (blog), October 28, 2015. https://www.calhealthreport.org/2015/10/27/failure-to-protect-should-victims-of-domestic-violence-face-child-abuse-charges/.

Bass, Ellen, and Laura Davis. *The Courage to Heal: A Guide for Women Survivors of Child Sexual Abuse: Featuring "Honoring the Truth, a Response to the Backlash."* 3rd ed., rev. up. New York: HarperPerennial, 1994.

Bazelon, Emily. "Abuse Cases, and a Legacy of Skepticism." *New York Times*, June 9, 2014. https://www.nytimes.com/2014/06/10/science/the-witch-hunt-narrative-are-we-dismissing-real-victims.html.

Beck, Allen, David Cantor, John Hartge, and Tim Smith. *Sexual Victimization in Juvenile Facilities Reported by Youth, 2012.* Washington, DC: Bureau of Justice Statistics, 2012.

Beck, Allen J., and Romana R. Rantala. *Sexual Victimization Reported by Juvenile Correctional Authorities, 2007–12.* Washington, DC: US Department of Justice, January 2016. https://www.hivlawandpolicy.org/sites/default/files/Sexual%20Victimization%20Reported%20by%20Juvenile%20Correctional%20Authorities,%202007-12.pdf.

Beck, Richard. *We Believe the Children: A Moral Panic in the 1980s.* 1st ed. New York: PublicAffairs, 2015.

Beckett, Katherine. "Culture and the Politics of Signification: The Case of Child Sexual Abuse." *Social Problems* 43, no. 1 (1996): 57–76.

Beier, Klaus M., Umut C. Oezdemir, Eliza Schlinzig, Anna Groll, Elena Hupp, and Tobias Hellenschmidt. "'Just Dreaming of Them': The Berlin Project for Primary Prevention of Child Sexual Abuse by Juveniles (PPJ)." *Child Abuse & Neglect* 52 (2016): 1–10.

Bell, Vikki. *Interrogating Incest: Feminism, Foucault, and the Law*. London and New York: Routledge, 1993.

Bennett, Natalie, and William O'Donohue. "The Construct of Grooming in Child Sexual Abuse: Conceptual and Measurement Issues." *Journal of Child Sexual Abuse* 23, no. 8 (2014): 957–76.

Berg, Chantal van den, Karin Beijersbergen, Paul Nieuwbeerta, and Anja Dirkzwager. "Sex Offenders in Prison: Are They Socially Isolated?" *Sexual Abuse: A Journal of Research and Treatment* 30, no. 7 (2017): 828–45.

Berlin, Fred S., Martin Malin, and Sharon Dean. "Effects of Statutes Requiring Psychiatrists to Report Suspected Sexual Abuse of Children." *American Journal of Psychiatry* 148, no. 4 (1991): 449–53.

Berrick, Jill Duerr. "Parental Involvement in Child Abuse Prevention Training: What Do They Learn?" *Child Abuse & Neglect* 12, no. 4 (1988): 543–53.

Best, Joel. *Threatened Children: Rhetoric and Concern about Child-Victims*. Chicago: University of Chicago Press, 1990.

Blackwell, Suzanne, and Fred Seymour. "Prediction of Jury Verdicts in Child Sexual Assault Trials." *Psychiatry, Psychology and Law* 21, no. 4 (2014): 567–76.

Bleyer, Jennifer. "Sympathy for the Deviant." *Psychology Today*, November 3, 2015. https://www.psychologytoday.com/articles/201511/sympathy-the-deviant.

Blinder, Alan. "What to Know about the Alabama Chemical Castration Law." *New York Times*, June 11, 2019. https://www.nytimes.com/2019/06/11/us/politics/chemical-castration.html.

Bomey, Nathan, Lindsay Schnell, and Cara Kelly. "Boy Scouts Files Chapter 11 Bankruptcy in the Face of Thousands of Child Abuse Allegations." *USA Today*, February 18, 2020. https://www.usatoday.com/in-depth/news/investigations/2020/02/18/boy-scouts-bsa-chapter-11-bankruptcy-sexual-abuse-cases/1301187001/.

Bonilla-Silva, Eduardo. "The Invisible Weight of Whiteness: The Racial Grammar of Everyday Life in Contemporary America." *Ethnic and Racial Studies* 35, no. 2 (2012): 173–94.

Bonnie, Richard J., and Elizabeth S. Scott. "The Teenage Brain: Adolescent Brain Research and the Law." *Current Directions in Psychological Science* 22, no. 2 (2013): 158–61.

Borgers, Natacha, Edith de Leeuw, and Joop Hox. "Children as Respondents in Survey Research: Cognitive Development and Response Quality 1." *Bulletin of Sociological Methodology/Bulletin de Méthodologie Sociologique* 66, no. 1 (2000): 60–75.

Bouffard, Jeff A., and LaQuana N. Askew. "Time-Series Analyses of the Impact of Sex Offender Registration and Notification Law Implementation and

Subsequent Modifications on Rates of Sexual Offenses." *Crime & Delinquency* 65, no. 11 (2017): 483–1512.

Bourdieu, Pierre. *Language and Symbolic Power.* Edited by John B. Thompson. Translated by Gino Raymond and Matthew Adamson. Cambridge: Harvard University Press, 2003.

Brackenridge, Celia H. "'. . . So What?' Attitudes of the Voluntary Sector towards Child Protection in Sports Clubs." *Managing Leisure* 7, no. 2 (2002): 103–23.

———. "'He Owned Me Basically . . .' Women's Experience of Sexual Abuse in Sport." *International Review for the Sociology of Sport* 32, no. 2 (1997): 115–30.

Braithwaite, Jeremy. "Colonized Silence: Confronting the Colonial Link in Rural Alaska Native Survivors' Non-Disclosure of Child Sexual Abuse." *Journal of Child Sexual Abuse* 27, no. 6 (2018): 589–611.

Brown, Donna M. "Evaluation of Safer, Smarter Kids: Child Sexual Abuse Prevention Curriculum for Kindergartners." *Child and Adolescent Social Work Journal* 34, no. 3 (2017): 213–22.

Brown, Leonard G., III, and Kevin Gallagher. "Mandatory Reporting of Abuse: A Historical Perspective on the Evolution of States' Current Mandatory Reporting Laws with a Review of the Laws in the Commonwealth of Pennsylvania." *Villanova Law Review* 59 (2015): 45.

Brown, Jocelyn, Patricia Cohen, Jeffrey G. Johnson, and Suzanne Salzinger. "A Longitudinal Analysis of Risk Factors for Child Maltreatment: Findings of a 17-Year Prospective Study of Officially Recorded and Self-Reported Child Abuse and Neglect." *Child Abuse & Neglect* 22, no. 11 (1998): 1065–78.

Brown, Steven. "City Officials Stoke Mob Mentality in Front of Sex Offender's Home." American Civil Liberties Union, October 24, 2018. https://www.aclu.org/blog/free-speech/rights-protesters/city-officials-stoke-mob-mentality-front-sex-offenders-home.

Budd, Kristen, and Scott A. Desmond. "Sex Offenders and Sex Crime Recidivism: Investigating the Role of Sentence Length and Time Served." *International Journal of Offender Therapy and Comparative Criminology* 58, no. 12 (2014): 1481–99.

Budd, Kristen M., and Christina Mancini. "Public Perceptions of GPS Monitoring for Convicted Sex Offenders: Opinions on Effectiveness of Electronic Monitoring to Reduce Sexual Recidivism." *International Journal of Offender Therapy and Comparative Criminology* 61, no. 12 (2017): 1335–53.

Bumby, Kurt M., and David J. Hansen. "Intimacy Deficits, Fear of Intimacy, and Loneliness among Sexual Offenders." *Criminal Justice and Behavior* 24, no. 3 (1997): 315–31.

Burch, Traci. "Skin Color and the Criminal Justice System: Beyond Black-White

Disparities in Sentencing." *Journal of Empirical Legal Studies* 12, no. 3 (2015): 395–420.

Buschmann, Christina. "Mandatory Fingerprinting of Public School Teachers: Facilitating Background Checks or Infringing on Individuals' Constitutional Rights?" *William & Mary Bill of Rights Journal* 11, no. 3 (2003): 1273–1307.

Butler, Edgar W., Hiroshi Fukarai, Jo-Ellan Dimitrius, and Richard Krooth. *Anatomy of the McMartin Child Molestation Case.* Lanham, MD: University Press of America, 2001.

Butt, Riazat. "Sex Abuse Rife in Other Religions, Says Vatican." *Guardian*, September 28, 2009. https://www.theguardian.com/world/2009/sep/28/sex-abuse-religion-vatican.

Button, Deeanna M., Matthew DeMichele, and Brian K. Payne. "Using Electronic Monitoring to Supervise Sex Offenders: Legislative Patterns and Implications for Community Corrections Officers." *Criminal Justice Policy Review* 20, no. 4 (2009): 414–36.

Caldwell, Michael F. "Quantifying the Decline in Juvenile Sexual Recidivism Rates." *Psychology, Public Policy, and Law* 22, no. 4 (2016): 414–26.

California Department of Corrections. "Laws Related to Sex Offender Parolees." Division of Adult Parole Operations (DAPO), 2020. https://www.cdcr.ca.gov/parole/sex-offender-laws/.

Calvert, James F., and Michelle Munsie-Benson. "Public Opinion and Knowledge about Childhood Sexual Abuse in a Rural Community." *Child Abuse & Neglect* 23, no. 7 (1999): 671–682.

Campbell, Bradley A., Tasha A. Menaker, and William R. King. "The Determination of Victim Credibility by Adult and Juvenile Sexual Assault Investigators." *Journal of Criminal Justice* 43, no. 1 (2015): 29–39.

Cantor, James M., and Ian V. McPhail. "Non-Offending Pedophiles." *Current Sexual Health Reports* 8, no. 3 (2016): 121–28.

Cavender, Gray. "Media and Crime Policy: A Reconsideration of David Garland's the Culture of Control." *Punishment & Society* 6, no. 3 (2004): 335–48.

Ceci, Stephen J., and Maggie Bruck. *Jeopardy in the Courtroom: A Scientific Analysis of Children's Testimony.* Washington, DC: American Psychological Association, 1996.

Cense, Marianne, and Celia H. Brackenridge. "Temporal and Developmental Risk Factors for Sexual Harassment and Abuse in Sport." *European Physical Education Review* 7, no. 1 (2001): 61–79.

Chaffin, Mark. "Our Minds Are Made Up—Don't Confuse Us with the Facts: Commentary on Policies Concerning Children with Sexual Behavior Problems and Juvenile Sex Offenders." *Child Maltreatment* 13, no. 2 (2008): 110–21.

———, Jill Levenson, Elizabeth Letourneau, and Paul Stern. "How Safe Are Trick-or-Treaters? An Analysis of Child Sex Crime Rates on Halloween." *Sexual Abuse: A Journal of Research and Treatment* 21, no. 3 (2009): 363–74.

Chalfin, Aaron, and Justin McCrary. "Criminal Deterrence: A Review of the Literature." *Journal of Economic Literature* 55, no. 1 (2017): 5–48.

Chamorro-Premuzic, Tomas. "How the Web Distorts Reality and Impairs Our Judgement Skills." *Guardian*, May 13, 2014. https://www.theguardian.com/media-network/media-network-blog/2014/may/13/internet-confirmation-bias.

Cheit, Ross E. "What Hysteria? A Systematic Study of Newspaper Coverage of Accused Child Molesters." *Child Abuse & Neglect* 27, no. 6 (2003): 607–23.

Cheung, Ariel. "Reduced Charges Common for Child Sex Assault." Post Crescent, January 25, 2015. https://www.postcrescent.com/story/news/local/2015/01/25/outagamie-county-child-sex-assaults-part-two/22179753/.

Child Welfare Information Gateway. *Mandatory Reporters of Child Abuse and Neglect*. Washington, DC: US Department of Health and Human Services, Children's Bureau, 2016. https://www.childwelfare.gov/pubpdfs/manda.pdf.

Children's Bureau/Administration on Children, Youth and Families/Administration for Children and Families/Health and Human Services. "Child Maltreatment 2016: Summary of Key Findings." Numbers and Trends. Washington, DC: Child Welfare Information Gateway, 2018. https://www.acf.hhs.gov/sites/default/files/cb/cm2016.pdf.

Christensen, Kim. "Scouts Employ Aggressive Tactics in Abuse Defense." *Los Angeles Times*, December 24, 2012. http://www.latimes.com/local/california/la-me-scouts-victims-2-story.html.

Christie, Nils. "The Ideal Victim." In *From Crime Policy to Victim Policy: Reorienting the Justice System*, edited by Ezzat A. Fattah, 17–30. London: MacMillan, 1990.

Clark, C. Brendan, Adam Perkins, Cheryl B. McCullumsmith, M. Aminul Islam, Erin E. Hanover, and Karen L. Cropsey. "Characteristics of Victims of Sexual Abuse by Gender and Race in a Community Corrections Population." *Journal of Interpersonal Violence* 27, no. 9 (2012): 1844–61.

Collings, Steven J. "Development, Reliability, and Validity for the Child Sexual Abuse Myth Scale." *Journal of Interpersonal Violence* 12, no. 5 (1997): 665–74.

Colorado Department of Public Safety. *Report on Safety Issues Raised by Living Arrangements for and Location of Sex Offenders in the Community*. Denver: Division of Criminal Justice, Colorado Department of Public Safety, 2004.

Colson, Marie-Hélène, Laurent Boyer, Karine Baumstarck, and Anderson D. Loundou. "Female Sex Offenders: A Challenge to Certain Paradigms." *Sexologies* 22, no. 4 (2013): 109–17.

Cortoni, Franca, and R. Karl Hanson. *A Review of the Recidivism Rates of Adult Female Sexual Offenders*. Ottawa: Correctional Service of Canada, May 2005. http://saratso.org/pdf/Corton_and_Hanson-2005.pdf.

Cossins, Anne. *Masculinities, Sexualities, and Child Sexual Abuse*. The Hague and Boston: Kluwer Law International, 2000.

Couture, Denise. "Texas Judge Allows Former Baylor Frat President to Sidestep Rape Charge." National Public Radio, December 11, 2018. https://www.npr.org/2018/12/11/675691750/texas-judge-sentences-former-baylor-frat-president-to-sidestep-rape-charge.

Coyne, Randall T. "Shooting the Wounded: First Degree Murder and Second Class Victims." *Oklahoma City University Law Review* 28 (2003): 93–117.

Crenshaw, Wesley B. "When Educators Confront Child Abuse: An Analysis of the Decision to Report." *Child Abuse & Neglect* 19, no. 9 (1995): 1095–1113.

Cross, Theodore P., Lisa M. Jones, Wendy A. Walsh, Monique Simone, David J. Kolko, Joyce Szczepanski, Tonya Lippert, et al. "Evaluating Children's Advocacy Centers' Response to Child Sexual Abuse." American Psychological Association, 2008. https://scholar.google.com/scholar?hl=en&as_sdt=0%2C36&q=Evaluating+Children's+Advocacy+Centers'+Response&btnG=.

Cross, Theodore P., Wendy A. Walsh, Monique Simone, and Lisa M. Jones. "Prosecution of Child Abuse: A Meta-Analysis of Rates of Criminal Justice Decisions." *Trauma, Violence, & Abuse* 4, no. 4 (2003): 323–40.

Cutajar, Margaret C., James R. P. Ogloff, and Paul E. Mullen. "Child Sexual Abuse and Subsequent Offending and Victimisation: A 45-Year Follow-up Study." Canberra, Australia: Criminology Research Council, 2011. http://citeseerx.ist.psu.edu/viewdoc/download?doi=10.1.1.421.9799&rep=rep1&type=pdf.

Cyr, Mireille, John Wright, Pierre McDuff, and Alain Perron. "Intrafamilial Sexual Abuse: Brother–Sister Incest Does Not Differ from Father–Daughter and Stepfather–Stepdaughter Incest." *Child Abuse & Neglect* 26, no. 9 (2002): 957–73.

Daly, Kathleen, Brigitte Bouhours, Roderic Broadhurst, and Nini Loh. "Youth Sex Offending, Recidivism and Restorative Justice: Comparing Court and Conference Cases." *Australian & New Zealand Journal of Criminology* 46, no. 2 (2013): 241–67.

Daro, Deborah A. "Prevention of Child Sexual Abuse." *Future of Children* 4, no. 2 (1994): 198–223.

Daugnault, Isabelle V., Mireille Cyr, and Martine Hébert. "Working with Non-Offending Parents in Cases of Child Sexual Abuse." In *The Wiley Handbook of What Works in Child Maltreatment: An Evidence-Based Approach to Assessment and Intervention in Child Protection*, edited by Louise Dixon, Daniel F. Perkins,

Catherine Hamilton-Giachritsis, and Leam A. Craig, 415–32. Hoboken, NJ: John Wiley & Sons, 2017.

De Francis, Vincent. *Protecting the Child Victim of Sex Crimes Committed by Adults: Final Report*. Denver, CO: American Humane Association, Children's Division, 1969.

Dell'Angela, Tracy. "Schools Embrace Parents' Help—after Background Check." *Chicago Tribune*, June 2002. https://www.chicagotribune.com/news/ct-xpm-2002-06-18-0206180164-story.html.

Denver, Megan, Garima Siwach, and Shawn D. Bushway. "A New Look at the Employment and Recidivism Relationship through the Lens of a Criminal Background Check." *Criminology* 55, no. 1 (2017): 174–204.

Devlin, Rachel. "'Acting out the Oedipal Wish': Father-Daughter Incest and the Sexuality of Adolescent Girls in the United States, 1941–1965." *Journal of Social History* 38, no. 3 (2005): 609–33.

deYoung, Mary. "The Devil Goes to Daycare: McMartin and the Making of a Moral Panic." *Journal of American Culture* 20, no. 1 (1997): 19–25.

Diocese of Victoria. "Misconduct Reporting." The Catholic Diocese of Victoria in Texas, 2019. https://victoriadiocese.org/misconduct-reporting.

Duane, Marina, Nancy La Vigne, Mathew Lynch, and Emily Reimal. "Criminal Background Checks." Washington, DC: The Urban Institute, 2017. https://www.urban.org/sites/default/files/publication/88621/2001174_criminal_background_checks_impact_on_employment_and_recidivism_1.pdf.

Dube, Shanta, Robert F. Anda, M. D. Whitfield, David W. Brown, Vincent J. Felitti, Maxia Dong, and Wayne H. Giles. "Long-Term Consequences of Childhood Sexual Abuse by Gender of Victim." *American Journal of Preventive Medicine* 28, no. 5 (2005): 430–38.

EchoHawk, Larry, and Tessa Meyer Santiago. "What Indian Tribes Can Do to Combat Child Sexual Abuse." *Tribal Law Journal* 4 (2004). http://lawschool.unm.edu/tlj/volumes/vol4/abuse/index.html.

Elliot, Michele, Kevin Browne, and Jennifer Kilcoyne. "Child Sexual Abuse Prevention: What Offenders Tell Us." *Child Abuse and Neglect* 19, no. 5 (1995): 579–94.

Ellman, Ira Mark, and Tara Ellman. "'Frightening and High': The Supreme Court's Crucial Mistake about Sex Crime Statistics." *Constitutional Commentary* 30 (2015): 495–508.

Everson, Mark D., and Barbara W. Boat. "False Allegations of Sexual Abuse by Children and Adolescents." *Journal of the American Academy of Child & Adolescent Psychiatry* 28, no. 2 (1989): 230–35.

Federal Bureau of Investigations. *June 2019 next Generation Identification System Fact Sheet*. Washington, DC: Federal Bureau of Investigations, 2019.

Felch, Jason, and Kim Christensen. "Boy Scout Files Reveal Repeat Child Abuse by Sexual Predators." *Los Angeles Times*, August 4, 2012. http://www.latimes.com/local/la-me-boyscouts-20120805-m-story.html.

Feld, Barry C. "Abolish the Juvenile Court: Youthfulness, Criminal Responsibility, and Sentencing Policy." *Journal of Criminal Law and Criminology* 88, no. 1 (1997): 68–136.

Fergusson, David M., Joseph M. Boden, and L. John Horwood. "Exposure to Childhood Sexual and Physical Abuse and Adjustment in Early Adulthood." *Child Abuse & Neglect* 32, no. 6 (2008): 607–19.

Filler, Daniel M. "Silence and the Racial Dimension of Megan's Law." *Iowa Law Review* 89 (2004): 1535–94.

Finkelhor, David. *Childhood Victimization: Violence, Crime and Abuse in the Lives of Young People.* New York: Oxford University Press, 2008.

———. *Sexually Victimized Children.* New York: Free Press, 1979.

———, and Lisa M. Jones. "Have Sexual Abuse and Physical Abuse Declined since the 1990s?" Durham, NH: Crimes against Children Research Center, 2012. http://scholars.unh.edu/ccrc/61/.

———, and N. Strapko. "Sexual Abuse Prevention Education: A Review of Evaluation Studies." In *Prevention of Child Maltreatment: Developmental and Ecological Processes*, edited by D. Willis, E. Holder, and M. Rosenberg. New York: Wiley, 1987.

———, Anne Shattuck, Heather A. Turner, and Sherry L. Hamby. "The Lifetime Prevalence of Child Sexual Abuse and Sexual Assault Assessed in Late Adolescence." *Journal of Adolescent Health* 55, no. 3 (2014): 329–33. http://www.sciencedirect.com/science/article/pii/S1054139X13008549.

———, Gerald Hotaling, I. A Lewis, and Christine Smith. "Sexual Abuse in a National Survey of Adult Men and Women: Prevalence, Characteristics, and Risk Factors." *Child Abuse & Neglect* 14, no. 1 (1990): 19–28.

———, Jennifer Vanderminden, Heather Turner, Sherry Hamby, and Anne Shattuck. "Child Maltreatment Rates Assessed in a National Household Survey of Caregivers and Youth." *Child Abuse & Neglect* 38, no. 9 (2014): 1421–35.

———, Kei Saito, and Lisa Jones. "Updated Trends in Child Maltreatment, 2018." Durham, NH: Crimes against Children Research Center, 2020. http://www.unh.edu/ccrc/pdf/CV203%20-%20Updated%20trends%202018_ks_df.pdf.

———, Nancy Asdigian, and Jennifer Dziuba-Leatherman. "The Effectiveness of Victimization Prevention Instruction: An Evaluation of Children's Responses to Actual Threats and Assaults." *Child Abuse & Neglect* 19, no. 2 (1995): 141–53.

———, Richard Ormrod, and Mark Chaffin. "Juveniles Who Commit Sex Offenses against Minors." *Juvenile Justice Bulletin.* Washington, DC: US Government Printing Office, 2009.

————, Richard Ormrod, Heather Turner, and Sherry L. Hamby. "The Victimization of Children and Youth: A Comprehensive National Survey." *Child Maltreatment* 10, no. 1 (2005): 5–25.

Flatow, Nicole. "Inside Miami's Hidden Tent City for 'Sex Offenders.'" ThinkProgress, October 23, 2014. https://thinkprogress.org/inside-miamis-hidden-tent-city-for-sex-offenders-5c9356a45d1f/.

Fontes, Lisa Aronson. "Sin Vergüenza: Addressing Shame with Latino Victims of Child Sexual Abuse and Their Families." *Journal of Child Sexual Abuse* 16, no. 1 (2007): 61–83.

Forliti, Amy. "Supreme Court Won't Hear Minnesota Sex Offender Case." *Twin Cities Pioneer Press*, October 2, 2017. https://www.twincities.com/2017/10/02/supreme-court-wont-hear-minnesota-sex-offender-case/.

Fortney, Timothy, Jill Levenson, Yolanda Brannon, and Juanita N. Baker. "Myths and Facts about Sexual Offenders: Implications for Treatment and Public Policy." *Sexual Offender Treatment* 2, no. 1 (2007): 1–15.

Foster, Jennifer M., and W. Bryce Hagedorn. "Through the Eyes of the Wounded: A Narrative Analysis of Children's Sexual Abuse Experiences and Recovery Process." *Journal of Child Sexual Abuse* 23, no. 5 (2014): 538–57.

Fox, Kathryn J. "Contextualizing the Policy and Pragmatics of Reintegrating Sex Offenders." *Sexual Abuse: A Journal of Research and Treatment* 29, no. 1 (2017): 28–50.

Freedman, Estelle B. "'Uncontrolled Desires': The Response to the Sexual Psychopath, 1920–1960." *Journal of American History* 74, no. 1 (1987): 83–106.

Freeman, Naomi J., Jeffrey C. Sandler, and Kelly M. Socia. "A Time-Series Analysis on the Impact of Sex Offender Registration and Community Notification Laws on Plea Bargaining Rates." *Criminal Justice Studies* 22, no. 2 (2009): 153–65.

Frenzel, Roy R., Reuben A. Lang, and Pierre Flor-Henry. "Sex Hormone Profiles in Pedophilic and Incestuous Men." *Annals of Sex Research* 3 (1990): 59–74.

Furby, Lita, Mark R. Weinrott, and Lyn Blackshaw. "Sex Offender Recidivism: A Review." *Psychological Bulletin* 105, no. 1 (1989): 3–30.

Fuselier, Daniel A., Robert L. Durham, and Sandy K. Wurtele. "The Child Sexual Abuser: Perceptions of College Students and Professionals." *Sexual Abuse: A Journal of Research and Treatment* 14, no. 3 (2002): 271–280.

Gartner, Richard B. "Talking about Sexually Abused Boys, and the Men They Become." *Psychology Today* (blog), January 30, 2011. http://www.psychologytoday.com/blog/psychoanalysis-30/201101/talking-about-sexually-abused-boys-and-the-men-they-become.

Garven, Sena, James M. Wood, Roy S. Malpass, and John S. Shaw. "More Than

Suggestion: The Effect of Interviewing Techniques from the McMartin Pre-school Case" *Journal of Applied Psychology* 83, no. 3 (1998): 347–59. http://eye-witness.utep.edu/Documents/Garven&98MoreThanSuggestion.pdf.

General Accounting Office. *Criminal History Records: Additional Actions Could Enhance the Completeness of Records Used for Employment-Related Background Checks*. Washington, DC, 2015. https://digitalcommons.ilr.cornell.edu/key_workplace/1393/.

Gibson, Laura E., and Harold Leitenberg. "Child Sexual Abuse Prevention Programs: Do They Decrease the Occurrence of Child Sexual Abuse?" *Child Abuse & Neglect* 24, no. 9 (2000): 1115–25.

Gies, Stephen V., Randy Gainey, Marcia I. Cohen, Eoin Healy, Dan Duplantier, Martha Yeide, Alan Bekelman, Amanda Bobnis, and Michael Hopps. *Monitoring High-Risk Sex Offenders with GPS Technology: An Evaluation of the California Supervision Program, Final Report*. Washington, DC: National Institute of Justice, 2012. https://pdfs.semanticscholar.org/6333/49d0abd658f9113f9299b-09bc7bb64c1f309.pdf.

Gilliam, Franklin D. "A New Dominant Frame: 'The Imperiled Child.'" Frameworks Institute, 2003.

Gilna, Derek. "Supreme Court Voids North Carolina Law Barring Sex Offenders from Facebook." Prison Legal News, June 30, 2017. https://www.prison legalnews.org/news/2017/jun/30/supreme-court-voids-north-carolina-law-barring-sex-offenders-facebook/.

Godbout, Natacha, John Briere, Stéphane Sabourin, and Yvan Lussier. "Child Sexual Abuse and Subsequent Relational and Personal Functioning: The Role of Parental Support." *Child Abuse & Neglect* 38, no. 2 (2014): 317–25.

Goldman, Juliette D. G., and Usha K. Padayachi. "Some Methodological Problems in Estimating Incidence and Prevalence in Child Sexual Abuse Research." *Journal of Sex Research* 37, no. 4 (2000): 305–14.

Gordon, Linda. "The Politics of Child Sexual Abuse: Notes from American History." *Feminist Review* 28 (1988): 56–64. https://www.jstor.org/stable/1394894?seq=1.

Gottfried, Mara H. "St. Paul Notification Meeting Wednesday to Detail 12 Predatory Offenders, Alarming Some Residents." *Twin Cities Pioneer Press*, September 24, 2018. https://www.twincities.com/2018/09/24/st-paul-no-tification-meeting-will-feature-12-predatory-offenders-raising-communi-ty-concerns/.

Government Accountability Office. *Selected Cases of Public and Private Schools That Hired or Retained Individuals with Histories of Sexual Misconduct*. Washington, DC: Government Accountability Office, 2010. https://www.gao.gov/products/GAO-11-200.

Graham, Lisa, Paul Rogers, and Michelle Davies. "Attributions in a Hypothetical Child Sexual Abuse Case: Roles of Abuse Type, Family Response and Respondent Gender." *Journal of Family Violence* 22, no. 8 (2007): 733–45.

Gramlich, John. "5 Facts about Crime in the U.S." *Pew Research Center* (blog), October 17, 2019. https://www.pewresearch.org/fact-tank/2019/10/17/facts-about-crime-in-the-u-s/.

Gray, Sandra, and Susan Rarick. "Exploring Gender and Racial/Ethnic Differences in the Effects of Child Sexual Abuse." *Journal of Child Sexual Abuse* 27, no. 5 (2018): 570–87.

Gross, Kimberly. "Framing Persuasive Appeals: Episodic and Thematic Framing, Emotional Response, and Policy Opinion." *Political Psychology* 29, no. 2 (2008): 169–92.

Group One. "Maine Child Care Workers Support New Background Checks." Group One, July 18, 2018. https://gp1.com/maine-child-care-workers-support-new-background-checks/.

Guerra, Jennifer. "Who's Allowed to Volunteer in Schools? It Depends." State of Opportunity, July 27, 2016. http://stateofopportunity.michiganradio.org/post/whos-allowed-volunteer-schools-it-depends.

Gusfield, Joseph R. "Constructing the Ownership of Social Problems: Fun and Profit in the Welfare State." *Social Problems* 36, no. 5 (1989): 431–41.

Hall, Linda. "Wooster Tent City: Sheltering Options Limited and Restricted for People with Series of Records." *Daily Record*, September 2, 2014. https://www.the-daily-record.com/article/20140902/NEWS/309029363.

Handy, Ariel B., Robyn A. Jackowich, Erik Wibowo, Thomas Wayne Johnson, and Richard J. Wassersug. "Gender Preference in the Sexual Attractions, Fantasies, and Relationships of Voluntarily Castrated Men." *Sexual Medicine* 4 (2016): 51–59. https://www.sciencedirect.com/science/article/pii/S2050116116000106.

Hansen, David J., Kurt M. Bumby, Lori M. Lundquist, Reginald M. Chandler, Peter T. Le, and Kristine T. Futa. "The Influence of Case and Professional Variables on the Identification and Reporting of Child Maltreatment: A Study of Licensed Psychologists and Certified Masters Social Workers." *Journal of Family Violence* 12, no. 3 (1997): 313–332.

Hanson, R. Karl, Arthur Gordon, Andrew J. R. Harris, Janice K. Marques, William Murphy, Vernon L. Quinsey, and Michael C. Seto. "First Report of the Collaborative Outcome Data Project on the Effectiveness of Psychological Treatment for Sex Offenders." *Sexual Abuse: A Journal of Research and Treatment* 14, no. 2 (2002): 169–94.

Hanson, R. Karl, and Kelly E. Morton-Bourgon. "The Accuracy of Recidivism Risk

Assessments for Sexual Offenders: A Meta-Analysis of 118 Prediction Studies."
Psychological Assessment 21, no. 1 (2009): 1–21.

————. "The Characteristics of Persistent Sexual Offenders: A Meta-Analysis of Recidivism Studies." *Journal of Consulting and Clinical Psychology* 73, no. 6 (2005): 1154–63.

Hardt, Jochen, and Michael Rutter. "Validity of Adult Retrospective Reports of Adverse Childhood Experiences: Review of the Evidence." *Journal of Child Psychology and Psychiatry* 45, no. 2 (2004): 260–73.

Harris, Andrew John Rawson, and Robert Karl Hanson. *Sex Offender Recidivism: A Simple Question.* Ottawa: Minister of Public Safety and Emergency Preparedness, 2004. https://www.publicsafety.gc.ca/cnt/rsrcs/pblctns/sx-ffndr-rcd vsm/index-en.aspx?wbdisable=true.

Harrison, Karen. "The High-Risk Sex Offender Strategy in England and Wales: Is Chemical Castration an Option?" *Howard Journal of Criminal Justice* 46, no. 1 (2007): 16–31.

Haugaard, Jeffrey J. "The Challenge of Defining Child Sexual Abuse." *American Psychologist* 55, no. 9 (2000): 1036–39.

Hauser, Christine, and Karen Zraick. "Larry Nassar Sexual Abuse Scandal: Dozens of Officials Have Been Ousted or Charged." *New York Times,* October 22, 2018. https://www.nytimes.com/2018/10/22/sports/larry-nassar-case-scandal.html.

Hawkes, Jeff. "After the Sandusky Case, a New Pennsylvania Law Creates Surge in Child Abuse Reports." LancasterOnline, February 20, 2015. https://lancasteronline.com/news/local/after-the-sandusky-case-a-new-pennsylvania-law-creates-surge/article_03541f66-b7a3-11e4-81cd-2f614d04c9af.html.

Hawkins, Russell, and Christy McCallum. "Effects of Mandatory Notification Training on the Tendency to Report Hypothetical Cases of Child Abuse and Neglect." *Child Abuse Review* 10, no. 5 (2001): 301–22.

Hayakawa, Alan. "'Wound Is So Deep': Kin of Victims Speak." Penn Live, December 16, 2007. https://www.pennlive.com/midstate/2007/12/alone_in_the_harrisburg_apartm.html.

Hayes, A. F. "Willingness to Express One's Opinion in a Realistic Situation as a Function of Perceived Support for That Opinion." *International Journal of Public Opinion Research* 13, no. 1 (March 1, 2001): 45–58.

Hazzard, Ann, Carol Webb, Carol Kleemeier, Lisa Angert, and Judy Pohl. "Child Sexual Abuse Prevention: Evaluation and One-Year Follow-Up." *Child Abuse & Neglect* 15, no. 1 (1991): 123–38.

Hébert, Martine, Francine Lavoie, and Nathalie Parent. "An Assessment of Outcomes Following Parents' Participation in a Child Abuse Prevention Program." *Violence and Victims* 17, no. 3 (2002): 355–72.

Helm, Rebecca K., Valerie F. Reyna, Allison A. Franz, Rachel Z. Novick, Sarah Dincin, and Amanda E. Cort. "Limitations on the Ability to Negotiate Justice: Attorney Perspectives on Guilt, Innocence, and Legal Advice in the Current Plea System." *Psychology, Crime & Law* 24, no. 9 (2018): 915–34.

Herek, Gregory. "Facts about Homosexuality and Child Molestation." University of California, Davis, 2013. https://psychology.ucdavis.edu/rainbow/html/facts_molestation.html.

Holmes, William C., and Gail B. Slap. "Sexual Abuse of Boys: Definition, Prevalence, Correlates, Sequelae, and Management." *JAMA* 280, no. 21 (1998): 1855–62.

Hoppe, Trevor. "Are Sex Offender Registries Reinforcing Inequality?" The Conversation, August 8, 2017. https://theconversation.com/are-sex-offender-registries-reinforcing-inequality-79818.

———. "Punishing Sex: Sex Offenders and the Missing Punitive Turn in Sexuality Studies." *Law & Social Inquiry* 41, no. 3 (2016): 573–94.

Howe, Allison C., Sharon Herzberger, and Howard Tennen. "The Influence of Personal History of Abuse and Gender on Clinicians' Judgments of Child Abuse." *Journal of Family Violence* 3, no. 2 (1988): 105–19.

Huguenor, Thomas. "Mother Deemed 'Sex Offender' for Violating Custody." Law Office of Huguenor Mattis AP, February 7, 2018. https://www.familylaw-sd.com/blog/when-sex-offender-registry-gets-it-wrong/.

Hunt, Mary E. "American Catholics: Time for a Stonewall Moment." *Pride Source* (blog), December 22, 2005. https://pridesource.com/article/16979/.

Institute for Work and Health. "Primary, Secondary and Tertiary Prevention," Institute for Work and Health, 2015. https://www.iwh.on.ca/what-researchers-mean-by/primary-secondary-and-tertiary-prevention.

International Association of Chiefs of Police. *Tracking Sex Offenders with Electronic Monitoring Technology: Implications and Practical Uses for Law Enforcement.* Alexandria, VA: International Association of Chiefs of Police, 2008. https://www.theiacp.org/sites/default/files/2018-08/TrackingOffenders.pdf.

Islam, Shafiqul. "Ideal Victims of Sexualized Violence: Why Is It Always Female?" *European Journal of Research in Social Sciences* 4, no. 8 (2016): 82–92.

Jackson, Rebecca L., and Derek T. Hess. "Evaluation for Civil Commitment of Sex Offenders: A Survey of Experts." *Sexual Abuse: A Journal of Research and Treatment* 19, no. 4 (2007): 425–48.

John Jay College of Criminal Justice. *The Nature and Scope of Sexual Abuse of Minors by Catholic Priests and Deacons in the United States, 1950–2002.* Washington, DC: United States Conference of Catholic Bishops, 2004. http://www.bishop-accountability.org/

reports/2004_02_27_JohnJay_revised/2004_02_27_John_Jay_Main_Report_
Optimized.pdf.

Johnson, Anne T. "Criminal Liability for Parents Who Fail to Protect." *Law &
Inequality: A Journal of Theory and Practice* 5 (1987): 359–92.

Judd, Alan. "Georgia's Juvenile Prisons: Assaults by Guards, Strip Searches,
Chaos." AJC, November 17, 2019. https://www.ajc.com/news/crime-law/
violence-permeates-youth-prisons/7YRQTDEnlT2ohGVEnjqybP/.

Jülich, Shirley. "Views of Justice among Survivors of Historical Child Sexual
Abuse: Implications for Restorative Justice in New Zealand." *Theoretical Criminology* 10, no. 1 (2006): 125–38.

Juvenile Law Center. "Juvenile Sex Offender Registry (SORNA)." Juvenile Law
Center, 2018. https://jlc.org/issues/juvenile-sex-offender-registry-sorna.

Kalichman, Seth C., and Mary E. Craig. "Professional Psychologists' Decisions to
Report Suspected Child Abuse: Clinician and Situation Influences." *Professional Psychology: Research and Practice* 22, no. 1 (1991): 84–89.

Kalichman, Seth C., Mary E. Craig, and Diane R. Follingstad. "Professionals'
Adherence to Mandatory Child Abuse Reporting Laws: Effects of Responsi-
bility Attribution, Confidence Ratings, and Situational Factors." *Child Abuse
& Neglect* 14, no. 1 (1990): 69–77.

Karp, David, and Jarrett B. Warshaw. "Their Day in Court: The Role of Murder
Victims in Decision Making." In *Wounds That Do Not Bind: Victim-Based Perspectives on the Death Penalty*, edited by James R. Acker and David R. Karp,
275–95. Durham, NC: Carolina Academic Press, 2006.

Katayama, Devin. "JCPS Background Checks Block Parents from Volunteering,
Even for Years-Old Offenses." 89.3 WFPL News Louisville, August 25, 2013.
http://wfpl.org/jcps-background-checks-block-parents-volunteering-even-
years-old-offenses/.

Katerndahl, David A., Sandra K. Burge, Nancy Kellogg, and Juan M. Parra. "Differences in Childhood Sexual Abuse Experience Between Adult Hispanic and
Anglo Women in a Primary Care Setting." *Journal of Child Sexual Abuse* 14, no.
2 (2005): 85–95.

Katz, Carmit, and Zion Barnetz. "Children's Narratives of Alleged Child Sexual
Abuse Offender Behaviors and the Manipulation Process." *Psychology of Violence* 6, no. 2 (2016): 223–32.

Katz-Schiavone, Stacey, Jill S. Levenson, and Alissa R. Ackerman. "Myths and Facts
about Sexual Violence: Public Perceptions and Implications for Prevention."
Journal of Criminal Justice and Popular Culture 15, no. 3 (2008): 291–311.

Kay, Judith. "Murder Victims' Families for Reconciliation: Story-Telling for Healing, as Witness, and in Public Policy." In *Handbook of Restorative Justice: A*

Global Perspective, edited by Dennis Sullivan and Larry Tifft, 230–45. New York: Routledge, 2006.

Keeter, Scott, Courtney Kennedy, Michael Dimock, Jonathan Best, and Pryton Craighill. "Gauging the Impact of Growing Nonresponse on Estimates from a National RDD Telephone Survey." *Public Opinion Quarterly* 70, no. 5 (2006): 759–79.

Keilman, John. "Penn State Scandal Spotlights Debate over Who Must Report Abuse." *Chicago Tribune*, November 11, 2011. https://www.chicagotribune.com/news/ct-xpm-2011-11-11-ct-met-mandated-reporters-20111111-story.html.

Kellogg, Nancy D., Juan M. Parra, and Shirley Menard. "Children with Anogenital Symptoms and Signs Referred for Sexual Abuse Evaluations." *Archives of Pediatrics & Adolescent Medicine* 152, no. 7 (1998): 634–41.

Kenny, Maureen C., and Adriana G. McEachern. "Racial, Ethnic, and Cultural Factors of Childhood Sexual Abuse: A Selected Review of the Literature." *Clinical Psychology Review* 20, no. 7 (2000): 905–22.

Kernsmith, Poco D., Sarah W. Craun, and Jonathan Foster. "Public Attitudes toward Sexual Offenders and Sex Offender Registration." *Journal of Child Sexual Abuse* 18, no. 3 (2009): 290–301.

Kiger, Patrick. "10 Unconventional Uses for GPS." HowStuffWorks, July 28, 2014. https://electronics.howstuffworks.com/10-unconventional-uses-gps.htm.

Kim, Bitna, Peter J. Benekos, and Alida V. Merlo. "Sex Offender Recidivism Revisited: Review of Recent Meta-Analyses on the Effects of Sex Offender Treatment." *Trauma, Violence, & Abuse* 17, no. 1 (2016): 105–17.

Kirby, Sandra L., Guylaine Demers, and Sylvie Parent. "Vulnerability/Prevention: Considering the Needs of Disabled and Gay Athletes in the Context of Sexual Harassment and Abuse." *International Journal of Sport and Exercise Psychology* 6, no. 4 (2008): 407–26.

Kirby, Sandra L., Lorraine Greaves, and Olena Hankivsky. *The Dome of Silence: Sexual Harassment and Abuse in Sport.* Halifax, Nova Scotia: Zed Books, 2008.

Kitzinger, Jenny. "Media Coverage of Sexual Violence against Women and Children." In *Women and Media: International Perspectives*, edited by Karen Ross and Carolyn M. Byerly, 13–38. Hoboken, NJ: Wiley-Blackwell, 2004.

———. "The Ultimate Neighbor from Hell? Stranger Danger and the Media Framing of Paedophiles." In *Social Policy, the Media and Misrepresentation*, edited by Bob Franklin, 207–21. New York: Routledge, 1999.

———. "Who Are You Kidding? Children, Power, and the Struggle against Sexual Abuse." In *Constructing and Reconstructing Childhood*, edited by Allison James and Alan Prout, 165–89. New York: Routledge, 1997.

———, and Paula Skidmore. "Playing Safe: Media Coverage of Child Sexual Abuse Prevention Strategies." *Child Abuse Review* 4 (1995): 47–56.

Kleemeier, Carol, Carol Webb, Ann Hazzard, and Judy Pohl. "Child Sexual Abuse Prevention: Evaluation of a Teacher Training Model." *Child Abuse & Neglect* 12, no. 4 (1988): 555–61.

Klein, Roger D., and Stacy Naccarato. "Broadcast News Portrayal of Minorities: Accuracy in Reporting." *American Behavioral Scientist* 46, no. 12 (2003): 1611–16.

Kochel, Tammy Rinehart, David B. Wilson, and Stephen D. Mastrofski. "Effect of Suspect Race on Officers' Arrest Decisions." *Criminology* 49, no. 2 (2011): 473–512.

———. "Effect of Suspect Race on Officers' Arrest Decisions." *Criminology* 49, no. 2 (May 1, 2011): 473–512.

Kofman, Ava. "Digital Jail: How Electronic Monitoring Drives Defendants into Debt." ProPublica, July 3, 2019. https://www.propublica.org/article/digital-jail-how-electronic-monitoring-drives-defendants-into-debt.

Kondracke, Morton. "Anita Bryant Is Mad about Gays." *New Republic* 176, no. 19 (1977): 13–15.

Koo, Kyo Chul, Geum Sook Shim, Hyoun Hee Park, Koon Ho Rha, Young Deuk Choi, Byung Ha Chung, Sung Joon Hong, and Jae Woo Lee. "Treatment Outcomes of Chemical Castration on Korean Sex Offenders." *Journal of Forensic and Legal Medicine* 20, no. 6 (2013): 563–66.

Kopplin, Zack. "Abused? You Can't Work at These Churches." The Daily Beast, April 15, 2016, http://www.thedailybeast.com/articles/2016/04/15/churches-ask-job-seekers-were-you-sexually-abused-as-a-child.

Kozlowski, Kim. "What MSU Knew: 14 Were Warned of Nassar Abuse." *Detroit News*, 2018. https://www.detroitnews.com/story/tech/2018/01/18/msu-president-told-nassar-complaint-2014/1042071001/.

Kroner, Daryl G., Jeremy F. Mills, and John R. Reddon. "A Coffee Can, Factor Analysis, and Prediction of Antisocial Behavior: The Structure of Criminal Risk." *International Journal of Law and Psychiatry* 28, no. 4 (2005): 360–74.

Lafree, Gary D., Barbara F. Reskin, and Christy A. Visher. "Jurors' Responses to Victims' Behavior and Legal Issues in Sexual Assault Trials." *Social Problems* 32, no. 4 (1985): 389–407.

Lageson, Sarah, and Christopher Uggen. "How Work Affects Crime—and Crime Affects Work—Over the Life Course." In *Handbook of Life-Course Criminology*, edited by Chris L. Gibson and Marvin D. Krohn, 201–12. New York: Springer New York, 2013.

Laurence, J., and C. Perry. "Hypnotically Created Memory among Highly Hypnotizable Subjects." *Science* 222, no. 4623 (1983): 523–24.

Lauritsen, Janet L. "How Families and Communities Influence Youth Victimization." *Juvenile Justice Bulletin*. Washington, DC: Office of Juvenile Justice and Delinquency Prevention, 2003. https://www.ncjrs.gov/pdffiles1/ojjdp/201629.pdf.

Lave, Tamara Rice. "Only Yesterday: The Rise and Fall of Twentieth Century Sexual Psychopath Laws." *Louisiana Law Review* 69 (2009): 549–91.

Lawrence, Linda L. "The Impact of Physician Training of Child Maltreatment Reporting: A Multi-Speciality Study." *Military Medicine* 165, no. 8 (2000): 607–11.

Lennard, Natasha. "Will the Prison Rape Epidemic Ever Have Its Weinstein Moment?" *The Intercept* (blog), November 21, 2017. https://theintercept.com/2017/11/21/prison-rape-sexual-assault-violence/.

Lepore, Jill. "The Rise of the Victims'-Rights Movement." *New Yorker*, May 14, 2018. https://www.newyorker.com/magazine/2018/05/21/the-rise-of-the-victims-rights-movement.

Letourneau, Elizabeth J. "Can Improved Health Care Access Reduce Sexual Violence?" *Psychology Today*, January 17, 2019. https://www.psychologytoday.com/blog/prevention-now/201901/can-improved-health-care-access-reduce-sexual-violence.

———, Jill S. Levenson, Dipankar Bandyopadhyay, Kevin S. Armstrong, and Debajyoti Sinha. "Effects of South Carolina's Sex Offender Registration and Notification Policy on Deterrence of Adult Sex Crimes." *Criminal Justice and Behavior* 37, no. 5 (2010): 537–52.

———, Jill S. Levenson, Dipankar Bandyopadhyay, Kevin S. Armstrong, and Debajyoti Sinha. "The Effects of Sex Offender Registration and Notification on Judicial Decisions." *Criminal Justice Review* 35, no. 3 (2010): 295–317.

———, Kevin S. Armstrong, Dipankar Bandyopadhyay, and Debajyoti Sinha. "Sex Offender Registration and Notification Policy Increases Juvenile Plea Bargains." *Sexual Abuse: A Journal of Research and Treatment* 25, no. 2 (2013): 189–207.

Levenson, Jill S., and Leo P. Cotter. "The Effect of Megan's Law on Sex Offender Reintegration." *Journal of Contemporary Criminal Justice* 21, no. 1 (2005): 49–66.

———, and Richard Tewksbury. "Collateral Damage: Family Members of Registered Sex Offenders." *American Journal of Criminal Justice* 34 (2009): 54–68.

———, Gwenda M. Willis, and David S. Prescott. "Adverse Childhood Experiences in the Lives of Male Sex Offenders: Implications for Trauma-Informed Care." *Sexual Abuse: A Journal of Research and Treatment* 28, no. 4 (2016): 340–59.

Levenson, Jill S., Yolanda N. Brannon, Timothy Fortney, and Juanita Baker. "Public Perceptions about Sex Offenders and Community Protection Policies." *Analyses of Social Issues and Public Policy* 7, no. 1 (2007): 137–61.

Levi, Ron. "The Mutuality of Risk and Community: The Adjudication of Community Notification Statutes" 29, no. 4 (2000): 578–601.

Levy, Robert. "The Dynamics of Child Sexual Abuse Prosecution: Two Florida Case Studies." *Journal of Law and Family Studies* 7 (2005): 57–109.

LexisNexis. "The Importance of Background Screening of Nonprofits: An Updated Briefing." White Paper. LexisNexis, 2009.

Lilienfeld, Scott O. "When Worlds Collide: Social Science, Politics, and the Rind et al. (1998) Child Sexual Abuse Meta-Analysis." *American Psychologist* 57, no. 3 (2002): 176–88.

Linden, Leigh, and Jonah E. Rockoff. "Estimates of the Impact of Crime Risk on Property Values from Megan's Laws." *American Economic Review* 98, no. 3 (2008): 1103–27.

Lisak, David, Lori Gardinier, Sarah C. Nicksa, and Ashley M. Cote. "False Allegations of Sexual Assault: An Analysis of Ten Years of Reported Cases." *Violence Against Women* 16, no. 12 (2010): 1318–34.

Loftus, Elizabeth F., and Edith Greene. "Warning: Even Memory for Faces May Be Contagious." *Law and Human Behavior* 4, no. 4 (1980): 323–34.

Loftus, Elizabeth F., and John C. Palmer. "Reconstruction of Automobile Destruction: An Example of the Interaction between Language and Memory." *Journal of Verbal Learning and Verbal Behavior* 13, no. 5 (October 1974): 585–89.

London, Kamala, Maggie Bruck, Stephen J. Ceci, and Daniel W. Shuman. "Disclosure of Child Sexual Abuse: What Does the Research Tell Us about the Ways That Children Tell?" *Psychology, Public Policy, and Law* 11, no. 1 (2005): 194–226.

Lovett, Kenneth. "Opponents of Child Victims Act for Adults Sexually Abused as Kids Mostly Operated in the Shadows to Kill the Bill." Daily News (New York), June 24, 2017. https://www.nydailynews.com/news/politics/child-victims-act-adults-sexually-abused-kids-quietly-dies-article-1.3274973.

Lundrigan, Samantha, Mandeep K. Dhami, and Kelly Agudelo. "Factors Predicting Conviction in Child Stranger Rape." *Child Abuse & Neglect* 101 (2020): 1–9.

Lynch, Mona. "Pedophiles and Cyber-Predators as Contaminating Forces: The Language of Disgust, Pollution, and Boundary Invasions in Federal Debates on Sex Offender Legislation." *Law & Social Inquiry* 27, no. 3 (2002): 529–57.

Lyon, Thomas D. and Julia A. Dente. "Child Witnesses and the Confrontation Clause." *Journal of Criminal Law and Criminology* 102, no. 4 (2012): 1181–1232.

Malesky, Alvin, and Jeanmarie Keim. "Mental Health Professionals' Perspectives on Sex Offender Registry Web Sites." *Sexual Abuse: A Journal of Research and Treatment* 13, no. 1 (2001): 53–63.

Malesky, L. Alvin. "Predatory Online Behavior: Modus Operandi of Convicted Sex Offenders Identifying Potential Victims and Contacting Minors over the Internet." *Journal of Child Sexual Abuse* 16, no. 2 (2007): 23–32.

Malkin, K., L. Johnston, and Celia H. Brackenridge. "A Critical Evaluation of Training Needs for Child Protection in UK Sports." *Managing Leisure* 5, no. 3 (2000): 151–60.

Martinson, Robert. "What Works? Questions and Answers about Prison Reform." *Public Interest* 35, no. Spring (1974): 22–54.

Martyniuk, Hallie, and Emily Dworkin. *Child Sexual Abuse Prevention: Programs for Children*. Harrisburg, PA: National Sexual Violence Resource Center, 2011. https://www.nsvrc.org/publications/child-sexual-abuse-prevention-programs-children.

Mathews, Ben, Xing Ju Lee, and Rosana E. Norman. "Impact of a New Mandatory Reporting Law on Reporting and Identification of Child Sexual Abuse: A Seven Year Time Trend Analysis." *Child Abuse & Neglect* 56 (2016): 62–79.

Matthews, Dona. "Call Children's Private Body Parts What They Are." *Psychology Today* (blog), 2017. https://www.psychologytoday.com/blog/going-beyond-intelligence/201703/call-children-s-private-body-parts-what-they-are.

Mauer, Marc. "Long-Term Sentences: Time to Reconsider the Scale of Punishment." *UMKC Law Review* 87 (2018): 113–30.

Maxey, Ron. "Sex Offenders Have a List of 'Don'ts' on Halloween Night, TDOC Officers Will Be Checking for Compliance." Commercial Appeal, October 12, 2018. https://www.commercialappeal.com/story/news/2018/10/12/tennessee-department-correction-officers-keep-eye-sex-offenders-halloween-night/1613989002/.

McElvaney, Rosaleen. "Disclosure of Child Sexual Abuse: Delays, Non-Disclosure and Partial Disclosure. What the Research Tells Us and Implications for Practice: Disclosure Patterns in Child Sexual Abuse." *Child Abuse Review* 24, no. 3 (2015): 159–69.

McGee, Robin A., and Susan L. Painter. "What If It Happens in My Family? Parental Reactions to a Hypothetical Disclosure of Sexual Abuse." *Canadian Journal of Behavioural Science/Revue canadienne des sciences du comportement* 23, no. 2 (1991): 228–40.

McGinn, Laura, Nicole Stone, Roger Ingham, and Andrew Bengry-Howell. "Parental Interpretations of 'Childhood Innocence': Implications for Early Sexuality Education." *Health Education* 116, no. 6 (2016): 580–94.

McGlynn, Clare, Nicole Westmarland, and Nikki Godden. "'I Just Wanted Him to Hear Me': Sexual Violence and the Possibilities of Restorative Justice." *Journal of Law and Society* 39, no. 2 (2012): 213–40.

McGrath, Patrick, Mario Cappelli, Dan Wiseman, Nadia Khalil, and Beth Allan. "Teacher Awareness Program on Child Abuse: A Randomized Controlled Trial." *Child Abuse & Neglect* 11, no. 1 (1987): 125–132.

McGreevy, Patrick. "Bill to Reduce Names on California's Sex Offender Registry Shelved." *LA Times*, September 1, 2017. https://www.latimes.com/politics/essential/la-pol-ca-essential-politics-updates-bill-to-reduce-names-on-california-s-1504292042-htmlstory.html.

———. "California Will Soon End Lifetime Registration of Some Sex Offenders under Bill Signed by Gov. Jerry Brown." *LA Times*, October 6, 2017. https://www.latimes.com/politics/essential/la-pol-ca-essential-politics-updates-bill-ending-lifetime-registry-of-sex-1507332406-htmlstory.html.

McGuffey, C. Shawn. "Engendering Trauma: Race, Class, and Gender Reaffirmation after Child Sexual Abuse." *Gender & Society* 19, no. 5 (2005): 621–43.

McGuire, Katherine, and Kamala London. "Common Beliefs about Child Sexual Abuse and Disclosure: A College Sample." *Journal of Child Sexual Abuse* 26, no. 2 (2017): 175–94.

McLeod, David Axlyn. "Female Offenders in Child Sexual Abuse Cases: A National Picture." *Journal of Child Sexual Abuse* 24, no. 1 (2015): 97–114.

McPherson, Lori. *Practitioner's Guide to the Adam Walsh Act*. Alexandria, VA: American Prosecutors Research Institute, 2007. https://www.smart.gov/pdfs/practitioner_guide_awa.pdf.

Mejia, Pamela, Andrew Cheyne, and Lori Dorfman. "News Coverage of Child Sexual Abuse and Prevention, 2007–2009." *Journal of Child Sexual Abuse* 21, no. 4 (2012): 470–87.

Mendelson, Tamar, and Elizabeth J. Letourneau. "Parent-Focused Prevention of Child Sexual Abuse." *Prevention Science* 16, no. 6 (2015): 844–52.

Meyer, Walter J., and Collier M. Cole. "Physical and Chemical Castration of Sex Offenders: A Review." *Journal of Offender Rehabilitation* 25, no. 3–4 (1997): 1–18.

Mikkelsen, Edwin J., Thomas G. Gutheil, and Margaret Emens. "False Sexual-Abuse Allegations by Children and Adolescents: Contextual Factors and Clinical Subtypes." *American Journal of Psychotherapy* 46, no. 4 (1992): 556–70.

Miller, Karen-Lee. "Purposing and Repurposing Harms: The Victim Impact Statement and Sexual Assault." *Qualitative Health Research* 23, no. 11 (2013): 1445–58.

Mills, David. "Oprah, Children's Crusader." *Washington Post*, November 13, 1991. https://www.washingtonpost.com/archive/lifestyle/1991/11/13/oprah-childrens-crusader/b388a5a3-85f4-41f1-89fe-93e31a940521/.

Min, Seong-Jae, and John C. Feaster. "Missing Children in National News Coverage: Racial and Gender Representations of Missing Children Cases." *Communication Research Reports* 27, no. 3 (2010): 207–16.

Minnesota Department of Corrections. "Residential Proximity & Sex Offense Recidivism in Minnesota." St. Paul: Minnesota Department of Corrections, 2007. https://ccoso.org/sites/default/files/import/SexOffenderReport-Proximity.pdf.

Mitchell, Kimberly J., Lisa Jones, David Finkelhor, and Janis Wolak. *Trends in Unwanted Sexual Solicitations: Findings from the Youth Internet Safety Studies*. Durham, NH: Crimes against Children Research Center, 2014. http://www.unh.edu/ccrc/pdf/Sexual%20Solicitation%201%20of%204%20YISS%20Bulletins%20Feb%202014.pdf.

Monahan, John, and Jennifer L. Skeem. "Risk Assessment in Criminal Sentencing." *Annual Review of Clinical Psychology* 12, no. 1 (2016): 489–513.

Morin, Brad. "Teachers, Staff Resent Fingerprint Law." *Ellsworth American*, November 25, 1999.

Morlino, Robert C. "Bishop Robert C. Morlino's Letter to the Faithful Regarding the Ongoing Sexual Abuse Crisis in the Church." *Diocese of Madison Catholic Herald*, August 18, 2018. http://www.madisoncatholicherald.org/bishopsletters/7730-letter-scandal.html.

Motivans, Mark, and Tracey Kychelhahn. "Federal Prosecution of Child Sex Exploitation Offenders, 2006." *Bureau of Justice Statistics Bulletin*, December 2007. https://www.bjs.gov/content/pub/pdf/fpcse006.pdf.

Munoz, Marco A. "Parental Volunteerism in Kindergarten: Assessing Its Impact in Reading and Mathematics Tests." *ERIC Document Reproduction Service*, no. ED464745 (2000): 1–11. https://eric.ed.gov/?id=ED464745.

Mustaine, Elizabeth Ehrhardt, and Richard Tewksbury. "Registered Sex Offenders, Residence, and the Influence of Race." *Journal of Ethnicity in Criminal Justice* 6, no. 1 (2008): 65–82.

———, Richard Tewksbury, and Kenneth M. Stengel. "Social Disorganization and Residential Locations of Registered Sex Offenders: Is This a Collateral Consequence?" *Deviant Behavior* 27, no. 3 (2006): 329–50.

Myers, John E. B. "A Short History of Child Protection in America." *Family Law Quarterly* 42, no. 3 (2008): 449–65.

Nadler, Janice, and Mary R. Rose. "Victim Impact Testimony and the Psychology of Punishment." *Cornell Law Review* 88 (2003): 419–56; *Northwestern Public Law Research Paper*, no. 3-2; *University of Texas Law, Public Law Research Paper*, no. 47. https://papers.ssrn.com/sol3/papers.cfm?abstract_id=377521.

Nagin, Daniel S. "Deterrence in the Twenty-First Century." *Crime and Justice* 42, no. 1 (2013): 199–263.

National Association of Criminal Defense Lawyers. "The Trial Penalty: The Sixth Amendment Right to Trial on the Verge of Extinction and How to Save It." *Federal Sentencing Reporter* 31, no. 4–5 (2018): 331–68.

National Center for Victims of Crime. "Victim Impact Statements." National Center for the Victims of Crime, 2011. https://members.victimsofcrime.org/help-for-crime-victims/get-help-bulletins-for-crime-victims/victim-impact-statements.

National Council of Juvenile and Family Court Justices. *Resolution Regarding Sex Offender Registration Requirements for Youth Younger Than Age 18*. Reno: National Council of Juvenile and Family Court Justices, 2018. https://www. ncjfcj.org/wp-content/uploads/2019/08/regarding-sex-offender-registra tion-requirements-for-youth-younger-than-age-18.pdf.

Nellis, Ashley. *Still Life: America's Increasing Use of Life and Long-Term Sentences*. Washington, DC: The Sentencing Project, 2017. https://www.sentencingproject.org/ publications/still-life-americas-increasing-use-life-long-term-sentences/.

Nellis, Mike. "Surveillance, Rehabilitation, and Electronic Monitoring: Getting the Issues Clear." *Criminology & Public Policy* 5, no. 1 (2006): 103–8.

Nickerson, Raymond S. "Confirmation Bias: A Ubiquitous Phenomenon in Many Guises." *Review of General Psychology* 2, no. 2 (1998): 175–220.

Noelle-Neumann, Elisabeth. "The Spiral of Silence: A Theory of Public Opinion." *Journal of Communication* 24, no. 2 (1974): 43–51.

Nunn, Kenneth B. "Race, Crime and the Pool of Surplus Criminality: Or Why the War on Drugs Was a War on Blacks." *Journal of Gender, Race and Justice* 6 (2002): 381.

Nurse, Anne M. "Coaches and Child Sexual Abuse Prevention Training: Impact on Knowledge, Confidence, and Behavior." *Children and Youth Services Review* 88 (2018): 395–400.

———. "Construction of the Offender in Child Sexual Abuse Prevention Training for Adults." *Journal of Criminal Justice Education* 28, no. 4 (2017): 598–615.

———. "Knowledge and Behavioral Impact of Adult Participation in Child Sexual Abuse Prevention: Evaluation of the Protecting God's Children Program." *Journal of Child Sexual Abuse* 26, no. 5 (2017): 608–24.

Okeke, Cameron, and Nancy G. La Vigne. "Restoring Humanity: Changing the Way We Talk about People Touched by the Criminal Justice System." Urban Institute, November 29, 2018. https://www.urban.org/urban-wire/restoring-hu manity-changing-way-we-talk-about-people-touched-criminal-justice-system.

Orloff, Leslye E., Mary Ann Dutton, Giselle Aguilar Hass, and Nawal Ammar. "Battered Immigrant Women's Willingness to Call for Help and Police Response." *UCLA Women's Law Journal* 13 (2003): 43.

Oswald, Zachary Edmonds. "'Off with His __': Analyzing the Sex Disparity in Chemical Castration Sentences." *Michigan Journal of Gender and Law* 19, no. 2 (2013): 472–503.

Owens, Caitlin, Stef W. Kight, and Harry Stevens. "Thousands of Migrant Youth Allegedly Suffered Sexual Abuse in U.S. Custody." Axios, February 26, 2019. https://www.axios.com/immigration-unaccompanied-minors-sexual-assaul t-3222e230-29e1-430f-a361-d959c88c5d8c.html.

Padgett, Kathy G., William D. Bales, and Thomas G. Blomberg. "Under Surveillance: An Empirical Test of the Effectiveness and Consequences of Electronic Monitoring." *Criminology & Public Policy* 5, no. 1 (2006): 61–91.

Paladino, Richard A. "The Adam Walsh Act as Applied to Juveniles: One Size Does Not Fit All." *Hofstra Law Review* 40, no. 1 (2014): 269–307.

Pantell, Robert H. "The Child Witness in the Courtroom." *Pediatrics* 139, no. 3 (2017): 1–9.

Paolucci, Elizabeth Oddone, Mark L. Genuis, and Claudio Violato. "A Meta-Analysis of the Published Research on the Effects of Child Sexual Abuse." *Journal of Psychology* 135, no. 1 (2001): 17-36.

Parent, Sylvie, and Guylaine Demers. "Sexual Abuse in Sport: A Model to Prevent and Protect Athletes." *Child Abuse Review* 20, no. 2 (2011): 120–33.

Park, Shelley M. "False Memory Syndrome: A Feminist Philosophical Approach." *Hypatia* 12, no. 2 (1997): 1–50.

Parton, Christine, and Nigel Parton. "Women, the Family and Child Protection." *Critical Social Policy* 8, no. 24 (1988): 38–49.

Paternoster, Ray, and Jerome Deise. "A Heavy Thumb on the Scale: The Effect of Victim Impact Evidence on Capital Decision Making." *Criminology* 49, no. 1 (2011): 129–61.

Patihis, Lawrence, Lavina Y. Ho, Ian W. Tingen, Scott O. Lilienfeld, and Elizabeth F. Loftus. "Are the 'Memory Wars' Over? A Scientist-Practitioner Gap in Beliefs about Repressed Memory." *Psychological Science* 25, no. 2 (2014): 519–30.

Payne, Brian K., and Matthew DeMichele. "Sex Offender Policies: Considering Unanticipated Consequences of GPS Sex Offender Monitoring." *Aggression and Violent Behavior* 16, no. 3 (2011): 177–87.

Payne, Brian K., and Randy R. Gainey. "A Qualitative Assessment of the Pains Experienced on Electronic Monitoring." *International Journal of Offender Therapy and Comparative Criminology* 42, no. 2 (1998): 149–63.

Pelisoli, Cátula, Steve Herman, and Débora Dalbosco Dell'Aglio. "Child Sexual Abuse Research Knowledge among Child Abuse Professionals and Laypersons." *Child Abuse & Neglect* 40 (2015): 36–47.

Peter, Tracey. "Exploring Taboos: Comparing Male- and Female-Perpetrated Child Sexual Abuse." *Journal of Interpersonal Violence* 24, no. 7 (2009): 1111–28.

Peterson, Cora, Curtis Florence, and Joanne Klevens. "The Economic Burden of Child Maltreatment in the United States, 2015." *Child Abuse & Neglect* 86 (2018): 178–83.

Petrunik, Michael, and Linda Deutschmann. "The Exclusion–Inclusion Spectrum in State and Community Response to Sex Offenders in Anglo-American and

European Jurisdictions." *International Journal of Offender Therapy and Comparative Criminology* 52, no. 5 (2008): 499–519.

Pew Research Center. "Questionnaire Design." *Pew Research Center Methods* (blog), 2020. https://www.pewresearch.org/methods/u-s-survey-research/questionnaire-design/.

Pfohl, Stephen J. "The 'Discovery' of Child Abuse." *Social Problems* 24, no. 3 (1977): 310–23.

Pittman, Nicole, Alison Parker, and Human Rights Watch (HRW). *Raised on the Registry: The Irreparable Harm of Placing Children in Sex Offenders Registries in the US*. New York: Human Rights Watch, 2013. https://www.hrw.org/sites/default/files/reports/us0513_ForUpload_1.pdf.

Platoff, Emma. "New Texas Law Keeps Sex Offenders out of College Dorms." *Texas Tribune*, September 25, 2017. https://www.texastribune.org/2017/09/25/books-sex-offenders-kept-out-campus-dorms/.

Plummer, Carol A. "The History of Child Sexual Abuse Prevention: A Practitioner's Perspective." *Journal of Child Sexual Abuse* 7, no. 4 (1999): 77–95.

Poche, C., P. Yoder, and R. Miltenberger. "Teaching Self-Protection to Children Using Television Techniques." *Journal of Applied Behavior Analysis* 21, no. 3 (1988): 253–61.

Porte, Ryan W. "Sex Offender Regulations and the Rule of Law: When Civil Regulatory Schemes Circumvent the Constitution." *Hastings Consititutional Law Quarterly* 45 (2018): 715–38.

Porter Decusati, Cheryl L., and James E. Johnson. "Parents as Classroom Volunteers and Kindergarten Students' Emergent Reading Skills." *Journal of Educational Research* 97, no. 5 (2004): 235–46.

Potts, Lawrence F. "The Youth Protection Program of the Boy Scouts of America." *Child Abuse & Neglect* 16, no. 3 (1992): 441–45.

Prescott, J. J., and Jonah E. Rockoff. "Do Sex Offender Registration and Notification Laws Affect Criminal Behavior?" *Journal of Law and Economics* 54, no. 1 (2011): 161–206.

Price, Vincent, David Tewskbury, and Elizabeth Powers. "Switching Trains of Thought: The Impact of News Frames on Readers' Cognitive Responses." *Communication Research* 24, no. 5 (1997): 481–506.

Privacy Rights Clearinghouse. "Employment Background Checks: A Jobseeker's Guide." Privacy Rights Clearinghouse, 2019. https://privacyrights.org/consumer-guides/employment-background-checks-jobseekers-guide.

———. "Volunteer Background Checks: Giving Back Without Giving Up on Privacy." Privacy Rights Clearinghouse, 2017. https://www.privacyrights.org/consumer-guides/volunteer-background-checks-giving-back-without-giving-privacy.

Psychology Today. "Cognitive Behavioral Therapy." *Psychology Today*, 2019. https://www.psychologytoday.com/basics/cognitive-behavioral-therapy.

Quas, Jodi A., and Gail S. Goodman. "Consequences of Criminal Court Involvement for Child Victims." *Psychology, Public Policy, and Law* 18, no. 3 (2012): 392–414.

Quas, Jodi A., David P. H. Jones, Simona Ghetti, Kristen W. Alexander, Robin Edelstein, Allison D. Redlich, and Ingrid M. Cordon. *Childhood Sexual Assault Victims: Long-Term Outcomes after Testifying in Criminal Court.* Vol. 70: *Monographs of the Society for Research in Child Development.* Washington, DC: Society for Research in Child Development, 2005.

Quas, Jodi A., William C. Thompson, and K. Alison Clarke-Stewart. "Do Jurors 'Know' What Isn't So about Child Witnesses?" *Law and Human Behavior* 29, no. 4 (2005): 425–56.

Quinn, James F., Craig J. Forsyth, and Carla Mullen-Quinn. "Societal Reaction to Sex Offenders: A Review of the Origins and Results of the Myths Surrounding Their Crimes and Treatment Amenability." *Deviant Behavior* 25, no. 3 (2004): 215–32.

RAINN. "Key Terms and Phrases." RAINN, 2019. https://www.rainn.org/articles/key-terms-and-phrases.

Rakoff, Jed S. "Why Innocent People Plead Guilty." *New York Review of Books*, November 20, 2014. https://www.nacdl.org/getattachment/8e5437e4-79b2-4535-b26c-9fa266de7de8/why-innocent-people-plead-guilty-_-jrakoff_ny-review-of-books-2014.pdf.

Randolph, M. K., and C. A. Gold. "Child Sexual Abuse Prevention: Evaluation of a Teacher Training Program." *School Psychology Review* 23, no. 3 (1994): 485–495.

Rassin, Eric, Anita Eerland, and Ilse Kuijpers. "Let's Find the Evidence: An Analogue Study of Confirmation Bias in Criminal Investigations." *Journal of Investigative Psychology and Offender Profiling* 7 (2010): 231–46.

Raz, Mical. "Unintended Consequences of Expanded Mandatory Reporting Laws." *Pediatrics* 139, no. 4 (2017): e20163511.

Reiman, Jeffrey H., and Paul Leighton. *The Rich Get Richer and the Poor Get Prison: Ideology, Class, and Criminal Justice.* 10th ed. New York: Routledge, 2012.

Renzema, Marc, and Evan Mayo-Wilson. "Can Electronic Monitoring Reduce Crime for Moderate to High-Risk Offenders?" *Journal of Experimental Criminology* 1, no. 2 (2005): 215–37.

Rheingold, Alyssa A., Kristyn Zajac, Jason E. Chapman, Meghan Patton, Michael de Arellano, Benjamin Saunders, and Dean Kilpatrick. "Child Sexual Abuse Prevention Training for Childcare Professionals: An Independent Multi-Site Randomized Controlled Trial of Stewards of Children." *Prevention Science* 16, no. 3 (2015): 374–85.

Richards, Kelly. "Born This Way? A Qualitative Examination of Public Perceptions of the Causes of Pedophilia and Sexual Offending against Children." *Deviant Behavior* 39, no. 7 (2018): 835–51.

Richardson, James T., Joel Best, and David Bromley. "Satanism as a Social Problem." In *The Satanism Scare*, edited by Richardson, Best, and Bromley, 3–17. New York: Routledge, 1991.

Rind, Bruce, Philip Tromovitch, and Robert Bauserman. "A Meta-Analytic Examination of Assumed Properties of Child Sexual Abuse Using College Samples." *Psychological Bulletin* 124, no. 1 (1998): 22–53.

Rindels, Michelle. "Nevada to Embark on New Sex Offender Registry System, but Critics Say It's Overly Harsh." *Nevada Independent*, September 2018. https://thenevadaindependent.com/article/nevada-to-embark-on-new-sex-offender-registry-system-but-critics-say-its-overly-harsh.

RiskAware. "State Legal Compliance." RiskAware, LLC, 2020. http://riskaware.com/resources/understanding-the-laws/state-legal-compliance/.

Rispens, Jan, Andre Aleman, and Paul Goudena. "Prevention of Child Sexual Abuse Victimization: A Meta-Analysis of School Programs." *Child Abuse & Neglect* 21, no. 10 (1997): 975–87.

Roberts, Andrea L., Margaret Rosario, Karestan C. Koenen, and S. Bryn Austin. "Childhood Gender Nonconformity: A Risk Indicator for Childhood Abuse and Posttraumatic Stress in Youth." *Pediatrics* 129, no. 3 (2012): 410–17.

Robinson, David, Jonathan Bandler, and Avram A. Billig. "Civil Commitment: The Cost of Locking up Sex Offenders." *Journal News.* June 8, 2017. https://www.lohud.com/story/news/investigations/2017/05/31/civil-commitment-sex-offenders/325390001/.

Rolfe, Shawn M., Richard Tewksbury, and Ryan D. Schroeder. "Homeless Shelters' Policies on Sex Offenders: Is This Another Collateral Consequence?" *International Journal of Offender Therapy and Comparative Criminology* 61, no. 16 (2017): 1833–49.

Rossetti, Stephen J. "The Impact of Child Sexual Abuse on Attitudes toward God and the Catholic Church." *Child Abuse & Neglect* 19, no. 12 (1995): 1469–81.

Rothman, Emily F., Deinera Exner, and Allyson L. Baughman. "The Prevalence of Sexual Assault against People Who Identify as Gay, Lesbian, or Bisexual in the United States: A Systematic Review." *Trauma, Violence, & Abuse* 12, no. 2 (2011): 55–66.

Roush, David W. "Staff Sexual Misconduct in Juvenile Justice Facilities: Implications for Work Force Training." *Corrections Today*, February 2008, 32–52.

Russell, Diana E. H. "The Incidence and Prevalence of Intrafamilial and Extrafamilial Sexual Abuse of Female Children." *Child Abuse & Neglect* 7, no. 2 (1983): 133–46.

Ryan, Gail. "Childhood Sexuality: A Decade of Study. Part 1—Research and Curriculum Development." *Child Abuse & Neglect* 24, no. 1 (2000): 33–48.

Sacco, Lynn. *Unspeakable: Father-Daughter Incest in American History*. Baltimore, MD: Johns Hopkins University Press, 2009.

Sample, Lisa L. *The Social Construction of the Sex Offender*. St. Louis: University of Missouri-St. Louis, 2001.

Sandler, Jeffrey C., Naomi J. Freeman, and Kelly M. Socia. "Does a Watched Pot Boil? A Time-Series Analysis of New York State's Sex Offender Registration and Notification Law." *Psychology, Public Policy, and Law* 14, no. 4 (2008): 284–302.

Sanghara, Kiranjeet K., and J. Clare Wilson. "Stereotypes and Attitudes about Child Sexual Abusers: A Comparison of Experienced and Inexperienced Professionals in Sex Offender Treatment." *Legal and Criminological Psychology* 11, no. 2 (2006): 229–44.

Saul, Janet, and Natalie C. Audage. "Preventing Child Sexual Abuse Within Youth-Serving Organizations: Getting Started on Policies and Procedures." Centers for Disease Control, 2007. https://www.cdc.gov/ViolencePrevention/pdf/PreventingChildSexualAbuse-a.pdf.

Saunders, Bernadette J., and Chris Goddard. "The Role of Mass Media in Facilitating Community Education and Child Abuse Prevention Strategies." *Child Abuse Prevention Issues*, no. 16 (2002).

Schober, Daniel J., Stephen B. Fawcett, and Jetta Bernier. "The Enough Abuse Campaign: Building the Movement to Prevent Child Sexual Abuse in Massachusetts." *Journal of Child Sexual Abuse* 21, no. 4 (2012): 456–69.

Schreiner, Bruce. "Judge Strikes down Kentucky's Internet Restrictions for Sex Offenders." *Courier Journal*, October 20, 2017. https://www.courier-journal.com/story/news/local/2017/10/20/judge-strikes-down-kentuckys-internet-restrictions-sex-offenders/786270001/.

Sedlak, Andrea J., Dana Schultz, Susan J. Wells, Peter Lyons, Howard J. Doueck, and Frances Gragg. "Child Protection and Justice Systems Processing of Serious Child Abuse and Neglect Cases." *Child Abuse & Neglect* 30, no. 6 (2006): 657–77.

———, Jane Mettenburg, Monica Basena, I. Peta, Karla McPherson, and A. Greene. *Fourth National Incidence Study of Child Abuse and Neglect (NIS-4)*. Washington, DC: US Department of Health and Human Services, Administration for Children and Families, and Office of Planning, Research, and Evaluation, and the Children's Bureau, 2010. http://cap.law.harvard.edu/wp-content/uploads/2015/07/sedlaknis.pdf.

Self, Zac. "This Is Where California Ranks on List of States with the Most Sex Offenders." KGTV San Diego, September 2, 2018. https://www.10news.com/news/california-ranks-high-on-list-of-states-with-most-sex-offenders.

Seto, Michael. *Internet-Facilitated Sexual Offending*. Washington, DC: Sex Offender Management Assessment and Planning Initiative, Office of Justice Programs, 2015.

Seto, Michael C. "Is Pedophilia a Sexual Orientation?" *Archives of Sexual Behavior* 41, no. 1 (2012): 231–36.

———. "Pedophilia." *Annual Review of Clinical Psychology* 5 (2009): 391–407.

———, James M. Cantor, and Ray Blanchard. "Child Pornography Offenses Are a Valid Diagnostic Indicator of Pedophilia." *Journal of Abnormal Psychology* 115, no. 3 (2006): 610–15.

Shackel, Rita Laura. "The Beliefs Commonly Held by Adults about Children's Behavioral Responses to Sexual Victimization." *Child Abuse & Neglect* 32, no. 4 (2008): 485–95.

Shure, Natalie. "Why Young Sexual Assault Victims Tell Incoherent Stories." *Atlantic*, February 5, 2014. https://www.theatlantic.com/national/archive/2014/02/why-young-sexual-assault-victims-tell-incoherent-stories/283613/.

Siegel, Jane A., and Linda M. Williams. "The Relationship between Child Sexual Abuse and Female Delinquency and Crime: A Prospective Study." *Journal of Research in Crime and Delinquency* 40, no. 1 (2003): 71–94.

Simmons, Clara, and Joshua Woods. "The Overrepresentation of White Missing Children in National Television News." *Communication Research Reports* 32, no. 3 (2015): 239–45.

Simon, Jonathan. *Governing through Crime: How the War on Crime Transformed American Democracy and Created a Culture of Fear*. Oxford: Oxford University Press, 2009.

———. "Managing the Monstrous: Sex Offenders and the New Penology." *Psychology, Public Policy, and Law* 4, no. 1/2 (1998): 452–67.

Simons, Dominique A., Sandy K. Wurtele, and Robert L. Durham. "Developmental Experiences of Child Sexual Abusers and Rapists." *Child Abuse & Neglect* 32, no. 5 (2008): 549–60.

Smith, Erica L., and Jessica Stroop. *Sexual Victimization Reported by Youth in Juvenile Facilities, 2018*. Washington, DC: US Department of Justice, Office of Justice Programs, 2018. https://www.bjs.gov/content/pub/pdf/svryjfi8.pdf.

Smith, James P. "The Long-Term Economic Impact of Criminalization in American Childhoods." *Crime & Delinquency* 65, no. 3 (2019): 422–44.

Smith, Steven R., and Robert G. Meyer. "Child Abuse Reporting Laws and Psychotherapy: A Time for Reconsideration." *International Journal of Law and Psychiatry* 7, no. 3–4 (1984): 351–66.

Sommers, Zach. "Missing White Woman Syndrome: An Empirical Analysis of

Race and Gender Disparities in Online News Coverage of Missing Persons." *Journal of Criminal Law and Criminology* 106, no. 2 (2017): 275–314.

Spraitz, Jason D., and Kendra N. Bowen. "Techniques of Neutralization and Persistent Sexual Abuse by Clergy: A Content Analysis of Priest Personnel Files from the Archdiocese of Milwaukee." *Journal of Interpersonal Violence* 31, no. 15 (2016): 2515–38.

State of California. "California Law." California Legislative Information, 2020. https://leginfo.legislature.ca.gov/faces/codes_displaySection.xhtml?sectionNum=288.7.&lawCode=PEN.

State of Massachusetts. "Massachusetts Law about Child Sexual Abuse." Mass.gov, 2020. https://www.mass.gov/info-details/massachusetts-law-about-child-sexual-abuse.

Steptoe, George, and Antoine Goldet. "Why Some Young Sex Offenders Are Held Indefinitely." The Marshall Project, January 27, 2016. https://www.themarshallproject.org/2016/01/27/why-some-young-sex-offenders-are-held-indefinitely.

Stolzenberg, Stacia N., and Thomas D. Lyon. "Evidence Summarized in Attorneys' Closing Arguments Predicts Acquittals in Criminal Trials of Child Sexual Abuse." *Child Maltreatment* 19, no. 2 (2014): 119–29.

Stroud, Delores D., Sonja L. Martens, and Julia Barker. "Criminal Investigation of Child Sexual Abuse: A Comparison of Cases Referred to the Prosecutor to Those Not Referred." *Child Abuse & Neglect* 24, no. 5 (2000): 689–700.

Summit, Roland C. "Abuse of the Child Sexual Abuse Accommodation Syndrome." *Journal of Child Sexual Abuse* 1, no. 4 (1992): 153–64.

———. "The Child Sexual Abuse Accommodation Syndrome." *Child Abuse & Neglect* 7 (1983): 177–93.

Sundt, Jody L., Francis T. Cullen, Brandon K. Applegate, and Michael G. Turner. "The Tenacity of the Rehabilitative Ideal: Have Attitudes Toward Offender Treatment Changed?" *Criminal Justice and Behavior* 25, no. 4 (1998): 426–42.

Talley, Tim. "Group Takes Aim at Oklahoma's Failure-to-Protect Law." Associated Press, September 29, 2018. https://apnews.com/45a6f24af72c4750ac141f3fe10b3bc9.

Talmon, Anat, and Karni Ginzburg. "'Body Self' in the Shadow of Childhood Sexual Abuse: The Long-Term Implications of Sexual Abuse for Male and Female Adult Survivors." *Child Abuse & Neglect* 76 (2018): 416–25.

Tavkar, Poonam, and David J. Hansen. "Interventions for Families Victimized by Child Sexual Abuse: Clinical Issues and Approaches for Child Advocacy Center-Based Services." *Aggression and Violent Behavior* 16, no. 3 (2011): 188–99.

Terry, Karen J, Margaret Leland Smith, Katarina Schuth, James R. Kelly, Brenda

Vollman, and Christina Massey. *"The Causes and Context of Sexual Abuse of Minors by Catholic Priests in the United States, 1950-2010: A Report Presented to the United States Conference of Catholic Bishops by the John Jay College Research Team."* Washington, DC: United States Conference of Catholic Bishops Communications, 2011. http://www.bishop-accountability.org/reports/2011_05_18_John_Jay_Causes_and_Context_Report.pdf

Tewksbury, Richard. "Collateral Consequences of Sex Offender Registration." *Journal of Contemporary Criminal Justice* 21, no. 1 (2005): 67–81.

———, and Kristen M. Zgoba. "Perceptions and Coping with Punishment: How Registered Sex Offenders Respond to Stress, Internet Restrictions, and the Collateral Consequences of Registration." *International Journal of Offender Therapy and Comparative Criminology* 54, no. 4 (2010): 537–51.

Tilly, Charles. *Credit and Blame.* Princeton: Princeton University Press, 2008. http://repository.umpwr.ac.id:8080/bitstream/handle/123456789/301/Credit%20and%20Blame.pdf?sequence=1&isAllowed=y.

Timpka, Toomas, Staffan Janson, Jenny Jacobsson, Örjan Dahlström, Armin Spreco, Jan Kowalski, Victor Bargoria, Margo Mountjoy, and Carl Göran Svedin. "Lifetime History of Sexual and Physical Abuse among Competitive Athletics (Track and Field) Athletes: Cross Sectional Study of Associations with Sports and Non-Sports Injury." *British Journal of Sports Medicine* 53, no. 22 (2018): 1–7.

Toftegaard Nielsen, Jan. "The Forbidden Zone: Intimacy, Sexual Relations and Misconduct in the Relationship between Coaches and Athletes." *International Review for the Sociology of Sport* 36, no. 2 (2001): 165–82.

Tollefson, Phoebe. "Prosecutors Seek to Restore Stronger Penalties for Sex Crimes against Children in Montana." *Billings Gazette*, February 9, 2019. https://billingsgazette.com/news/state-and-regional/crime-and-courts/prosecutors-seek-to-restore-stronger-penalties-for-sex-crimes-against/article_578453ed-f51d-53be-8708-3636723a3c68.html.

Tolman, Arielle W. "Sex Offender Civil Commitment to Prison Post-Kingsley." *Northwestern University Law Review* 113, no. 1 (2018): 115–91.

Tonry, Michael. "Prosecutors and Politics in Comparative Perspective." *Crime and Justice* 41, no. 1 (2012): 1–33.

Topping, K. J., and I. G. Barron. "School-Based Child Sexual Abuse Prevention Programs: A Review of Effectiveness." *Review of Educational Research* 79, no. 1 (2009): 431–63.

Tripodi, Stephen J., Johnny S. Kim, and Kimberly Bender. "Is Employment Associated with Reduced Recidivism? The Complex Relationship Between Employment and Crime." *International Journal of Offender Therapy and Comparative Criminology* 54, no. 5 (2010): 706–20.

Turner, Daniel, Martin Rettenberger, Lena Lohmann, Reinhard Eher, and Peer Briken. "Pedophilic Sexual Interests and Psychopathy in Child Sexual Abusers Working with Children." *Child Abuse & Neglect* 38, no. 2 (2014): 326–35.

Turner, Susan, Alyssa W. Chamberlain, Jesse Jannetta, and James Hess. "Does GPS Improve Recidivism among High Risk Sex Offenders? Outcomes for California's GPS Pilot for High Risk Sex Offender Parolees." *Victims & Offenders* 10, no. 1 (2015): 1–28.

Uggen, Christopher. "Ex-Offenders and the Conformist Alternative: A Job Quality Model of Work and Crime." *Social Problems* 46, no. 1 (February 1999): 127–51.

United States Courts. *Overview of Probation and Supervised Release Conditions.* Washington, DC: Administrative Office of the United States Courts Probation and Pretrial Services Office, 2016. http://www.uscourts.gov/services-forms/computer-internet-restrictions-probation-supervised-release-conditions.

United States Department of Justice. *Prison Rape Elimination Act: Prisons and Jail Standards.* Washington, DC: United States Department of Justice, 2012. https://bja.ojp.gov/sites/g/files/xyckuh186/files/media/document/PREA-Prison-Jail-Standards.pdf.

US Census Bureau. *Overview of Race and Hispanic Origin: 2010.* Washington, DC: US Department of Commerce Economics and Statistics Administration, 2011. https://www.census.gov/prod/cen2010/briefs/c2010br-02.pdf.

US House of Representatives. *Adam Walsh Reauthorization Act of 2017.* Washington, DC: US House of Representatives, 2017. https://www.congress.gov/congressional-report/115th-congress/house-report/142/1.

Van Horn, Joan, Mara Eisenberg, Carol McNaughton Nicholls, Jules Mulder, Stephen Webster, Caroline Paskell, Ashley Brown, Jeantine Stam, Jane Kerr, and Natalie Jago. "Stop It Now! A Pilot Study into the Limits and Benefits of a Free Helpline Preventing Child Sexual Abuse." *Journal of Child Sexual Abuse* 24, no. 8 (2015): 853–72.

Victor, Jeffrey. "Satanic Cult Rumors as Contemporary Legend." *Western Folklore* 49, no. 1 (1990): 51–81.

Visher, Christy A. "Incapacitation and Crime Control: Does a 'Lock 'Em up' Strategy Reduce Crime?" *Justice Quarterly* 4, no. 4 (1987): 513–43.

Volkwein, Karin A. E., Frauke I. Schnell, Dennis Sherwood, and Anne Livezey. "Sexual Harassment in Sport: Perceptions and Experiences of American Female Student-Athletes." *International Review for the Sociology of Sport* 32, no. 3 (1997): 283–95.

Volkwein-Caplan, Karin, Frauke Schnell, Shannon Devlin, Michelle Mitchell, and Jennifer Sutera. "Sexual Harassment of Women in Athletics vs. Academia." In *Sexual Harassment and Abuse in Sport: International Research and Policy*

Perspectives, edited by Celia H. Brackenridge and Kari Fasting, 91–110. Chicago: Whiting & Birch, 2002.

Vries Robbé, Michiel de, Ruth E. Mann, Shadd Maruna, and David Thornton. "An Exploration of Protective Factors Supporting Desistance from Sexual Offending." *Sexual Abuse* 27, no. 1 (2015): 16–33.

Walsh, Wendy A., Lisa M. Jones, Theodore P. Cross, and Tonya Lippert. "Prosecuting Child Sexual Abuse: The Importance of Evidence Type." *Crime & Delinquency* 56, no. 3 (2010): 436–54.

Walsh, Wendy A., Tonya Lippert, Meredyth Goldberg Edelson, and Lisa M. Jones. "Length of Time to Resolve Criminal Charges of Child Sexual Abuse: A Three-County Case Study." *Behavioral Sciences & the Law* 33, no. 4 (2015): 528–45.

Walster, Elaine. "Assignment of Responsibility for an Accident." *Journal of Personality and Social Psychology* 3, no. 1 (1966): 73–79.

Ward, Tony, and Thomas Keenan. "Child Molesters' Implicit Theories." *Journal of Interpersonal Violence* 14, no. 8 (1999): 821–38.

Warner, Carolyn M. "The Politics of Sex Abuse in Sacred Hierarchies: A Comparative Study of the Catholic Church and the Military in the United States." *Religions* 10, no. 4 (2019): 281–309.

Warren, Deirdre M., and Katrina R. Bloch. "Framing Same-Sex Marriage: Media Constructions of California's Proposition 8." *Social Science Journal* 51, no. 4 (2014): 503–13.

Washington State Institute for Public Policy. *Washington State's Community Notification Law: 15 Years of Change*. Olympia: Washington State Institute for Public Policy, 2006. https://www.wsipp.wa.gov/ReportFile/936/Wsipp_Washington-States-Community-Notification-Law-15-Years-of-Change_Full-Report.pdf.

Websdale, Neil. "Predators: The Social Construction of 'Stranger Danger' in Washington State as a Form of Patriarchal Ideology." In *Making Trouble: Cultural Constructions of Crime, Deviance, and Control*, edited by Jeff Ferrell and Neil Websdale. New York: Aldine de Gruyter, 1996.

Webster, Michelle Waul, and Julie Whitman. *Who's Lending a Hand? A National Survey of Nonprofit Volunteer Screening Practices*. Washington, DC: The National Center for Victims of Crime, 2008.

Weinberger, Linda E., Shoba Sreenivasan, Thomas Garrick, and Hadley Osran. "The Impact of Surgical Castration on Sexual Recidivism Risk Among Sexually Violent Predatory Offenders." *Journal of the American Academy of Psychiatry and the Law* 33, no. 1 (2005): 21.

Weis, Lois. "Identity Formation and the Processes of 'Othering': Unraveling Sexual Threads." *Journal of Educational Foundations* 9, no. 1 (1995): 17–33.

Weiss, Kenneth J., and Julia Curcio Alexander. "Sex, Lies, and Statistics: Inferences from the Child Sexual Abuse Accommodation Syndrome." *Journal of the American Academy of Psychiatry and the Law* 41, no. 3 (2013): 412–20.

Wendell, Bryan. "Youth Protection: 'Two-Deep Leadership' vs. 'No One-on-One Contact.'" *Scouting Magazine*, January 19, 2018. https://blog.scoutingmagazine.org/2018/01/19/whats-the-difference-between-two-deep-leadership-and-no-one-on-one-contact/.

White, Codi, Dianne C. Shanley, Melanie J. Zimmer-Gembeck, Kerryann Walsh, Russell Hawkins, Katrina Lines, and Haley Webb. "Promoting Young Children's Interpersonal Safety Knowledge, Intentions, Confidence, and Protective Behavior Skills: Outcomes of a Randomized Controlled Trial." *Child Abuse & Neglect* 82 (2018): 144–55.

Widom, C. S., and S. Morris. "Accuracy of Adult Recollections of Childhood Victimization." *Psychological Assessment* 9, no. 34–46 (1997): 34–46.

Wiley, Tisha R. A., and Bette L. Bottoms. "Effects of Defendant Sexual Orientation on Jurors' Perceptions of Child Sexual Assault." *Law and Human Behavior* 33, no. 1 (2009): 46–60.

Williams, Katria S., and David M. Bierie. "An Incident-Based Comparison of Female and Male Sexual Offenders." *Sexual Abuse: A Journal of Research and Treatment* 27, no. 3 (2015): 235–57.

Williams, L. M. "Recall of Childhood Trauma: A Prospective Study of Women's Memories of Child Sexual Abuse." *Journal of Consulting and Clinical Psychology* 62 (1994): 1167–76.

Williams, Rebecca, Steven M. Gillespie, Ian A. Elliott, and Hilary J. Eldridge. "Characteristics of Female Solo and Female Co-Offenders and Male Solo Sexual Offenders against Children." *Sexual Abuse* 31, no. 2 (2019): 151–72.

Willis, Gwenda M., and Randolph C. Grace. "Assessment of Community Reintegration Planning for Sex Offenders: Poor Planning Predicts Recidivism." *Criminal Justice and Behavior* 36, no. 5 (2009): 494–512.

Wilson, Helen W., and Cathy Spatz Widom. "Does Physical Abuse, Sexual Abuse, or Neglect in Childhood Increase the Likelihood of Same-Sex Sexual Relationships and Cohabitation? A Prospective 30-Year Follow-Up." *Archives of Sexual Behavior* 39, no. 1 (2010): 63–74.

Wilson, R. J., F. Cortoni, and A. J. McWhinnie. "Circles of Support & Accountability: A Canadian National Replication of Outcome Findings." *Sexual Abuse: A Journal of Research and Treatment* 21, no. 4 (2009): 412–30.

Windham, Craig, and Patricia Hudsen. "Study of Past Participants in the Protecting God's Children Program." Virtus Program, November 1, 2010.

Wortley, Richard, and Stephen Smallbone. "A Criminal Careers Typology of Child Sexual Abusers." *Sexual Abuse: A Journal of Research and Treatment* 26, no. 6 (2014): 569–585.

Wright, Richard G. "Sex Offender Post-Incarceration Sanctions: Are There Any Limits." *New England Journal on Crime and Civil Confinement* 34 (2008): 17–50.

Wurtele, Sandy K., Laura C. Kast, Cindy L. Miller-Perrin, and P.A. Kondrick. "Comparison of Programs for Teaching Personal Safety Skills to Preschoolers." *Journal of Consulting and Clinical Psychology* 57, no. 4 (1989): 505–11.

Wurtele, Sandy K., and Maureen C. Kenny. "Partnering with Parents to Prevent Childhood Sexual Abuse." *Child Abuse Review* 19, no. 2 (2010): 130–52.

Yoder, Steven. "Registered Sex Offenders in the United States and Its Territories per 100,000 Population." The Appeal, 2019. https://theappeal.org/why-sex-offender-registries-keep-growing-even-as-sexual-violence-rates-fall/.

Yung, Corey Rayburn. "Civil Commitment for Sex Offenders." *AMA Journal of Ethics* 15, no. 10 (2013): 873–77.

Zevitz, Richard G., and Mary Ann Farkas. "Sex Offender Community Notification: Examining the Importance of Neighborhood Meetings." *Behavioral Sciences and the Law* 18 (2000): 393–408.

Zgoba, Kristen, Philip Witt, Melissa Dalessandro, and Bonita Veysey. *Megan's Law: Assessing the Practical and Monetary Efficacy*. Trenton, NJ: The Research & Evaluation Unit, Office of Policy and Planning, New Jersey Department of Corrections, 2008. https://www.ncjrs.gov/App/Publications/abstract.aspx?ID=247350.

Zimring, Franklin E., Alex R. Piquero, and Wesley G. Jennings. "Sexual Delinquency in Racine: Does Early Sex Offending Predict Later Sex Offending in Youth and Young Adulthood?" *Criminology & Public Policy* 6, no. 3 (2007): 507–34.

www.ingramcontent.com/pod-product-compliance
Lightning Source LLC
Chambersburg PA
CBHW052121270326
41930CB00012B/2713

* 9 7 8 1 6 4 3 1 5 0 3 2 1 *